Raffael Buff

Using Additional Information in Streaming Algorithms

Anchor Academic
Publishing

Buff, Raffael: Using Additional Information in Streaming Algorithms, Hamburg, Anchor Academic Publishing 2016

Buch-ISBN: 978-3-96067-094-0
PDF-eBook-ISBN: 978-3-96067-594-5
Druck/Herstellung: Anchor Academic Publishing, Hamburg, 2016
Covermotiv: © pixabay.de

Bibliografische Information der Deutschen Nationalbibliothek:
Die Deutsche Nationalbibliothek verzeichnet diese Publikation in der Deutschen Nationalbibliografie; detaillierte bibliografische Daten sind im Internet über http://dnb.d-nb.de abrufbar.

Bibliographical Information of the German National Library:
The German National Library lists this publication in the German National Bibliography. Detailed bibliographic data can be found at: http://dnb.d-nb.de

© Anchor Academic Publishing, Imprint der Diplomica Verlag GmbH
Hermannstal 119k, 22119 Hamburg
http://www.diplomica-verlag.de, Hamburg 2016
Printed in Germany

Abstract

Streaming problems are algorithmic problems that are mainly characterized by their massive input streams. Because of these data streams, the algorithms for these problems are forced to be space-efficient, as the input stream length generally exceeds the available storage. In this thesis, the two streaming problems *most frequent item* and *number of distinct items* are studied in detail relating to their algorithmic complexities, and it is compared whether the verification of solution hypotheses has lower algorithmic complexity than computing a solution from the data stream. For this analysis, we introduce some concepts to prove space complexity lower bounds for an approximative setting and for hypothesis verification.

For the most frequent item problem which consists in identifying the item which has the highest occurrence within the data stream, we can prove a linear space complexity lower bound for the deterministic and probabilistic setting. This implies that, in practice, this streaming problem cannot be solved in a satisfactory way since every algorithm has to exceed any reasonable storage limit. For some settings, the upper and lower bounds are almost tight, which implies that we have designed an almost optimal algorithm. Even for small approximation ratios, we can prove a linear lower bound, but not for larger ones. Nevertheless, we are not able to design an algorithm that solves the most frequent item problem space-efficiently for large approximation ratios. Furthermore, if we want to verify whether a hypothesis of the highest frequency count is true or not, we get exactly the same space complexity lower bounds, which leads to the conclusion that we are likely not able to profit from a stated hypothesis.

The number of distinct items problem counts all different elements of the input stream. If we want to solve this problem exactly (in a deterministic or probabilistic setting) or approximately with a deterministic algorithm, we require once again linear storage size which is tight to the upper bound. However, for the approximative and probabilistic setting, we can enhance an already known space-efficient algorithm such that it is usable for arbitrarily small approximation ratios and arbitrarily good success probabilities. The hypothesis verification leads once again to the same lower bounds.

However, there are some streaming problems that are able to profit from additional information such as hypotheses, as e.g., the median problem.

i

Acknowledgement

I would like to thank Prof. Juraj Hromkovič for the interesting thesis topic. I especially value that he always wanted to discuss the proofs and their concepts to understand and evaluate the basis of the thesis, instead of just observing rough overviews or summaries.

A big thanks goes to my advisors Hans-Joachim Böckenhauer and Dennis Komm for all the discussions, guidelines and helpful comments on the content and how to structure this thesis. I really appreciate their constructive inputs on the optimal degree of formalism, especially for the definitions, and that they made sure that the mathematical formulas and algorithm concepts are described well enough to have a good readability.

Last but not least, I would like to thank my friends Sonja Bachl and Marco Poltera for proofreading my thesis and identifying all my lingual shortcomings such that the reader is now able to focus on the content.

Contents

List of Figures

List of Tables

Chapter 1

Introduction

The title of this thesis, *Using Additional Information in Streaming Algorithms*, presses for three simple questions: What is a *streaming algorithm*? What is meant by the all-encompassing *additional information*? And what can additional information be *used for* in streaming algorithms? We address these questions in the following.

What is a *streaming algorithm*? A streaming algorithm processes massive data streams to compute a certain function on these data. From a practical point of view, a data stream means that these data are successively generated and not completely known upfront. The streaming algorithm processes the generated data piecewise to calculate intermediate and final results for a given streaming problem. Furthermore, streaming algorithms may only read the streaming data once because, generally, they cannot store the entire data stream, as the massive stream length often exceeds the possible storage capacity. Facing these conditions, the basic question is whether a streaming problem can be solved within practical time and space boundaries or not. Generally, a poly-logarithmic space complexity in relation to the data stream size is considered practical. The time needed to process a current data value is also required to be low, as otherwise the new values generated have to be cached in the meantime, i.e., stored, which might on the other side exceed the allowed storage size because queues build up when incoming data stream exceeds processing capacity. The study of streaming problems includes both the identification of streaming algorithms solving the streaming problem with a certain space and time complexity and the analysis of lower bounds on the required intermediate storage size to successively calculate a certain function on the data stream. The following examples illustrate the kind of thoughts and analysis necessary to construct an algorithm that solves a streaming problem.

As an example, a simple streaming problem is the identification of the maximal integer value within a massive data stream of integers. Let us assume that this data stream contains 10^8 numbers, each with any integer value between one and 10^9. Of course, one can easily solve this problem with an algorithm that simply tracks the highest already known value. At the end, after reading all 10^8 values, this algorithm outputs the highest observed value between one and 10^9. This algorithm would only require small storage to encode this highest value.

A slightly more complex example would be the calculation of the k-th highest

1

value within this same data stream. Once again one could store the already known, now k highest values and would therefore use k times more storage than for the simple streaming problem above. For small k, e.g., $k < 100$, this is generally still practical. A more difficult streaming problem is, e.g., the calculation of the most frequent value, i.e., the value which occurs the most within the data stream. Here, one cannot easily generate a streaming algorithm using sub-linear storage. Furthermore, we will later present a proof that shows that this problem requires at least linear storage.

With the technique of *communication complexity*, we will be able to prove space complexity lower bounds, which imply that any possible algorithm that solves a certain streaming problem requires at least a certain space size. If the identified algorithm requires the same amount of bits for its storage as the proven lower bound, we have found an optimal algorithm in relation to the space complexity. If there is a gap between the upper and lower bound, it might be possible to find an algorithm with a lower space complexity.

These types of analyses - finding time and space efficient algorithms to solve a streaming problem and proving necessary space complexities - are the core of the study of streaming algorithms. This leads to the second question:

What is meant by the all-encompassing *additional information*? Additional information may help solve a certain streaming problem. One possible usage of this additional information is when it represents a *solution hypothesis*. This means that the streaming algorithm receives a solution hypothesis upfront, e.g., that the number 20 appears within the data stream the most with a frequency of 39 times. Now the streaming problem is transformed from a general solution search problem to the decision problem of verifying whether this hypothesis is true for the given input stream. For this decision problem of hypothesis verification, one can similarly analyze the possible space and time complexities.

For the hypothesis verification, a streaming algorithm has to verify any possible hypothesis for a certain input stream. This type of problem is relevant, if we have a powerful but untrusted source. Then, we may calculate a solution hypothesis with this source solving the general streaming problem and verify the hypothesis with an eventually more space and time efficient algorithm.

What can additional information be *used for* in streaming algorithms? The concepts of streaming problems with and without additional information are compared. Namely, the possible algorithms and proofs for both the general solution search problem and the hypothesis verification problem determine whether the additional information is helpful, i.e., the required time and space complexities are lower. In some cases, the additional information is useless for solving the streaming problem with lower algorithmic complexities.

More specifically, this thesis introduces some concepts to evaluate, whether the hypothesis verification is significantly easier than the general solution search problem. Here, *easier* means that the algorithm to verify the hypothesis is faster or requires less storage than the algorithm for the general solution search problem requires in the optimal case. Additionally, some streaming problems are stated where the hypothesis verification is equally difficult as the general streaming problem, which means that the additional information is not useful for the streaming algorithm at all.

1.1 Overview and Structure of the Thesis

The goal of this thesis is to analyze the impact of additional information (more specifically, a hypothesis of the solution) on the algorithmic space complexities of several streaming problems.

To this end, different streaming problems are analyzed and compared. The two problems *most frequent item* and *number of distinct items*, with many configurations of different result accuracies and probabilities, are deeply studied. Both lower and upper bounds for the space and time complexity for deterministic and probabilistic environments are analyzed with respect to possible improvements due to additional information. The general solution search problem is compared to the decision problem where a solution hypothesis has to be satisfied.

Figure 1.1 illustrates this approach, which is explained in more detail in the following. Based on this illustration, the following different layers are described: Streaming problems (gray boxes), decision vs. search problems (dark blue boxes), deterministic vs. probabilistic settings (light blue boxes), exact solutions vs. approximations (yellow boxes) and lower vs. upper bounds of algorithmic complexities (orange boxes).

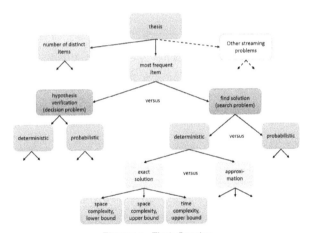

Figure 1.1. Thesis Overview

Streaming Problems: The following streaming problems are analyzed. The goal of the *most frequent item problem* is to identify the value which is most frequent within a data stream $x = (x_1, x_2, \ldots, x_n)$. The streaming problem *number of distinct items* identifies the amount of different values, i.e., the size of the subset of the data stream without any duplications. As sketched in the last section of this thesis, the introduced approach and technique to analyze upper and lower bounds that are used to analyze the two streaming problems can be used for further streaming problems as well.

Decision vs. Search Problems: Our aim is to prove or disprove the possible benefits of additional information (in the form of a solution hypothesis) for solving one of the mentioned streaming problems. Therefore, the best possible algorithms with respect to space and time complexity are identified for both the search problem, where the optimal solution has to be found and for the decision problem, where one has to verify or refuse a certain solution hypothesis. One can verify that the decision problem is not more complex than the search problem because, for the decision problem, one can always compute the solution as in the search problem and compare it to the hypothesis. Therefore, the question is, whether the decision problem (with additional information, i.e., a hypothetical solution) has a smaller complexity, and if so, by how much.

Deterministic vs. Probabilistic Approaches: Deterministic algorithms differ from probabilistic ones in both the result accuracy and the required time and space complexity. Therefore, the impact of additional information (i.e., a solution hypothesis) is compared for both deterministic and probabilistic algorithms.

Exact Solutions vs. Approximations: Streaming optimization problems such as the most frequent item problem may allow an approximation of the solution. Identifying an exact solution and allowing approximative results yield fundamentally different implications on the time and space complexities of its streaming algorithms.

Lower vs. Upper Bounds: For a certain streaming problem and its configuring setting (decision or search problem, deterministic or probabilistic approach, and exact solution or approximation), the best possible algorithms with respect to space and time complexity are identified. Concrete algorithms deliver upper bounds. Furthermore, formal proofs lead to space complexity lower bounds for certain streaming problems.

Structure of the Thesis

After this introduction, Chapter 2 discusses an overview of the literature providing similar topics. Chapter 3 introduces and describes the relevant definitions. Chapter 4 covers the approaches to prove space complexity lower bounds. Chapter 5 and Chapter 6 contain the detailed analysis of the *most frequent item problem* and the *distinct item problem*. The summary of the results, the thesis conclusion and an outlook on possible future work is given in Chapter 7.

Chapter 2

Related Work

In this chapter, we introduce some relevant papers, articles and books for the topic of this thesis. We first state some related work on streaming problems and algorithms. To prove space complexity lower bounds, we use the technique of communication complexity. Therefore, we state some resources about communication complexity and its usage on other problems. At last, we list five papers on the two analyzed streaming problems, the *most frequent item problem* and the *number of distinct items problem*.

Streaming Problems and Algorithms: There are different resources addressing the area of streaming problems and data streams. Aggarwal [Agg07] gives a brief overview of the characteristics of a data stream and lists several interesting streaming problems. Babcock et al. [BBD+02] study data streams from a more practical point of view, including optimized database queries and time measures. A more formal and theoretical analysis of some streaming problems is given by Muthukrishnan [Mut05]. The doctoral thesis by Prakash about *Efficient Delegation Algorithms for Outsourcing Computations on Massive Data Stream* [Pra15] is a recommended literature because it introduces the relevant parts of streaming problems, their characteristics and their analysis including lower-bound proofs.

Communication Complexity: For a significant analysis of streaming problems, we have to prove space complexity lower bounds, besides designing efficient streaming algorithms. For these proofs, we will use the technique of communication complexity, which was originally introduced by Yao [Yao79]. The principles of communication complexity are introduced in detail later on, namely, in Chapter 4. A more broad and formal introduction is given by Hromkovič [Hro97]. A more practical resource on communication complexity is given by Roughgarden [Rou15], which focusses on *communication complexity for algorithm designers*. Halstenberg and Reischuk [HR88] introduce different *communication complexity models* and Kremet et al. [KNR01] focus on one of these models, the *one-round communication complexity*, which is also the basis for the lower-bound proofs of the two analyzed streaming problems. Babai et al. [BFS86] introduce different communication complexity classes. Yao [Yao83], Paturi and Simon [PS84], as well as Ablayev [Abl96] wrote useful papers on proving lower bounds in a probabilistic setting. For our lower bound proofs in a randomized setting, we will use the theorems by Ablayev [Abl96].

Based on the communication complexity theory, there are different papers illustrating the usage of this technique. As an example, Kalyanasundaram and Schnitger [KS92] analyze the *probabilistic communication complexity of set intersection*. The *distributional complexity of disjointness* is analyzed by Razborov [Raz92]. Munro and Paterson [MP80] focus on *selection and sorting with limited storage* and the *approximate counting of inversions in a data stream* is studied by Ajatai et al. [AJKS02]. Indyk and Woodruff [IW05] analyze the optimality of frequency moment algorithms.

Most Frequent Item and Number of Distinct Items Problem: The two studied streaming problems of this thesis are analyzed in several resources. Carmode and Hadjieleftheriou [CH09] as well as Manku and Motwani [MM12] give concrete implementations of algorithms for the most frequent item problem. The paper *Space Complexity of Approximating the Frequency Moments* by Alon et al. [AMS99] introduces an efficient algorithm for the number of distinct items problems and analyzes the space complexity lower bounds of both streaming problems for a deterministic and probabilistic setting. Karp et al. [KSP03] as well as Trevisan and Williams [TW12] state further lower bounds for the most frequent item problem for some conditions of the input values.

The relevant results of these resources are gathered in detail in the corresponding chapters of the streaming problems, namely in Chapter 5 for the most frequent item problem and in Chapter 6 for the number of distinct items problem.

Chapter 3

Definitions

Before we can start analyzing concrete streaming algorithms with respect to space and time complexity, we first have to formally define what a streaming algorithm is. Yet before, a definition for a streaming problem has to be provided. Additionally, in the following chapters we will often use special cases of streaming problems or algorithms – these special cases are also introduced here. Therefore, this chapter contains several basic definitions for streaming problems and algorithms.

First, the general definitions for streaming problems, algorithms and their special cases are given (Section 3.1, Section 3.2). Then, for streaming algorithms, we introduce how the time and space complexities are identified (Section 3.3). The problem characteristics *success probability* and *approximation ratio* are explained (Section 3.4). Definitions on solvability (Section 3.5) and a few basic calculations for further analysis (Section 3.6) conclude this chapter.

3.1 Streaming Problems and Algorithms

In this section, streaming problems and algorithms are introduced and formally defined. First, the general definition of a *streaming problem* is explained and then, two special cases are defined: The *streaming counting problem* and the *streaming decision problem*. All analyzed streaming problems can be reduced to one of these two. The general definition of the streaming problem is introduced to show the similarity of these two cases and to avoid duplications of definitions and theorems that are valid for both cases. These formal definitions are required to allow the mathematical analysis of space complexity lower bounds.

As outlined in the introduction (Chapter 1), a streaming problem is mainly characterized by the enormous size of the data stream as its input. As we will see in the following definition, this input stream is defined as a sequence of n input values, where n represents a very large number. The set of feasible output values defines which outputs are allowed for every possible input stream. Finally, the problem function defines which one of the feasible output values is the optimal or correct one for a certain input stream. All of this together leads to the following definition.

Definition 3.1. *A **streaming problem** $\mathcal{S}$ is a triple $(\mathcal{X}, \mathcal{Y}, f)$ containing a class of input streams $\mathcal{X}$, where each input stream $x^j \in \mathcal{X}$ is a sequence of n input values, i.e., $x^j = (x_1^j, \ldots, x_n^j)$, with $n \in \mathbb{N}^+$. The second element of the triple is a class of feasible output sets $\mathcal{Y} = \{\mathcal{Y}_{x^1}, \ldots, \mathcal{Y}_{x^d}\}$ with $d = |\mathcal{X}|$, where every input stream $x^j \in \mathcal{X}$ has a corresponding feasible output set $\mathcal{Y}_{x^j}$. Additionally, the streaming problem contains a problem function $f \colon \mathcal{X} \to \mathcal{Y}_x^*$, where, for every input stream $x \in \mathcal{X}$, one or more values from the feasible output set are indicated as optimal or correct output value, namely $f(x) \subseteq \mathcal{Y}_x$.*

With this general definition of a streaming problem, one can either define a classical optimization problem or a decision problem. For optimization problems, one has to be defined how good non-optimal output values are, such that this metric can be optimized. For a decision problem, the problem function can simply be interpreted as determining the correct decisions.

As an illustration of this definition, the simple streaming problem from above (Chapter 1), in which the task was simply to identify the maximum integer value within the input stream, could be formally defined as follows.

- Input streams: Each input stream $x = (x_1, \ldots, x_n) \in \mathcal{X}$ contains a series of n integers between 0 and a fixed $m \in \mathbb{N}^+$, namely, $x_i \in \{0, \ldots, m\}$.

- Feasible output sets: For every input stream $x \in \mathcal{X}$, the corresponding output set allows every integer between 0 and m, namely $\mathcal{Y}_x = \{0, \ldots, m\} \in \mathcal{Y}$.

- Problem function: For every certain input stream $x \in \mathcal{X}$, it defines the optimal or correct output value from the feasible output set $\mathcal{Y}_x = \{0, \ldots, m\}$, which is $f(x) = \max\{x_i \mid 1 \leq i \leq n\}$.

With this definition of $\mathcal{X}$, $\mathcal{Y}$, and f, we defined a streaming problem $\mathcal{S} = (\mathcal{X}, \mathcal{Y}, f)$, that searches for the maximum value in an input stream. The introduced formalism seems to be too complicated for such a simple problem. But for more complicated problems, this level of formalism is required to identify algorithms that solve it and, especially, to prove some space complexity lower bounds.

Now, we will distinguish two special cases of the general streaming problem, the *streaming counting problem* and the *streaming decision problem*.

First, we will introduce the streaming counting problem. In counting problems, we deal with series of integers as input streams and integers as output values, and the aim is always to evaluate some counting function. Some examples of streaming counting problems are the sum of all input values, their median, or the most frequent item.

A streaming counting problem has input streams with n integer values from the set from 1 to $m \in \mathbb{N}^+$. The resulting counting value of an input stream is an integer between 0 and a fixed value $s(n, m)$, which depends on the input stream length and its values. This result size is specific to each streaming problem.

We will describe a few examples of how $s(n, m)$ could be defined to illustrate its usage. To find a maximum number and its position within the input stream, $s(n, m) = \max\{n, m\}$ is a reasonable result size, as higher values are not possible. To identify the most frequent item within the input streams, $s(n, m) = n$ seems suitable, as an item cannot occur more often than n times. To sum up all numbers within the input stream, $s(n, m) = nm$ is a meaningful result size. Now, the feasible output values of an input stream are any possible counting values between 0 and $s(n, m)$.

The problem function is just the counting function on the input stream, which is the core of a certain counting problem. The goal of a streaming algorithm is to produce this optimal value or, in some cases, a good approximation of this optimal value. We can capture this in the following definition.

Definition 3.2. *A **streaming counting problem** $\mathcal{S}_\# = (\mathcal{X}, \mathcal{Y}, f, s)$ is a streaming problem $\mathcal{S} = (\mathcal{X}, \mathcal{Y}, f)$ together with a result-size function $s(n, m) \in \mathbb{N}^+$ with the following additional constraints: The input streams $x = (x_1, \ldots, x_n) \in \mathcal{X}$ have input values $x_i \in \{1, \ldots, m\}$, with $m \in \mathbb{N}^+$. For every feasible input stream $x \in \mathcal{X}$, the possible output values are $y \in \mathcal{Y}_x$ with $y \in \{0, \ldots, s(n, m)\}$. The problem function defines, for every input stream $x \in \mathcal{X}$, exactly one counting value $y \in \mathcal{Y}_x$ as the optimal counting result.*

An example of a streaming counting problem is the frequency moment.

Definition 3.3. *For every $k \in \mathbb{N}$, we define the **frequency moment** F_k of a streaming counting problem $\mathcal{S}_\# = (\mathcal{X}, \mathcal{Y}, f, s)$ as*

$$F_k := \sum_{j=1}^{m} (f_j)^k,$$

where f_j counts the frequency of the item j in the input stream, namely,

$$f_j := \left| \{ i \mid 1 \leq i \leq n \text{ and } x_i = j \} \right|.$$

F_0 counts the number of distinct items within the input stream, F_1 counts the input stream length, namely $F_1(x) = n$ and F_∞ is defined as the most frequent item, namely, $F_\infty := \max_{j=1}^{m} f_j$.

Note that, indeed, we have a relation between the general definition of the frequency moment f_k for $f \in \mathbb{N}$ and F_∞ because

$$\sqrt[k]{F_k} \xrightarrow{k \to \infty} F_\infty = \max_{1 \leq j \leq m} f_j.$$

Besides the streaming counting problem, the second special case is the streaming decision problem. The only constraint for this streaming problem type is that the problem function defines exactly one feasible output value as correct. A general streaming problem might have several optimal output values, as, e.g., the streaming problem answering the question: Which is the shortest path from one point to another? Therefore, the streaming decision problem is defined as follows.

Definition 3.4. *A **streaming decision problem** $\mathcal{S}_{decision} = (\mathcal{X}, \mathcal{Y}, f)$ is a streaming problem with the constraint that the problem function defines, for every possible input stream, exactly one feasible output value as the correct one.*

A binary streaming decision problem allows only two different feasible output values, namely $\mathcal{Y}_x := \{0, 1\}$. For every input stream, either 0 or 1 is the correct decision.

With the general and the two specialized definitions of a streaming problem, we will now discuss streaming algorithms, which may solve a certain streaming problem. Just like any classical algorithm, a streaming algorithm also produces a feasible output value for every possible input stream. As known from the introduction, streaming problems have massive data streams, which can only be read once, as the size of the entire input generally exceeds the storage limit. Now, a streaming algorithm can be understood as a series of n update-algorithm computations, in which every update-algorithm computation processes one input value and modifies the intermediate storage. This intermediate storage is a binary string of maximal size $d \in \mathbb{N}^+$ that has in total 2^d different states. Of course, a concrete implementation of a streaming algorithm does not have to store all d bits, e.g., when the first half of the bit string is only containing zeros. Therefore, the set of all storage states contains the empty bit string λ, the bit string "1" and all possible combinations of bit strings of length at most d which have a "1" at the beginning. Formally, this cache set is defined as:

$$\mathcal{C} = \{\lambda, 1\} \cup \Big\{(1, x) \mid x \in \{0, 1\}^i \text{ and } 1 \leq i \leq d - 1\Big\}.$$

As required, the different storage states have a size of 2^d, because,

$$|\mathcal{C}| = |\{\lambda, 1\}| + \left(\sum_{i=1}^{d-1} 2^i\right) = 2 + (2^d - 2) = 2^d.$$

The initial cache state is the empty bit string λ. During the algorithm execution, this cache can be used to store intermediate results. Finally, after considering all n input values, an output algorithm transforms the last cache state into a feasible output value of the streaming problem. This leads to the following definition of a streaming algorithm.

Definition 3.5. *A **streaming algorithm** $\mathcal{A} = (\mathcal{A}_{update}, \mathcal{A}_{output})$ for a streaming problem $\mathcal{S} = (\mathcal{X}, \mathcal{Y}, f)$ contains an update algorithm $\mathcal{A}_{update}$ such that $\mathcal{A}_{update}(c_{i-1}, x_i) = c_i$ and an output algorithm $\mathcal{A}_{output}$ such that $\mathcal{A}_{output}(c_n) = y \in \mathcal{Y}$.*

For an input stream $x \in \mathcal{X}$, the algorithm $\mathcal{A}$ computes a feasible output value $y = \mathcal{A}(x)$ using the following approach: First, the cache $c_0 \in \mathcal{C}$ is empty, namely $c_0 = \lambda$. Iteratively, all n inputs values are processed with the update algorithm $\mathcal{A}_{update}$, namely, for all $i \in (1, \ldots, n), c_i := \mathcal{A}_{update}(c_{i-1}, x_i)$. Then, the output value $y \in \mathcal{Y}_x$ is generated as $y := \mathcal{A}_{output}(c_n)$.

This means, the streaming algorithm $\mathcal{A}$ computes a series of intermediate cache storages $c_i \in \mathcal{C}$. The first update algorithm computation processes an empty cache state $c_0 = \lambda$ and the first input value $x_1 \in (x_1, \ldots, x_n) = x$, namely $\mathcal{A}_{update}(c_0, x_1) = c_1$. The next update computation processes the second input value, namely $\mathcal{A}_{update}(c_1, x_2) = c_2$. This is analogously repeated, until the last input value is processed, namely $\mathcal{A}_{update}(c_{n-1}, x_n) = c_n$.

We write $\mathcal{A}_{update}^k(c_i, x) = c_{i+k}$ to indicate that the update algorithm is executed k times on the starting cache state c_i, using the input values $(x_{i+1}, \ldots, x_{i+k})$. The input values have to be a substream of the input stream, namely $(x_{i+1}, \ldots, x_{i+k})$ is a substream of $(x_1, \ldots, x_n) = x$. One can therefore conclude that,

$$\mathcal{A}(x) = \mathcal{A}_{output}(c_n) = \mathcal{A}_{output}(\mathcal{A}_{update}^n(c_0, x)) = \mathcal{A}_{output}(\mathcal{A}_{update}^n(\lambda, x)).$$

We say that a streaming algorithm $\mathcal{A}$ *solves* a certain streaming problem $\mathcal{S}$ if $\mathcal{A}$ is a streaming algorithm for $\mathcal{S}$ as defined above. This implies that for every input stream $x \in \mathcal{X}$ of the streaming problem, the streaming algorithm computes a feasible output value, namely $\mathcal{A}(x) \in \mathcal{Y}_x$ for all $x \in \mathcal{X}$.

We assume, that the streaming algorithm knows the input stream size n.

The definition of *streaming problem* and *streaming algorithm* are leaned on the idea by Komm [Kom15], Prakash [Pra15], and Muthukrishnan [Mut05]. The definition of the frequency moment is based on the results by Alon et al. [AMS99].

3.2 Determinism and Randomization

Streaming problems can be solved by streaming algorithms that are either deterministic or probabilistic. For any input stream, a deterministic streaming algorithm produces the same intermediate cache states and final results in every computation. Therefore, Definition 3.5 defines a **deterministic streaming algorithm** $\mathcal{A}^{det}$. The next definition will demonstrate the essential difference between deterministic and probabilistic streaming algorithms.

Probabilistic algorithms use random decisions in their computations. Randomization is modelled by a random bit string. This random bit string contains a finite number of random bits, which are used for the algorithm's computation. The number of random bits depends on the input stream size n. Therefore, we define the length of the random bit string of at most $d(n) \in \mathbb{N}^+$. For the computation of a probabilistic algorithm $\mathcal{A}^{prob}$, both update and output algorithm may use some random bits $b \in \mathcal{B} = \bigcup_{l=0}^{d(n)} \{0, 1\}^l$. The number of consumed random bits at an update step or in the output algorithm can vary, based on the input stream and on previous random decisions. But the sum of all consumed random bits is limited by $d(n)$. The consequence of the use of these random bits is that the algorithm does not necessarily always produce the same cache states or the same final results. We define a probabilistic streaming algorithm as follows.

Definition 3.6. *A streaming algorithm $\mathcal{A}^{prob}$ for a streaming problem $\mathcal{S} = (\mathcal{X}, \mathcal{Y}, f)$ is called **probabilistic** if the algorithm uses, within the update or output computations, a random bit string b of length $l \leq d(n) \in \mathbb{N}^+$, namely $b \in \{0, 1\}^l$. The term $\mathcal{A}^{prob}(x)$ defines a probability distribution over all feasible output values $y \in \mathcal{Y}_x$, namely, for all $y \in \mathcal{Y}_x$, we have $0 \leq \Pr[y = \mathcal{A}^{prob}(x)] \leq 1$ and $\sum_{y \in \mathcal{Y}_x} \Pr[y = \mathcal{A}^{prob}(x)] = 1$.*

Note, that $\Pr[\ldots]$ is the used notation to indicate the probability of a certain event according to the given probability distribution.

As described, probabilistic algorithms do not necessarily always produce the same results for a fixed input stream $x \in \mathcal{X}$. We define the deterministic streaming algorithm $\mathcal{A}_b$ that uses an already generated random bit string b and produces the output $\mathcal{A}_b(x) = \mathcal{A}(x, b) = y \in \mathcal{Y}_x$. One can see that $\mathcal{A}^{prob}(x)$ computes the same probability distribution as the set of deterministic algorithms $\mathcal{A}(x, b)$ where the bit string $b \in \mathcal{B}$ is chosen uniformly at random. Using a random bit string of size $l \leq d(n)$, the probability of producing a certain output value $y \in \mathcal{Y}_x$ is defined by the probability distribution and can be calculated by identifying the number of different random bit strings which lead to the corresponding output value. Namely,

$$\Pr[y = \mathcal{A}^{prob}(x)] = \frac{|\{b \mid b \in \mathcal{B} \text{ and } y = \mathcal{A}(x, b)\}|}{2^l}.$$

For a probabilistic streaming algorithm $\mathcal{A}^{prob}$ for a decision problem $\mathcal{S}_{decision}$, the two special cases *one-sided* and *two-sided Monte Carlo algorithm* are defined.

Monte Carlo algorithms require the streaming decision problem to have binary decision values, i.e., there are only two possible decision values $\mathcal{Y}_x = \{0, 1\}$. In the following, these two types of algorithms are introduced.

Monte Carlo Algorithms

We call a probabilistic algorithm $\mathcal{A}^{prob}$ for a binary streaming decision problem $\mathcal{S}_{decision}$, in which there are only two decision possibilities, namely $\mathcal{Y}_x = \{0, 1\}$ for all input streams $x \in \mathcal{X}$, to be a *Monte Carlo algorithm* if we have a certain required success probability. This probabilistic streaming algorithm has to identify the correct decision with a probability of at least $\frac{1}{2}$. We further distinguish between the *one-sided Monte Carlo algorithm* and the *two-sided Monte Carlo algorithm*.

A one-sided Monte Carlo algorithm allows false positives, but never false negatives. This means that if the correct decision is one ($f(x) = 1$), then the algorithm always has to indicate this result. However, if the correct decision is zero ($f(x) = 0$), then the algorithm is required to produce this result at least in every second computation on average. This leads to the following definition.

Definition 3.7. *Let $\mathcal{A}^{prob}$ be a probabilistic streaming algorithm for a binary streaming decision problem $\mathcal{S}_{decision}$ with $\mathcal{Y}_x = \{0, 1\}$. We call $\mathcal{A}^{prob}$ a **one-sided Monte Carlo algorithm** if, for all $x \in \mathcal{X}$ with $f(x) = 1$, $\Pr[f(x) = \mathcal{A}^{prob}(x)] = 1$ and for all $x \in \mathcal{X}$ with $f(x) = 0$, $\Pr[f(x) = \mathcal{A}^{prob}(x)] \geq \frac{1}{2}$.*

Two-sided Monte Carlo algorithms are similar to one-sided algorithms, but now both false positives and false negatives are allowed. However, the probability of identifying the correct decision has to be at least $\frac{2}{3}$. Therefore, we have the following definition.

Definition 3.8. *Let $\mathcal{A}^{prob}$ be a probabilistic streaming algorithm for a binary streaming decision problem $\mathcal{S}_{decision}$ with $\mathcal{Y}_x = \{0, 1\}$. We call $\mathcal{A}^{prob}$ a **two-sided Monte Carlo algorithm** if, for all $x \in \mathcal{X}$, $\Pr[f(x) = \mathcal{A}^{prob}(x)] \geq \frac{2}{3}$.*

The definition of a probabilistic streaming algorithm is leaned on the results by Hromkovič [Hro97], Definition 2.5.5.1 on randomized protocols. The definition on 1- and 2-sided Monte Carlo algorithms are similar to the Definition 2.5.5.4 in [Hro97]

3.3 Space and Time Complexity

A streaming algorithm $\mathcal{A}$ for a streaming problem $\mathcal{S}$ can be analyzed with respect to its space and time complexity. The space complexity states the maximal number of required bits in the storage over the entire computation. As stated in the definition of a streaming algorithm (Definition 3.5), the algorithm is a composition of an update algorithm, which is executed n times for every input value and an output algorithm. Each update algorithm computation produces an intermediate result $c_i \in \mathcal{C}$, which is stored in the cache. The space complexity is the maximal number of bits required to store the intermediate results and the output value in the cache. We use the notation of $|c_i|$ and $|y|$ to represent the required number of bits to store the content of the cache state c_i and the output value y. Note, that $|c_i|$ and $|y|$ are not the absolute values, as both do not have to be numbers. Formally, we define the space complexity of a streaming algorithm $\mathcal{A}$ and a certain input stream $x \in \mathcal{X}$ as follows,

$$
\begin{aligned}
\text{space}(\mathcal{A}, x) &= \max\left\{ |c_1|, |c_2|, \ldots, |c_{n-1}|, |y| \right\} \\
&= \max\left\{ |\mathcal{A}_{update}(\lambda, x_1)|, |\mathcal{A}_{update}^2(\lambda, x)|, |\mathcal{A}_{update}^3(\lambda, x)|, \right. \\
&\qquad \left. \ldots, |\mathcal{A}_{update}^n(\lambda, x)|, |\mathcal{A}(x)| \right\}.
\end{aligned}
$$

The overall space complexity of a streaming algorithm is simply the worst case space complexity on all possible input streams with the corresponding stream length n, i.e.,

$$
\text{space}(\mathcal{A}) = \max\left\{ \text{space}(\mathcal{A}, x) \mid x \in \mathcal{X} \right\}.
$$

With the space complexity analysis of a streaming algorithm, one has an upper bound of the space complexity of the streaming problem $\mathcal{S}$. The space complexity of the streaming problem is the space complexity of the best streaming algorithm solving the problem, i.e.,

$$
\text{space}(\mathcal{S}) = \min\left\{ \text{space}(\mathcal{A}) \mid \mathcal{A} \text{ solves } \mathcal{S} \right\}.
$$

We conclude with this definition of the space complexity approximation.

Definition 3.9. *For any streaming algorithm $\mathcal{A}$ that solves $\mathcal{S}$, we define the **space complexity** as follows.*

$$
\text{space}(\mathcal{S}) \leq \text{space}(\mathcal{A}) = \max\left\{ \text{space}(\mathcal{A}, x) \mid x \in \mathcal{X} \in \mathcal{S} \right\}.
$$

We have seen how the space complexity of a streaming algorithm $\mathcal{A}$ can be evaluated. On the other hand, the time complexity indicates the required computation time. Time complexity analysis is always done using the big-$\mathcal{O}$ notation. Basic mathematical operations such as comparison, addition, or multiplication on values with a fixed size are made within $\mathcal{O}(1)$ time steps. These basic mathematical operations on numbers relative to n, i.e., $i \in \{1, \ldots, n\}$, require a time complexity of $\mathcal{O}(\log(n))$. Similarly, computations on the input values of a streaming counting problem with input values $x_i \in \{1, \ldots, m\}$ have a time complexity of $\mathcal{O}(\log(m))$.

Read or write requests to the storage of (current) size k require $\mathcal{O}(\log(k))$ time steps for a random-access storage.

With these time measures, the time complexities of the update and output-algorithms can be identified. Formally, time$(\mathcal{A}_{update})$ and time$(\mathcal{A}_{output})$ are the sum of the individual basic time measures. The update time complexities indicate the required time for processing a single input value. For the time complexity analysis of a streaming algorithm, we are interested in two different measures. First, the worst-case time complexity for a single update algorithm basically indicates how fast the individual input values of an input stream can be evaluated or, in other words, how fast they might arrive.

Definition 3.10. *We define the **update time complexity** of a streaming algorithm as the worst-case time complexity of a single update algorithm execution, which is,*

$$\text{update-time}(\mathcal{A}) = \max\{\text{time}(\mathcal{A}_{update}(c_{i-1}, x_i)) \mid$$
$$1 \leq i \leq n, c_{i-1} \in \mathcal{C} \text{ and } x_i \in x \in \mathcal{X}\}.$$

Second, the overall time complexity is the sum of all update time complexities and the output time complexity. For a fixed input stream $x \in \mathcal{X}$, this is:

$$\text{time}(\mathcal{A}, x) = \sum_{i=1}^{n} \text{time}(\mathcal{A}_{update}(c_{i-1}, x_i))$$
$$+ \text{time}(\mathcal{A}_{output}(c_n)).$$

We state the second definition on the time complexity.

Definition 3.11. *The overall **time complexity** is the worst-case time complexity for any possible input streams $x \in \mathcal{X}$:*

$$\text{time}(\mathcal{A}) = \max\{\text{time}(\mathcal{A}, x) \mid x \in \mathcal{X}\}.$$

For probabilistic algorithms, the worst-case time complexities state the maximal required time for any possible random decision $b \in \mathcal{B}$.

3.4   Approximation Ratio and Success Probability

In this section, the approximation ratio for streaming counting problems is introduced, which defines the approximation of an output value, compared to the optimal output value. Afterwards, the success probability for probabilistic algorithms is defined that renders the probability that the algorithm produces the optimal output value or one within an acceptable approximation ratio. With approximation ratio and success probability, the deterministic, exact streaming problem can be modified to get a deeper analysis and a more differentiated understanding of the usefulness of additional information.

Approximation Ratio of a Streaming Counting Problem

A streaming algorithm $\mathcal{A}$ (a deterministic or probabilistic one) for a streaming counting problem $\mathcal{S}_{\#}$ (see Definition 3.2) may produce results with a tolerated approximation of the optimal output value. We will first introduce how one can identify the approximation ratio of a given streaming algorithm for a streaming maximization problem.

Basically, the approximation ratio stands for the fraction between the optimal result and the output value produced by the streaming algorithm. The approximation ratio α may have any value $\alpha \in \mathbb{R}, \alpha \geq 1$, where an approximation ratio of $\alpha = 1$ implies an optimal result. In more general terms, the lower the approximation ratio, the more accurate the result.

Suppose we are given a deterministic streaming algorithm $\mathcal{A}^{det}$ that solves a streaming counting problem $\mathcal{S}_{\#} = (\mathcal{X}, \mathcal{Y}, f, s)$. Then, for a certain input stream $x \in \mathcal{X}$ and the output value $\mathcal{A}^{det}(x) = y \in \mathcal{Y}_x$, we define the approximation value for this specific input stream as the fraction between the produced output value and the optimal value, namely,

$$approx(\mathcal{A}^{det}, x) = \max\left\{ \frac{f(x)}{\mathcal{A}^{det}(x)}, \frac{\mathcal{A}^{det}(x)}{f(x)} \right\}.$$

The max-clause is used for both the approximation value below the optimal output value (first term) and the approximation values above the optimal output value (second term). We observe that if and only if the streaming algorithm produces the optimal value, the approximation value is 1. Furthermore, we define the approximation ratio over all input streams as follows.

Definition 3.12. *Let $\mathcal{A}^{det}$ be a deterministic streaming algorithm for a streaming counting problem $\mathcal{S}_{\#} = (\mathcal{X}, \mathcal{Y}, f, s)$. The **approximation ratio** is the maximal approximation value among all possible input streams, which is,*

$$\text{approx-rate}(\mathcal{A}^{det}, \mathcal{X}) = \max\{approx(\mathcal{A}^{det}, x) \mid x \in \mathcal{X}\}$$
$$= \max\left\{ \frac{f(x)}{\mathcal{A}^{det}(x)}, \frac{\mathcal{A}^{det}(x)}{f(x)} \middle| x \in \mathcal{X} \right\}.$$

We observe that this definition of the approximation ratio may always allow approximative output values both above and below the optimal output value. Sometimes, only a 1-sided approximation with feasible output values below the optimal result is allowed. Then, we define the approximation value only with output values below the optimal result as valid. This is formally defined as follows.

Definition 3.13. *Let $\mathcal{A}^{det}$ be a deterministic streaming algorithm for a streaming counting problem $\mathcal{S}_{\#} = (\mathcal{X}, \mathcal{Y}, f, s)$. The **1-sided approximation ratio** is the maximal 1-sided approximation value among all possible input streams, which is,*

$$\text{1-sided-approx-rate}(\mathcal{A}^{det}, \mathcal{X}) = \max\{\text{1-sided-approx}(\mathcal{A}^{det}, x) \mid x \in \mathcal{X}\} \text{ with}$$

$$\text{1-sided-approx}(\mathcal{A}^{det}, x) = \begin{cases} \frac{f(x)}{\mathcal{A}^{det}(x)}, & \text{if } \mathcal{A}^{det}(x) \leq f(x) \\ \infty, & \text{else.} \end{cases} \tag{3.1}$$

This definition of the 1-sided approximation ratio assumes that the streaming counting problem is a maximization problem. With the second case of (3.1), we ensure feasible output values below the optima one, as the approximation ratio is infinite and, as a consequence, useless.

Corollary 3.1. *For a certain deterministic streaming algorithm $\mathcal{A}^{det}$ that solves a streaming counting problem $\mathcal{S}_\#$ with an approximation ratio* approx-rate$(\mathcal{A}^{det}, \mathcal{X}) = 1$, *$\mathcal{A}^{det}$ always produces an optimal output result for every possible input stream $x \in \mathcal{X}$.*

For a probabilistic streaming algorithm $\mathcal{A}^{prob}$, we can determine a success probability for any fixed approximation ratio $\alpha \geq 1$, which is introduced in the following. For a single computation, which uses a certain random bit string $b \in \mathcal{B}$, we can similarly define the approximation value,

$$approx(\mathcal{A}^{prob}, x, b) = \max\left\{ \frac{f(x)}{\mathcal{A}^{prob\cdot}(x,b)}, \frac{\mathcal{A}^{prob}(x,b)}{f(x)} \right\}.$$

Based on this approximation value of a single computation, we will see in the following how one can evaluate the lowest approximation ratio for a fixed success probability such that the success probability is still given. Some streaming algorithms have the possibility to produce an arbitrarily good approximation ratio $\alpha = 1 + \varepsilon$ for any small $\varepsilon > 0$.

Success Probability

Besides the approximation ratio, we introduce the success probability. For a probabilistic streaming algorithm $\mathcal{A}^{prob}$ that solves a certain streaming counting problem $\mathcal{S}_\#$, we define the success ratio as the probability that $\mathcal{A}^{prob}$ produces a result within the tolerated approximation ratio. We define, for a fixed input stream $x \in \mathcal{X}$, the set of all output values within the approximation ratio $\alpha \geq 1$ as $\tilde{\mathcal{Y}}_x^\alpha$, which is,

$$\tilde{\mathcal{Y}}_x^\alpha = \left\{ y \mid y \in \mathcal{Y}_x \text{ and } \frac{f(x)}{\alpha} \leq y \leq f(x) \cdot \alpha \right\}.$$

Given a probabilistic streaming algorithm $\mathcal{A}^{prob}$ for a streaming counting problem $\mathcal{S}_\#$ and a fixed approximation ratio $\alpha \geq 1$, the success probability to produce an output value within the tolerated approximation is the sum of all individual probabilities, that $\mathcal{A}^{prob}$ outputs any $\tilde{y}_x \in \tilde{\mathcal{Y}}_x$. Therefore,

$$success(\mathcal{A}^{prob}, x, \alpha) = pr\left[\frac{f(x)}{\alpha} \leq \mathcal{A}^{prob}(x) \leq f(x) \cdot \alpha \right]$$
$$= \sum_{\tilde{y}_x \in \tilde{\mathcal{Y}}_x^\alpha} pr\left[\mathcal{A}^{prob}(x) = \tilde{y}_x \right].$$

Similarly to the approximation ratio, we can define the success probability of a probabilistic streaming algorithm for a streaming counting problem as the lowest success ratio among all possible input streams.

Definition 3.14. *For a probabilistic streaming algorithm $\mathcal{A}^{prob}$ solving a streaming counting problem $\mathcal{S}_\# = (\mathcal{X}, \mathcal{Y}, f, s)$ and an approximation ratio $\alpha \geq 1$, the **success probability** for the streaming counting problem is defined as,*

$$success\text{-}probability(\mathcal{A}^{prob}, \mathcal{X}, \alpha) = \min\{success(\mathcal{A}^{prob}, x, \alpha) \mid x \in \mathcal{X}\}.$$

If and only if the success probability is 1, then the probabilistic streaming algorithm always produces a result within the allowed approximation ratio. We use the notation $S_{\alpha,p}$ to indicate a streaming problem with an approximation ratio of $\alpha \geq 1$ and a success probability of $p \leq 1$.

Similarly to the case of a streaming counting problem, we can define the success probability for a probabilistic streaming algorithm $\mathcal{A}^{prob}$ on a streaming decision problem $S_{decision}$. As we do not have approximation ratios because streaming decision problem just distinguish between correct and wrong decisions, the success probability just measures the minimum probability to produce the correct result over all possible input streams.

Definition 3.15. *For a probabilistic streaming algorithm $\mathcal{A}^{prob}$ solving a streaming decision problem $S_{decision} = (\mathcal{X}, \mathcal{Y}, f)$, the **success probability** for the streaming decision problem is defined as,*

$$\text{success-probability}(\mathcal{A}^{prob}, \mathcal{X}) = \min\left\{ \Pr[\mathcal{A}^{prob}(x) = f(x)] \mid x \in \mathcal{X} \right\}.$$

As stated before, studies of approximation ratios of $\alpha > 1$ for streaming decision problems are meaningless. Here, we are only interested in the success probabilities of exact solutions using the same formulas as above but simply with $\alpha = 1$. Generally, a probabilistic streaming algorithm $\mathcal{A}^{prob}$ for a streaming decision problem $S_{decision}$ is required to have a fixed success probability of at least $p > \frac{1}{2}$. Otherwise it is possible that a wrong decision may be amplified more often than the correct one. An exception is the 1-sided Monte Carlo algorithm, as there are only two possible values and the wrong decision cannot be amplified, as false negatives are not allowed.

In a deterministic environment, the study of different success probabilities other than 1 is obviously not meaningful, as deterministic streaming algorithms do not use any random bits.

3.5 Solvability

In this section, some measures are introduced by which a certain streaming algorithm can be identified as practical or useful. As explained in the introduction, the algorithm cannot store the entire input stream and compute the entire function in the last final output algorithm. It was also stated that the required space complexity should be sub-linear. But what does this mean in detail?

We will recall the definition from the well-known complexity class *POLYLOG* and use this measure to classify the required space complexity of a streaming algorithm as *space-efficient* (if it is poly-logarithmic) or *not space-efficient* (if it is not poly-logarithmic). If a space-efficient algorithm for a certain streaming problem has a poly-logarithmic time complexity for each update algorithm computation, we then call the corresponding streaming problem *efficiently solvable*. If we can prove that any possible streaming algorithm that solves a certain streaming problem has either a not space-efficient space complexity or any update algorithm computation has a time complexity outside the poly-logarithmic class, we then call this streaming problem *not efficiently solvable*.

Later, this classification of streaming problems into efficiently solvable and not efficiently solvable will be very helpful to distinguish different streaming problems and the possible advantage of additional information like hypothesis verification. Now we will introduce these categories more formally.

First, we recall: A streaming algorithm $\mathcal{A}$ is said to *solve* a streaming problem $\mathcal{S}_{\alpha,p}$ with an approximation ratio $\alpha \geq 1$ and a success probability $p \leq 1$ if, for every possible input stream $x \in \mathcal{X}$, it writes an output value within the approximation ratio with at least the according success probability. Streaming decision problems always have an approximation ratio of $\alpha = 1$ to ensure correct decisions.

As a basis: The poly-logarithmic complexity class $POLYLOG(n)$ includes all algorithms $\mathcal{A}$, where there exists a $d \in \mathbb{N}^+$, such that *time-complexity*$(\mathcal{A}) \in \mathcal{O}(\log^d(n))$ and *space-complexity*$(\mathcal{A}) \in \mathcal{O}(\log^d(n))$. The word *polylogarithmic* is standardized by NIST and , for example, listed in the dictionary of algorithms and data structures by Sant [San04].

Definition 3.16. *A streaming algorithm $\mathcal{A}$ for a streaming problem $\mathcal{S} = (\mathcal{X}, \mathcal{Y}, f)$ with input streams $x \in \mathcal{X}$ of length $n = |x|$ is said to be* **space-efficient***, if* space$(\mathcal{A}, \mathcal{X}) \in POLYLOG(n)$. *On the other hand, if* space$(\mathcal{A}, \mathcal{X}) \notin POLYLOG(n)$, *the streaming algorithm $\mathcal{A}$ for $\mathcal{S}$ is called* **not space-efficient***.*

A streaming problem $\mathcal{S}$ is said to be **efficiently solvable** *if there exists a space-efficient streaming algorithm $\mathcal{A}$ that solves the streaming problem $\mathcal{S}$ and each update algorithm computation has* time$(\mathcal{A}_{update}) \in POLYLOG(n)$ *and the output algorithm has* time$(\mathcal{A}_{output}) \in POLYLOG(n)$.

A streaming problem $\mathcal{S}$ is said to be **not efficiently solvable** *if, for any possible streaming algorithm $\mathcal{A}$ that solves $\mathcal{S}$, either* space$(\mathcal{A}, \mathcal{X}) \notin POLYLOG(n)$ *or there exists an update algorithm computation such that* time$(\mathcal{A}_{update}) \notin POLYLOG(n)$.

Of course, to prove that a streaming problem is not efficiently solvable by verifying that the time complexity of a certain update algorithm is outside the poly-logarithmic class is very difficult, as hardly any time-complexity lower bound proofs exist. Therefore, the later presented proofs of streaming problems being not efficiently solvable are made by disproving space-efficiency.

3.6 Basic Calculations

For several analyses, the binomial coefficient $\binom{n}{k}$ has to be approximated. We will provide the used approximation at this point, so that this proof and calculation does not have to be repeated. The main content of this approximation is described in [Dob10] in Exercise 2.151, a) and b).

Lemma 3.1 (Dobrushkin [Dob10], Exercise 2.151, b). *For any $n, k \in \mathbb{N}^+$ with $0 < k < n$:*

$$\left(\frac{n}{k}\right)^k < \binom{n}{k} < \frac{n^n}{k^k \cdot (n-k)^{n-k}}.$$

Lemma 3.2 (Dobrushkin [Dob10], Exercise 2.151, a). *For any $n \in \mathbb{N}^+$,*

$$\frac{2^n}{\sqrt{2n}} < \binom{n}{n/2} < \frac{2^n}{\sqrt{1.5n+1}}.$$

Lemma 3.3. *For any $n \in \mathbb{N}^+$,*

$$\binom{n}{n/2-1} > \frac{2^n \cdot \sqrt{2n}}{2n+4}.$$

Proof. We prove this lemma by starting from the result of Lemma 3.2, which is $\frac{2^n}{\sqrt{2n}} < \binom{n}{n/2}$. Using a simple relation between $\binom{n}{n/2-1}$ and $\binom{n}{n/2}$ will lead to the above stated approximation:

$$\binom{n}{n/2-1} = \frac{n!}{(n/2-1)! \cdot (n/2+1)!} \qquad \text{definition of binomial coefficient}$$

$$= \frac{n! \cdot (n/2)}{(n/2)! \cdot (n/2)! \cdot (n/2+1)} \qquad \text{basic transformation}$$

$$= \binom{n}{n/2} \cdot \frac{n/2}{n/2+1} \qquad \text{definition of binomial coefficent}$$

Therefore, we can replace the left side of the claim using the equality,

$$\binom{n}{n/2-1} = \binom{n}{n/2} \cdot \frac{n/2}{n/2+1} \qquad \text{transformation from above}$$

$$= \binom{n}{n/2} \cdot \frac{n}{n+2} \qquad \text{basic transformation}$$

$$> \frac{2^n \cdot n}{\sqrt{2n} \cdot (n+2)} \qquad \text{Lemma 3.2}$$

$$= \frac{2^n \cdot \sqrt{2n}}{2n+4}. \qquad \text{basic transformation} \qquad \square$$

Next, we want to approximate $\binom{n}{n/4}$. The proof for this approximation is a bit more complicated, as the stated approximation for the general case $\binom{n}{k}$ (Lemma 3.1) leads to a very bad approximation, namely,

$$\binom{n}{\frac{n}{4}} > \left(\frac{n}{\frac{n}{4}}\right)^{\frac{n}{4}} = 4^{\frac{n}{4}} = 2^{0.5n} \ll 2^{0.915n} \approx \binom{n}{\frac{n}{4}}$$

With the approach of the following, hand-made proof, we can achieved the last approximation, namely, $2^{0.915n}$ and one can similarly verify the referenced exercise from the literature used in Lemma 3.1 and Lemma 3.2.

Lemma 3.4. *For any $n > 100, n = 4 \cdot l, l \in \mathbb{N}^+$,*

$$\binom{n}{n/4} > \frac{0.916}{\sqrt{n}} \cdot 2^{n \cdot (\frac{1}{2} + \log_2(4/3))} > \frac{0.916}{\sqrt{n}} \cdot 2^{0.915n}.$$

Proof. First, we have to recall the *Stirling formula* for the approximation of the faculty,

$$\sqrt{2\pi n} \cdot \left(\frac{n}{e}\right)^n \leq n! \leq \sqrt{2\pi n} \cdot \left(\frac{n}{e}\right)^n \cdot e^{\frac{1}{12n}}.$$

With the *Stirling formula* we get the following approximation.

$$\binom{n}{n/4} = \frac{n!}{(\frac{n}{4})! \cdot (\frac{3n}{4})!} \tag{3.2}$$

$$\geq \frac{\sqrt{2\pi n} \cdot (\frac{n}{e})^n}{\left(\sqrt{2\pi \frac{n}{4}} \cdot (\frac{(\frac{n}{4})}{e})^{\frac{n}{4}} \cdot e^{\frac{4}{12n}}\right) \cdot \left(\sqrt{2\pi \frac{3n}{4}} \cdot (\frac{\frac{n}{4}}{e})^{\frac{3n}{4}} \cdot e^{\frac{4}{12 \cdot 3n}}\right)} \tag{3.3}$$

$$= \frac{\sqrt{2\pi n} \cdot (\frac{n}{e})^n}{\left(\sqrt{\pi \frac{n}{2}} \cdot (\frac{n}{4e})^{\frac{n}{4}} \cdot e^{\frac{1}{3n}}\right) \cdot \left(\sqrt{\pi \frac{3n}{2}} \cdot (\frac{3n}{4e})^{\frac{3n}{4}} \cdot e^{\frac{1}{9n}}\right)} \tag{3.4}$$

$$= \frac{\sqrt{2\pi n} \cdot (\frac{n}{e})^n}{\frac{\sqrt{3}}{2}\pi n \cdot (\frac{n}{4e})^n \cdot 3^{\frac{3n}{4}} \cdot e^{\frac{4}{9n}}} = \frac{\frac{\sqrt{2\pi n} \cdot n^n}{e^n}}{\frac{\sqrt{3}\pi n \cdot n^n \cdot 3^{\frac{3n}{4}} \cdot e^{\frac{4}{9n}}}{2 \cdot (4e)^n}} \tag{3.5}$$

$$= \frac{\sqrt{2\pi n} \cdot n^n \cdot 2 \cdot (4e)^n}{e^n \cdot \sqrt{3}\pi n \cdot n^n \cdot 3^{\frac{3n}{4}} \cdot e^{\frac{4}{9n}}} = \frac{\sqrt{2\pi n} \cdot 2 \cdot 4^n}{\sqrt{3}\pi n \cdot 3^{\frac{3n}{4}} \cdot e^{\frac{4}{9n}}} \tag{3.6}$$

After replacing the binomial coefficient with the corresponding faculties (3.2), we approximate these faculties using the Stirling approximation from above (3.3). (3.4) and (3.5) are some basic mathematical transformations to simplify the term. The end of (3.5) leads to the possibility of transforming the double fraction to a simple fraction in (3.6), in which in the last term equal parts are cancelled.

Some parts of this remaining term can now be simply approximated. These are $\sqrt{2\pi} > 2.506$, and $\sqrt{3} \cdot \pi < 5.442$. Furthermore, for any $n > 100$, one can easily verify that $e^{\frac{4}{9n}} < 1.005$. Therefore, we can use this approximations to make the term simpler:

$$\binom{n}{n/4} \geq \frac{\sqrt{2\pi n} \cdot 2 \cdot 4^n}{\sqrt{3}\pi n \cdot 3^{\frac{3n}{4}} \cdot e^{\frac{4}{9n}}} \qquad \text{approx. as above}$$

$$> \frac{2 \cdot 2.506 \cdot \sqrt{n} \cdot 4^n}{5.442 \cdot n \cdot 3^{\frac{3n}{4}} \cdot 1.005} \qquad \text{using new single approx.}$$

$$> 0.916 \cdot \frac{\sqrt{n} \cdot 4^n}{n \cdot 3^{0.75n}} \qquad \text{basic transformations}$$

$$= 0.916 \cdot \frac{\sqrt{n} \cdot 4^{0.25n}}{n} \cdot \frac{4^{0.75n}}{3^{0.75n}} \qquad \text{split } 4^n \text{ into } 4^{0.25n} \cdot 4^{0.75n}$$

$$= 0.916 \cdot \frac{2^{0.5n}}{\sqrt{n}} \cdot \left(\frac{4}{3}\right)^{0.75n} \qquad \text{basic transformations}$$

Now, one can transform $\frac{4}{3} = 2^{log_2\left(\frac{4}{3}\right)} > 2^{0.415}$. With this approximation we can prove the statement of the lemma:

$$\binom{n}{n/2} > 0.916 \cdot \frac{2^{0.5n}}{\sqrt{n}} \cdot \left(\frac{4}{3}\right)^{0.75n} \qquad \text{approx. as above}$$

$$= \frac{0.916}{\sqrt{n}} \cdot 2^{n \cdot \left(\frac{1}{2} + \log_2(4/3)\right)} \qquad \text{replace } \left(\frac{4}{3}\right) \text{ as explained}$$

$$> \frac{0.916}{\sqrt{n}} \cdot 2^{0.915n} \qquad \text{final, basic transformation} \qquad \square$$

Chapter 4

Lower Bounds on Space Complexity

For every streaming problem $\mathcal{S}$, we want to analyze both upper and lower bounds for the achievable space complexity. For the upper bound, one has to find a certain streaming algorithm that solves $\mathcal{S}$. Such an algorithm can afterwards be analyzed with respect to its required space and time complexities. To prove a lower bound on the space complexity, the technique of communication complexity theory is used, which is described by Hromkovič [Hro97] or in the initial paper by Yao [Yao79].

4.1 Introduction to Communication Complexity

Communication complexity is a study area that tries to identify the required communication for a distributed algorithmic problem. The most common model is the two-computer model, in which two distributed computers have to calculate a certain function value. Both computers have a part of the input value and have unbounded computation power and storage resources, but a limited communication channel to each other. The main question is: How many communication bits do the two computers have to exchange to calculate the function value for a given input value separation? With this model, it is possible to mathematically analyze lower bounds on the communication complexity.

One special type of the communication complexity is the one-way communication. In this model, we have two computers, named as the left one C_L and the right one C_R, both having a part of the input value. In the one-way communication model, only the left computer is allowed to communicate to the other computer. To evaluate a certain function on the distributed input value, the left computer processes its input value part and transmits some communication. The right computer uses this communication and the second input value part to compute the function.

Obviously, if the left computer transmits its whole input value part, the right computer can easily evaluate the correct output value, as it has unbounded storage and computation resources. For some functions, the output value can be computed with a significantly lower communication complexity. For example, if one wants to identify the highest integer of a certain set of integers as input values, that is distributed among the two computers, the left computer can just communicate its maximal integer and the right computer outputs the correct output value easily. With this approach, we have a space complexity of one integer instead of communicating the whole input value part.

For this model of one-way communication, we can define a fooling set that allows us to prove a certain communication complexity lower bound. The idea of a fooling set is to list some input value candidates, that force any algorithm to use different communications from C_L to C_R in order to distinguish these input value candidates. This concept of one-way communication between two computers can be transformed to a streaming problem setting where we can prove a certain space complexity lower bound. In the following, we will define two fooling set concepts and prove in the following section why these fooling sets imply a space complexity lower bound for streaming problems.

But first, we have to define the deterministic one-way communication more formally: For the two computers C_L and C_R we may introduce a fooling set $\mathcal{F}$ containing d input values $I^i \in \mathcal{X}$, where $\mathcal{X}$ is the set of all feasible input values and each $I^i = (I^i_L, I^i_R)$ has an input value partition on the two computers C_L and C_R, where I^i_L is assigned to C_L and I^i_R to C_R. The first kind of fooling set approach is described in detail by Ablayev [Abl96], and the second one by Hromkovič [Hro97].

One can define a fooling set for the one-way communication complexity as the combination of a set of *representatives* and a *test set*. The representatives are located at the left computer, the tests at the right one. Such a combination is called a *fooling set* if, for every two representatives, there is at least one test such that the communication from C_L to C_R has to be different. This is the case if the correct algorithm has to compute two different output values for these two representatives combined with the same test entry. This communication complexity concept can be used to prove space complexity lower bounds for streaming problems. Formally, a fooling set for a streaming problem is defined as follows.

Definition 4.1. *For a streaming problem* $\mathcal{S} = (\mathcal{X}, \mathcal{Y}, f)$, *a **fooling set** $\mathcal{F} = (\mathcal{F}_L, \mathcal{F}_R)$ contains a set of representatives* $\mathcal{F}_L = \{I^1_L, \ldots, I^d_L\}$ *and a test set* $\mathcal{F}_R = \{I^1_R, \ldots, I^{d'}_R\}$, *such that each combination of representative and test is an input stream, i.e.,* $\forall I^i_L \in \mathcal{F}_L, \forall I^j_R \in \mathcal{F}_R \colon (I^i_L, I^j_R) \in \mathcal{X}$. $\mathcal{F} = (\mathcal{F}_L, \mathcal{F}_R)$ *is a fooling set for $\mathcal{S}$ if*

$$\forall I^i_L, I^j_L \in \mathcal{F}_L \text{ with } I^i_L \neq I^j_L \colon \exists I^v_R \in \mathcal{F}_R \text{ s.t. } f(I^i_L, I^v_R) \neq f(I^j_L, I^v_R).$$

We call $\mathcal{F}_R$ a *test* for the representatives $\mathcal{F}_L$ if $\mathcal{F} = (\mathcal{F}_L, \mathcal{F}_R)$ is a fooling set for the given streaming problem.

In the second approach, the space complexity lower bound is calculated using the matrix rank from an output value matrix. Similarly to the first approach, a *matrix fooling set* defines two input value sets for the left and the right computer. The output value matrix defines, for every possible combination of input values from the left and the right computer, the result of a correct algorithm, namely the problem function f of the streaming problem $\mathcal{S}$. The rank of this output value matrix defines the space complexity lower bound. The following definition gives a more formal description.

Definition 4.2. *For a streaming problem* $S = (\mathcal{X}, \mathcal{Y}, f)$, *the **matrix fooling set** $\mathcal{F} = (\mathcal{F}_L, \mathcal{F}_R)$ contains two input sets $\mathcal{F}_L = \{I_L^1, \ldots, I_L^{d''}\}$ and $\mathcal{F}_R = \{I_R^1, \ldots, I_R^{d'}\}$, such that each combination is an input stream, i.e., $\forall I_L^i \in \mathcal{F}_L, \forall I_R^j \in \mathcal{F}_R: (I_L^i, I_R^j) \in \mathcal{X}$. The result matrix $\mathcal{M}$ with the entries of $\mathcal{F}_L$ as rows and $\mathcal{F}_R$ as columns is defined as $\mathcal{M}(i,j) = f(I_L^i, I_R^j)$.*

The rank of the result matrix $d = \mathrm{rank}(\mathcal{M})$ is the fooling set size.

With a *matrix fooling set* of rank d, we have d independent columns and, as a consequence, d different input value parts that have to be distinguished from the right computer C_R, and therefore we have an equivalent situation as with a *fooling set* of size d from the first approach.

Based on these two approaches, with a fooling set $\mathcal{F}$ with either size d in the first approach or a result matrix of rank d in the second approach, a communication complexity lower bound of at least $\log_2(d)$ between these two computers is proven. We define $|\mathcal{F}| := |\mathcal{F}_L| = d$ for the first approach and $|\mathcal{F}| := \mathrm{rank}(\mathcal{M}) = d \leq \max\{|\mathcal{F}_L|, |\mathcal{F}_R|\}$ for the second approach.

4.2 Lower Bound for General Streaming Problems

In the following, we show how the techniques of communication complexity can be used for lower bounds on the space complexity of deterministic and probabilistic streaming problems that require an exact result or may allow approximative output values.

Lower Bound for an Exact Deterministic Streaming Problem

With the following theorem, one can prove space complexity lower bounds for an exact deterministic streaming problem, i.e., the approximation ratio is $\alpha = 1$ and the success probability is $p = 1$. Such problems are abbreviated by $S_{1,1}$.

Theorem 4.1. *A fooling set $\mathcal{F}$ of size $|\mathcal{F}| = d$ for a streaming problem S proves, for an exact (approximation ratio $\alpha = 1$) and deterministic (success probability $p = 1$) setting, a space complexity lower bound of size*

$$\mathrm{space}(S_{1,1}) \geq \log_2(d) = \log_2(|\mathcal{F}|).$$

Proof. An input stream $x = (x_1, \ldots, x_n) \in \mathcal{X}$ for a streaming problem S can be split into two sub-streams $x' = (x_1, \ldots, x_l)$ and $x'' = (x_{l+1}, \ldots, x_n)$ for any input stream cut $l \in \{1, \ldots, n-1\}$. The streaming algorithm is forced to process first the sub-stream x' and only then x''. Thus, it can be understood as one-way communication from a (left) computer processing x', which then transmits its intermediate storage $c_l \in \mathcal{C}$ to a (right) computer that processes the second sub-stream x'' and generates the final output value.

Or in other words, the first (left) computer C_L is given the input values $I_L = (x_1, \ldots, x_l) \in \mathcal{F}_L$, and the second (right) computer C_R is given the input values $I_R = (x_{l+1}, \ldots, x_n) \in \mathcal{F}_R$, for any input stream cut $l \in \{1, \ldots, n-1\}$. The communication complexity lower bound for this distributed problem with a cut and the two computers C_L and C_R allow to bound the minimally required space after reading $(x_1, \ldots, x_l)$ to compute the correct result for S.

Therefore, a fooling set of size $|\mathcal{F}| = d$ for the distributed two-computer model with any cut l implies a space complexity lower bound for the streaming problem $\mathcal{S}$ of size $\mathrm{space}(\mathcal{S}_{1,1}) \geq \log_2(d)$.   □

This deterministic lower bound is now extended to cases where randomization is allowed to compute the result.

Lower Bound for an Exact Probabilistic Streaming Problem

The following space complexity lower bounds (Theorem 4.2 and Theorem 4.3) for probabilistic (streaming) problems were introduced by Ablayev [Abl96]. As this thesis uses a slightly different notation than the referred paper, the theorems are restated using our notation.

The first result states that the probabilistic space complexity lower bound is in the logarithmic order of the deterministic one.

Theorem 4.2 (Ablayev [Abl96], Theorem 4). *Let $\mathcal{S}$ be a (streaming) problem with a fooling set $\mathcal{F} = (\mathcal{F}_L, \mathcal{F}_R)$ according to the first approach with representatives $\mathcal{F}_L$ and a test set $\mathcal{F}_R$. The exact probabilistic (streaming) problem (approximation ratio $\alpha = 1$) with a success probability $p > \frac{1}{2}$ has a space complexity lower bound of,*

$$\mathrm{space}(\mathcal{S}_{1,p}) \geq \log_2(\mathrm{space}(\mathcal{S}_{1,1})) - \log_2\left(\log_2\left(\frac{2 \cdot p + 1}{2 \cdot p - 1}\right)\right) - 1$$

$$\geq \log_2(\log_2(|\mathcal{F}_L|)) - \log_2\left(\log_2\left(\frac{2 \cdot p + 1}{2 \cdot p - 1}\right)\right) - 1.$$

For success probabilities that are not very close to $\frac{1}{2}$, the second term of this lower bound is insignificant. Therefore, we state the following corollary.

Corollary 4.1. *Let $\mathcal{S}$ be a (streaming) problem with a fooling set $\mathcal{F} = (\mathcal{F}_L, \mathcal{F}_R)$ according to the first approach with representatives $\mathcal{F}_L$ and test $\mathcal{F}_R$. The exact probabilistic (streaming) problem (approximation ratio $\alpha = 1$) with a success probability $p \geq 0.505$ has a space complexity lower bound of,*

$$\mathrm{space}(\mathcal{S}_{1,p}) \geq \log_2(\mathrm{space}(\mathcal{S}_{1,1})) - 4 \geq \log_2(\log_2(|\mathcal{F}_L|)) - 4.$$

Proof. This corollary can easily be verified by evaluating the second term of Theorem 4.2 with success probabilities of $p \geq 0.505$.   □

The next theorem proves a lower bound on the probabilistic space complexity that is sometimes closer to the deterministic one. For this purpose, it is required that the test set is minimal. The minimality of the test is proven when it is shown that every test entry has to be used to verify the fooling set. Or in other words, the test set is minimal if the removal of just one test entry would make it impossible to justify the fooling set.

Theorem 4.3 (Ablayev [Abl96], Theorem 1). *Let S be a (streaming) problem with a fooling set $\mathcal{F} = (\mathcal{F}_L, \mathcal{F}_R)$ according to the first approach with representatives $\mathcal{F}_L$ and a minimal test set $\mathcal{F}_R$. The exact probabilistic (streaming) problem (approximation ratio $\alpha = 1$) with success probability $p > \frac{1}{2}$ has a space complexity lower bound of*

$$\text{space}(S_{1,p}) \geq \text{space}(S_{1,1}) \cdot \left(1 - \frac{|\mathcal{F}_R|}{\text{space}(S_{1,1})} \cdot h(p)\right) - 1$$

$$\geq \log_2(|\mathcal{F}_L|) \cdot \left(1 - \frac{|\mathcal{F}_R|}{\log_2(|\mathcal{F}_L|)} \cdot h(p)\right) - 1,$$

with $h(p) = -p \cdot \log_2(p) - (1-p) \cdot \log_2(1-p)$.

As stated above, we have to verify the minimality of the test set to use this theorem. We can do this by showing that any single test is required. This means literally that for any test (4.1), there are two representatives (4.2) such that the streaming problem result for these two representatives and the test is different (usual fooling set condition, (4.3)) and for all other tests (4.4), the streaming problem would generate the same result for the two representatives (4.5). Then, if we would exclude this test element (4.1), it will no longer be a fooling set because of this representative pair (4.2). Or, formally, a fooling set $\mathcal{F} = (\mathcal{F}_L, \mathcal{F}_R)$ for a streaming problem S has a minimal test set if:

$\forall I_R^v \in \mathcal{F}_R,$	For all elements of the test set,	(4.1)
$\exists I_L^i, I_L^j \in \mathcal{F}_L, I_L^i \neq I_L^j$	there are two different representatives,	(4.2)
s.t. $\left(S(I_L^i, I_R^v) \neq S(I_L^j, I_R^v)\right)$	such that the cache states have to be different.	(4.3)
and $\forall I_R^{v'} \in (\mathcal{F}_R \setminus I_R^v):$	And for all other tests,	(4.4)
$S(I_L^i, I_R^{v'}) = S(I_L^j, I_R^{v'})\big)$	they are not required to be different.	(4.5)

The term (4.3) literally states, that the intermediate storage after l input values is forced to have a different cache state after processing I_L^i, or I_L^j, as different output values have to be generated with the same test element. On the opposite, (4.5) implies, that the cache state for the other test elements is not required to be different. We have this alleviated formulation because it is possible that with different intermediate storage cache states the algorithm will produce the same output value for a certain test entry v'.

We can conclude, that with a space complexity lower bound proof for an exact deterministic streaming problem using the first approach with a set of representatives and tests, we can prove a space complexity lower bound for an exact probabilistic streaming problem with a success probability $p > \frac{1}{2}$ using the theorems above. Besides these two theorems, Ablayev [Abl96] states some further lower bound proofs, which are not used in this thesis and therefore not introduced and explained here. However, they might be useful for further analysis as well.

This summary explicitly states that the above lower bound proofs are only valid for exact solutions, i.e., with an approximation ratio of $\alpha = 1$. In the following, we will introduce an approach to get space complexity lower bounds in an approximative setting.

Lower Bound for an Approximative Deterministic Streaming Problem

The existence of a fooling set implies a space complexity lower bound because it forces the right computer to distinguish the different representatives or the second part of the update computations to presume different cache states. If a streaming algorithm is allowed to produce an approximative result, some of these representatives are not necessarily required to be distinguished as these might have different optimal output values that might still be within a given approximation ratio. Therefore, we have to implement this approximation ratio into the fooling set.

For this purpose, we define an α-fooling set that forces the different representatives to differ more from each other.

Definition 4.3. *For a streaming problem $\mathcal{S} = (\mathcal{X}, \mathcal{Y}, f)$ and a fixed approximation ratio $\alpha \geq 1$, an α-fooling set $\mathcal{F}^\alpha = (\mathcal{F}_L^\alpha, \mathcal{F}_R^\alpha)$ contains a set of representatives $\mathcal{F}_L^\alpha = \{I_L^1, \ldots, I_L^d\}$ and a test set $\mathcal{F}_R^\alpha = \{I_R^1, \ldots, I_R^{d'}\}$, such that each combination of representative and test is an input stream, i.e., $\forall I_L^i \in \mathcal{F}_L^\alpha, I_R^j \in \mathcal{F}_R^\alpha : (I_L^i, I_R^j) \in \mathcal{X}$. $\mathcal{F}^\alpha$ is an α-fooling set for $\mathcal{S}$ if,*

$$\forall I_L^i, I_L^j \in \mathcal{F}^\alpha \text{ with } I_L^i \neq I_L^j : \exists I_R^v \in \mathcal{F}_R^\alpha \text{ such that}$$

$$\frac{f(I_L^i, I_R^v)}{f(I_L^j, I_R^v)} < \frac{1}{\alpha} \text{ or } \frac{f(I_L^i, I_R^v)}{f(I_L^j, I_R^v)} > \alpha.$$

If the fraction between the problem function values $f(I_L^i, I_R^v)$ and $f(I_L^j, I_R^v)$ are separated by a factor of more than α, i.e., smaller than $\frac{1}{\alpha}$ or larger than α, then we have the same situation as with the inequality of the normal fooling set, that the algorithm has to store two different cache states, to calculate for both representatives the correct output value.

One can easily see that a 1-fooling set (which demands an exact solution as the approximation ratio is 1) is equal to the common fooling set from above using the first approach.

With the definition of an α-fooling set, we can derive the following space complexity lower bound.

Theorem 4.4. *Let $\mathcal{S}_\# = (\mathcal{X}, \mathcal{Y}, f, s)$ be a streaming counting problem with an α-fooling set $\mathcal{F}^\alpha = (\mathcal{F}_L^\alpha, \mathcal{F}_R^\alpha)$ for a fixed $\alpha \geq 1$. The α-approximative deterministic streaming counting problem $\mathcal{S}_{\alpha,1}$ (approximation ratio α, success probability $p = 1$) with a 1-sided approximation (see Definition 3.13) has a space complexity lower bound of,*

$$\text{space}(\mathcal{S}_{\alpha,1}) \geq \log_2(|\mathcal{F}^\alpha|) = \log_2(|\mathcal{F}_L^\alpha|).$$

Proof. As explained above, an α-fooling set contains entries such as the typical fooling set which force any algorithm to change its cache states, even when the algorithm may allow a 1-sided approximation of α. Following the proof of Theorem 4.1, the space complexity lower bound for $\mathcal{S}_{\alpha,1}$ is also proven. □

Recall, the 1-sided approximation allows only approximations below the optimal output values, as defined in Definition 3.13. For the 2-sided approximation that allows approximative output values both above and below the optimal one, we can prove the same lower bound only for a smaller approximation ratio.

Theorem 4.5. *Let* $\mathcal{S}_\# = (\mathcal{X}, \mathcal{Y}, f, s)$ *be a streaming counting problem with an α-fooling set* $\mathcal{F}^\alpha = (\mathcal{F}^\alpha_L, \mathcal{F}^\alpha_R)$ *for a fixed $\alpha \geq 1$. The $\sqrt{\alpha}$-approximative deterministic streaming counting problem* $\mathcal{S}_{\sqrt{\alpha},1}$ *(approximation ratio $\sqrt{\alpha}$, success probability $p = 1$) with a 2-sided approximation (see Definition 3.12) has a space complexity lower bound of,*

$$\text{space}(\mathcal{S}_{\sqrt{\alpha},1}) \geq \log_2(|\mathcal{F}^\alpha|) = \log_2(|\mathcal{F}^\alpha_L|).$$

Proof. If an approximation algorithm may compute results both above and below the optimal output value, an α-fooling set implies for an allowed approximation ratio of $\sqrt{\alpha}$, that the cache states between any two representatives of the α-fooling set is forced to be different, because $\sqrt{\alpha}^2 = \alpha$.

Or, in other words, if a streaming algorithm wants to approximate two optimal output values a and b, with $b > a \cdot \alpha$, as given from the α-fooling set, it cannot approximate both, a and b, with just one intermediate value k, that is $a \leq k \leq b$, and an approximation ratio $\sqrt{\alpha}$, because

$$\forall k \in (a,b): \ \max\left\{\frac{k}{a}, \frac{b}{k}\right\} > \sqrt{\alpha}, \text{ because}$$

$$\frac{b}{k} > \sqrt{\alpha} \text{ if } k \leq a \cdot \sqrt{\alpha} \text{ as } b > a \cdot \alpha \text{ and otherwise, } \frac{k}{a} > \sqrt{\alpha} \text{ if } k > a \cdot \sqrt{\alpha}. \qquad \square$$

In the last part of this section, we will argue how the theorems for probabilistic space complexity lower bounds from Ablayev [Abl96] are also valid for an approximative environment.

Lower Bound for an Approximative Probabilistic Problem

Based on an α-fooling set for a streaming counting problem $\mathcal{S}_\#$ and a deterministic space complexity lower bound space($\mathcal{S}_{\alpha,1}$) for 1-sided approximations (see Theorem 4.4) or space($\mathcal{S}_{\sqrt{\alpha},1}$) for 2-sided approximations (see Theorem 4.5), one can apply Theorem 4.2 and Theorem 4.3 to prove α-approximative, or, $\sqrt{\alpha}$-approximative probabilistic space complexity lower bounds for success probabilities of $p > \frac{1}{2}$.

The general fooling set is mainly a formal definition of *forcing the left computer to a different communication* for the communication complexity model or *forcing the cache states to be different* after processing l input values for the streaming problem model. In an approximative setting, this is analogously achieved with the formally defined α-fooling set. One can in addition apply the same proof idea by Ablayev [Abl96] on the α-fooling set to justify the correctness of the usage of Theorem 4.2 and Theorem 4.3.

As stated below Theorem 4.3, in a probabilistic setting, the test set is required to be minimal. This minimality of an α-fooling set can similarly be verified with the following expression.

$$\forall I_R^v \in \mathcal{F}_R, \qquad \text{For all elements of the test set,} \qquad (4.6)$$

$$\exists I_L^i, I_L^j \in \mathcal{F}_L, I_L^i \neq I_L^j \qquad \text{there are two different representatives,} \qquad (4.7)$$

$$\text{s.t.} \left(\left(\frac{f(I_L^i, I_R^v)}{f(I_L^j, I_R^v)} < \frac{1}{\alpha} \right. \right. \qquad \begin{array}{l}\text{such that the cache states}\\ \text{have to be different}\end{array} \qquad (4.8)$$

$$\left. \text{or } \frac{f(I_L^i, I_R^v)}{f(I_L^j, I_R^v)} > \alpha \right) \qquad \text{as stated above in Definition 4.3.} \qquad (4.9)$$

$$\text{and } \left(\forall I_R^{v'} \in (\mathcal{F}_R \setminus I_R^v): \qquad \text{And for all other tests,} \qquad (4.10)$$

$$\left. \frac{1}{\alpha} \leq \frac{f(I_L^i, I_R^{v'})}{f(I_L^j, I_R^{v'})} \leq \alpha \right) \right) \qquad \text{they are not required to be different.} \qquad (4.11)$$

In the following section, we will address the approach to prove space complexities for hypothesis verification.

4.3 Lower Bounds for Hypotheses Verifications

In this thesis, the algorithmic complexities of some general streaming problems are compared to the space complexities of hypothesis verification. A *streaming hypothesis verification problem* verifies a certain solution hypothesis, namely whether the streaming problem function outputs the stated hypothesis for a certain input stream. It is therefore a *binary streaming decision problem*, which is defined in Definition 3.4. Contrary to a classical decision problem, we can consider the approximation ratio of the general streaming problem in the hypothesis verification by adapting the streaming problem function such that it indicates a hypothesis as correct when it is within the approximation ratio of the general streaming problem function.

Hypothesis verification needs to verify, for every possible input stream and feasible output value as hypothesis, whether this hypothesis is correct or not. We can identify the following space complexity dependency between the general streaming problem and the hypothesis verification,

$$\text{space(General } \mathcal{S}) \geq \text{space(Verify all possible hypotheses for } \mathcal{S}).$$

Let us assume we have a certain streaming algorithm $\mathcal{A}$ that solves a general streaming problem $\mathcal{S}$. We can easily adapt this algorithm such that it compares the final output value with the stated hypothesis and then indicates the correctness of it. However, it might be possible that the verification of a hypothesis requires less storage as, e.g., the indication of an inequality of two bit strings if we know the position of the differing bit as hypothesis. That is why space(General $\mathcal{S}$) $\geq$ space(Verify all possible hypothesis for $\mathcal{S}$).

We can formally define a fooling set for proving space complexity lower bounds if we want to verify all possible solution hypotheses.

Definition 4.4. *For a streaming problem* $\mathcal{S} = (\mathcal{X}, \mathcal{Y}, f)$, *a* **hypothesis fooling set** $\mathcal{F}^{HYP} = (\mathcal{F}_L^{HYP}, \mathcal{F}_R^{HYP})$ *contains a set of representatives* $\mathcal{F}_L^{HYP} = \{I_L^1, \ldots, I_L^d\}$ *and a test set* $\mathcal{F}_R^{HYP} = \{I_R^1, \ldots, I_R^{d'}\}$. *Each representative* $I_L^i \in \mathcal{F}_L^{HYP}$ *contains a solution hypothesis, followed by an input stream part as in the normal fooling set, i.e.,* $I_L^i = (y^i, \tilde{x}^i)$ *with* $y^i \in \mathcal{Y}_x$ *and* $\tilde{x}^i$ *is a substream of* $x \in \mathcal{X}$. *Each combination of representative and test contains an input stream, i.e.,* $\forall I_L^i = (y^i, \tilde{x}^i) \in \mathcal{F}_L^{HYP}, \forall I_R^j \in \mathcal{F}_R : (\tilde{x}^i, I_R^j) \in \mathcal{X}$. $\mathcal{F}^{HYP} = (\mathcal{F}_L^{HYP}, \mathcal{F}_R^{HYP})$ *is a hypothesis fooling set for* $\mathcal{S}$ *if,*

$$I_L^i = (y^i, \tilde{x}^i), I_L^j = (y^j, \tilde{x}^j) \in \mathcal{F}_L^{HYP} \text{ with } I_L^i \neq I_L^j : \exists I_R^v \in \mathcal{F}_R^{HYP} \text{ such that}$$
$$\left(y^i = f(\tilde{x}^i, I_R^v) \right) \not\Leftrightarrow \left(y^j = f(\tilde{x}^j, I_R^v) \right).$$

The two terms $\left(y^i = f(\tilde{x}^i, I_R^v) \right)$ *and* $\left(y^j = f(\tilde{x}^j, I_R^v) \right)$ *are Boolean terms that are either true (i.e., 1) or false (i.e., 0).*

The inequality from the definition above literally states that the cache states after processing the two representatives have to be different because the right computer or the second part of the update computations with the test I_R^v have to decide on a correct hypothesis, i.e., 1, for one representative and on false, i.e., 0, for the other representative.

Similarly to Theorem 4.1, we have proven a space complexity lower bound of space$\left(\mathcal{S}_{1,1}^{HYP}\right) \geq \log_2(|\mathcal{F}_L^{HYP}|)$ for the hypothesis verification of a streaming problem $\mathcal{S}_{1,1}$, if we can define a hypothesis fooling set $\mathcal{F}^{HYP} = (\mathcal{F}_L^{HYP}, \mathcal{F}_R^{HYP})$.

To use Theorem 4.3 for proving space complexity lower bounds in a probabilistic setting, we additionally have to verify the minimality of the test set. Similarly to the test set minimality verification of a normal fooling set, we can verify this minimality by showing this term:

$$\forall I_R^v \in \mathcal{F}_R, \qquad\qquad \text{For all elements of the test set,} \qquad (4.12)$$

$$\exists I_L^i = (y^i, \tilde{x}^i), I_L^j = (y^j, \tilde{x}^j) \qquad \text{there are two different} \qquad (4.13)$$

$$\in \mathcal{F}_L, I_L^i \neq I_L^j \qquad\qquad \text{representatives,} \qquad (4.14)$$

$$\text{s.t. } \left(\left(y^i = f(\tilde{x}^i, I_R^v)\right) \not\Longleftrightarrow \right. \qquad \text{such that the cache states} \qquad (4.15)$$

$$\left(y^j = f(\tilde{x}^j, I_R^v)\right) \qquad\qquad \text{have to be different.} \qquad (4.16)$$

$$\text{and } \forall I_R^{v'} \in (\mathcal{F}_R \setminus I_R^v): \qquad \text{And for all other tests,} \qquad (4.17)$$

$$\left(y^i = f(\tilde{x}^i, I_R^{v'})\right) \Longleftrightarrow \qquad \text{they are not required} \qquad (4.18)$$

$$\left.\left(y^j = f(\tilde{x}^j, I_R^{v'})\right)\right) \qquad\qquad \text{to be different.} \qquad (4.19)$$

Additionally, we require a further definition of a hypothesis fooling set for the approximative environment.

Definition 4.5. *For a streaming problem $\mathcal{S} = (\mathcal{X}, \mathcal{Y}, f)$ and a fixed approximation ratio $\alpha \geq 1$, a* **hypothesis α-fooling set** *$\mathcal{F}^{HYP,\alpha} = (\mathcal{F}_L^{HYP,\alpha}, \mathcal{F}_R^{HYP,\alpha})$ contains a set of representatives $\mathcal{F}_L^{HYP,\alpha} = \{I_L^1, \ldots, I_L^d\}$ and a test set $\mathcal{F}_R^{HYP,\alpha} = \{I_R^1, \ldots, I_R^{d'}\}$. Each representative $I_L^i \in \mathcal{F}_L^{HYP,\alpha}$ contains a solution hypothesis, followed by an input stream part as in the normal α-fooling set, i.e., $I_L^i = (y^i, \tilde{x}^i)$ with $y^i \in \mathcal{Y}_x$ and $\tilde{x}^i \subseteq x \in \mathcal{X}$. Each combination of representative and test contains an input stream, i.e., $\forall I_L^i = (y^i, \tilde{x}^i) \in \mathcal{F}_L^{HYP,\alpha}, \forall I_R^j \in \mathcal{F}_R^{HYP,\alpha} : (\tilde{x}^i, I_R^j) \in \mathcal{X}. \; \mathcal{F}^{HYP,\alpha} = (\mathcal{F}_L^{HYP,\alpha}, \mathcal{F}_R^{HYP,\alpha})$ is a hypothesis α-fooling set for $\mathcal{S}$ if,*

$$I_L^i = (y^i, \tilde{x}^i), I_L^j = (y^j, \tilde{x}^j) \in \mathcal{F}_L^{HYP,\alpha} \text{ with } I_L^i \neq I_L^j : \; \exists I_R^v \in \mathcal{F}_R^{HYP,\alpha} \text{ such that}$$

$$\left(\frac{1}{\alpha} \leq \frac{f(\tilde{x}^i, I_R^v)}{y^i} \leq \alpha\right) \not\Longleftrightarrow \left(\frac{1}{\alpha} \leq \frac{f(\tilde{x}^j, I_R^v)}{y^j} \leq \alpha\right).$$

Once again, the two terms at the left and the right side of the inequality above are Boolean terms that are either true (i.e., 1) or false (i.e., 0).

The inequality from the definition above literally states that the cache states after processing the two representatives have to be different because the right computer or the second part of the update computation with the test I_R^v have to decide on a correct hypothesis, i.e., 1, for one representative, because the hypothesis is within the approximation ratio, and false, i.e., 0, for the other representative, because it is outside the approximation ratio.

Again, similarly to Theorem 4.4 and Theorem 4.5, we can prove a space complexity lower bound of space$\left(\mathcal{S}_{\alpha,1}^{HYP}\right) \geq \log_2(|\mathcal{F}_L^\alpha|)$ for the hypothesis verification of a streaming problem with a 1-sided approximation ratio of α, or a 2-sided approximation ratio or $\sqrt{\alpha}$, respectively, if we can define a hypothesis α-fooling set $\mathcal{F}^{HYP,\alpha} = (\mathcal{F}_L^{HYP,\alpha}, \mathcal{F}_R^{HYP,\alpha})$.

Similarly as above, we can verify the minimality of the set by showing the following.

$\forall I_R^v \in \mathcal{F}_R,$	For all elements of the test set,	(4.20)
$\exists I_L^i = (y^i, \tilde{x}^i), I_L^j = (y^j, \tilde{x}^j)$	there are two different	(4.21)
$\in \mathcal{F}_L, I_L^i \neq I_L^j$	representatives,	(4.22)
s.t. $\left(\left(\dfrac{1}{\alpha} \le \dfrac{f(\tilde{x}^i, I_R^v)}{y^i} \le \alpha \right) \not\Longleftrightarrow$	such that the cache states have to be different	(4.23)
$\left(\dfrac{1}{\alpha} \le \dfrac{f(\tilde{x}^j, I_R^v)}{y^j} \le \alpha \right)$	as stated above in Definition 4.5.	(4.24)
and $\forall I_R^{v'} \in (\mathcal{F}_R \setminus I_R^v):$	And for all other tests,	(4.25)
$\left(\dfrac{1}{\alpha} \le \dfrac{f(\tilde{x}^i, I_R^{v'})}{y^i} \le \alpha \right) \Longleftrightarrow$	they are not required to be different,	(4.26)
$\left(\dfrac{1}{\alpha} \le \dfrac{f(\tilde{x}^j, I_R^{v'})}{y^j} \le \alpha \right) \Big)$	because both hypotheses are true or false	(4.27)

With these two definitions of hypothesis fooling sets, we can prove space complexity lower bounds for hypothesis verification on exact and approximative streaming problems. With Theorem 4.2 and Theorem 4.3, we can also prove lower bounds in a probabilistic setting.

In the following two chapters, we will analyze the streaming problems *most frequent item* and *number of distinct items* and use these techniques and concepts to prove space complexity lower bounds.

Chapter 5

Most Frequent Item Problem

In this chapter, the streaming problem of computing the most frequent item is analyzed. Some already known upper and lower bound proofs from the literature are presented and enhanced with more exact bounds.

After the problem definition, the general streaming problem with several different approximation ratios and success probabilities is analyzed first. Then, the hypothesis verification is analyzed, in which, for every input stream, every possible solution hypothesis has to be verified. At the end, the results are summed up and the insights are described.

5.1 General Streaming Problem Analysis

The general streaming counting problem *most frequent item problem* $\mathcal{S}_{F_\infty}$ is defined as follows.

Definition 5.1. *The counting problem **most frequent item** $\mathcal{S}_{F_\infty} = (\mathcal{X}, \mathcal{Y}, f, s)$ has input values $x = (x_1, \ldots, x_n) \in \mathcal{X}$ containing n numbers with $x_i \in \{1, \ldots, m\}$. The result size function is $s(n, m) = n$, which implies that the feasible output values are $\mathcal{Y}_x = \{0, \ldots, n\}$. The problem function f defines the most frequent item over items $j \in \{1, \ldots, m\}$:*

$$f(x) = f((x_1, \ldots, x_n)) = \max_{1 \le j \le m} \left| \left\{ i \mid i \in \{1, \ldots, n\} \text{ and } x_i = j \right\} \right|.$$

The most frequent item problem $\mathcal{S}_{F_\infty}$ is therefore a frequency moment (Definition 3.3) with $k = \infty$.

For the analysis, we assume, for ease of presentation, that n and m are even. If n or m would be odd, then the proofs would often lead to the exact same results and sometimes affect the space complexity by an additive constant value (but not by a factor). As these effects are normally negligible and the proofs are less complicated, we are presuming that they are even. In the following subsections, the most frequent item problem is analyzed with respect to different approximation ratios and success probabilities.

Exact Deterministic Most Frequent Item Problem

First, the exact deterministic most frequent item streaming problem is analyzed. With a success probability of 1, an exact solution (approximation ratio $\alpha = 1$) has to be found. After some already known upper and lower bounds, more exact bounds are introduced. We use the notation of $\mathcal{S}_{F_\infty,1,1}$ for the exact deterministic most frequent item problem.

Known Bounds from the Literature

There are three different lower bounds already known for the exact deterministic case. These are stated in the next three theorems.

Theorem 5.1 (Alon et al. [AMS99]). *The streaming problem* $\mathcal{S}_{F_\infty,1,1}$ *has, for any* $\frac{m}{2} \le n \le 2m$, *a space complexity lower bound of*

$$\text{space}\left(\mathcal{S}_{F_\infty,1,1}^{\frac{m}{2} \le n \le 2m}\right) \in \Omega(m).$$

This theorem states that the required space complexity is at least a constant amount of bit for every possible item. Note that the condition $n \ge \frac{m}{2}$ is not stated in the original paper. It is only stated, that $n \le 2m$ and, in another theorem of this paper, with the condition of $n = \frac{m}{2}$ this lower bound of $\Omega(m)$ is also stated. The paper did not indicate a lower bound condition on n (such as $n \ge \frac{m}{2}$), as they assumed that n is of the order of m, even though they did not officially mention it. Of course, for very small n, e.g., for $n \in \Theta(\sqrt{m})$, this lower bound of $\Omega(m)$ is wrong, as the complete input stream only requires $\Theta(n \cdot \log(m)) = \Theta(\sqrt{m} \cdot \log(m))$ which is less than linear storage bits. For the purpose of correctness, we added the lower bound condition of $n \ge \frac{m}{2}$. The proof from this paper can be extended, such that this space complexity lower bound order is given for any $n \in \Theta(m)$.

Theorem 5.2 (Karp et al. [KSP03]). *The streaming problem* $\mathcal{S}_{F_\infty,1,1}$ *has, for any* $n > 4m$, *a space complexity lower bound of*

$$\text{space}\left(\mathcal{S}_{F_\infty,1,1}^{n>4m}\right) \in \Omega\left(m \cdot \log\left(\frac{n}{m}\right)\right).$$

For the given condition, the lower bound complexity order of Theorem 5.1 is increased by the factor $\log(\frac{n}{m})$.

Theorem 5.3 (Trevisan and Williams [TW12]). *The streaming problem* $\mathcal{S}_{F_\infty,1,1}$ *has, for any* $m > n^2$, *a space complexity lower bound of*

$$\text{space}\left(\mathcal{S}_{F_\infty,1,1}^{m>n^2}\right) \in \Omega(n \cdot \log(m)).$$

This theorem states, that if $m > n^2$, we are required to store the data in the same complexity order as the entire input size, which is $\Theta(n \cdot \log(m))$ bits.

These three lower bounds prove the impracticability of any concrete implementation of an exact, deterministic algorithm. That is why the literature did not study upper bounds in detail besides the trivial one of $\mathcal{O}(m \cdot \log(n))$, which is achieved with a simple histogram storage, that counts the frequency of any item. One exemplary realisation is described by Indyk and Woodruff [IW05]. Unfortunately, these lower bounds are only given in the Ω-notation, but not with an exact bound. Later, we will compare these algorithms with the ones for hypothesis verification. To get better insights from this comparison, we are interested in exact upper and lower bounds, which are given below.

Enhanced Upper Bounds

First, we introduce a trivial streaming algorithm solving the streaming problem $\mathcal{S}_{F_{\infty,1,1}}$ with a space complexity of $\mathcal{O}(m \cdot \log(n))$. Then, we will show how to decrease it with a simple trick to $\mathcal{O}(n \cdot \log(\frac{n}{m}))$, which is, for $n > 4m$, of the same order as the lower bound from Theorem 5.2 and therefore solves the problem optimally, up to constant factors.

Theorem 5.4. *The streaming problem $\mathcal{S}_{F_{\infty,1,1}}$ has, for any $n, m \in \mathbb{N}^+$, a space complexity upper bound of*

$$\operatorname{space}\left(\mathcal{S}_{F_{\infty,1,1}}\right) \leq m \cdot \lceil \log_2(n) \rceil \in \mathcal{O}(m \cdot \log(n)).$$

Proof. This upper bound can be achieved with a trivial algorithm that stores the frequency for every possible item $j \in \{1, \ldots, m\}$.

Therefore, any cache state $c \in \mathcal{C}$ requires $m \cdot \lceil \log_2(n) \rceil$ bits, in which the first $\lceil \log_2(n) \rceil$ bits are the binary representation of the frequency of the item 1. The next $\lceil \log_2(n) \rceil$ bits are the binary representation of the frequency of the item 2. This is continued until the m-th item. The initial cache state is empty. The update algorithm $\mathcal{A}_{update}$ processes a single input stream value $x_i \in \{1, \ldots, m\}$ by incrementing the binary representation of the value $j = x_i$ by one. After the computation of the update algorithm on a complete input stream, the cache state represents the frequency for each item $j \in \{1, \ldots, m\}$, namely the number of its occurrences in the input stream. The output algorithm just outputs the highest frequency count.

Obviously, this algorithm solves the most frequent item streaming problem deterministically and exactly. Furthermore, in order to represent all possible cache states, this algorithm requires $m \cdot \lceil \log_2(n) \rceil$ bits. $\qquad \square$

Now, we will use the technique of self-delimitation to decrease the order of the upper bound space complexity. We observe that, for a fixed input stream, many bits will never be used with the algorithm of Theorem 5.4, as it is impossible that all m items count from zero to n. With this insight, we can find the following better upper bound.

Theorem 5.5. *The streaming problem $\mathcal{S}_{F_{\infty,1,1}}$ has, for any $n \geq m$, a space complexity upper bound of*

$$\operatorname{space}\left(\mathcal{S}_{F_{\infty,1,1}}^{n \geq m}\right) \leq 2m \cdot \left(\left\lceil \log_2\left(\frac{n}{m}\right)\right\rceil + 1\right) - 2 \in \mathcal{O}\left(m \cdot \log\left(\frac{n}{m}\right)\right).$$

Proof. With a similar approach, the algorithm will count the frequency of every item $j \in \{1, \ldots, m\}$. But now, we will not allocate upfront $\lceil \log_2(n) \rceil$ bits for every item, but will count each item frequency with the least required amount of bits. Of course, we need to have some delimiter to indicate whether a new frequency count starts. Therefore, we define the bit-tuples "00" and "01" as counting values for the frequency counts and "10" as delimiter. The initial cache state is empty once again, but the first update procedure will store $(m-1)$ delimiters to the intermediate storage. With each input value processed, the corresponding frequency representation is increased using the two binary representatives "00" and "01". Finally, the output algorithm delivers the maximal frequency, namely the highest integer represented by the original, binary representation.

This algorithm also finds the optimal output value, as the frequency count is strictly enumerated. Next, we have to argue why the total amount of required cache bits is at most $2m \cdot \left(\lceil \log_2(\frac{n}{m}) \rceil + 1\right) - 2$. First, the delimiters require $(2m - 2)$ bits, as every one of the $(m - 1)$ delimiters requires two bits, i.e., "10". The n input values can have any possible distribution over the m different items. In the most space-efficient way, all n input values are all the same item, then, we require $\lceil \log_2(n) \rceil$ bit pairs only at one position, and all other items do not require any further bits. If, e.g., the half of this frequency is now separated on other items, we require only one bit pair less to store the new frequency, namely, $\lceil \log_2(\frac{n}{2}) \rceil$, but the other items require more than one bit pair. Therefore, the total amount of bits to store all frequency counts is increased. In the extreme case, the worst space-efficient storage occurs when the n input values are distributed equally likely on all items. Then, each position requires $\lceil \log_2(\frac{n}{m}) \rceil$ bit pairs, which in total amounts to $2m \cdot \lceil \log_2(\frac{n}{m}) \rceil$ bits. With these completely balanced frequency counts, we cannot increase the size of storage bits by modifying the frequencies of the individual items, because we only require 1 additional bit pair if we raise the frequency to the next higher power of two, which reduces the amount of bit pairs to represent another frequency count. Therefore, we have in the worst case the following number of total bits:

$$2m - 2 + 2m \cdot \left\lceil \log_2\left(\frac{n}{m}\right) \right\rceil = 2m \cdot \left(\left\lceil \log_2\left(\frac{n}{m}\right) \right\rceil + 1\right) - 2 \in \Omega\left(m \cdot \log\left(\frac{n}{m}\right)\right). \quad \square$$

This self-delimitation technique allows to have an upper bound which is of the same complexity order as the given lower bound in Theorem 5.2. For a detailed analysis, an exact space complexity lower bound is required. Such an exact lower bound is given in the following part, but first, we will further improve this upper bound. The above described realization of a streaming algorithm using the self-delimitation technique has some space inefficiency, as, e.g., the bit-tuple "11" is never used. If we include three of the four bit-tuples for the counting value, we can get a more space efficient representation, as we are currently only using the two tuples "00" and "01". More generally, if the factor $\frac{n}{m}$ is large, the delimiter can be chosen more efficiently, e.g., with a bit-triple that uses "000" to "110" as frequency counting values zero to seven and "111" as the delimiter.

Theorem 5.6. *The streaming problem* $\mathcal{S}_{F_{\infty,1,1}}$ *has, for any* $n \geq m$ *and any delimiter size* $d \geq 2, d \in \mathbb{N}^+$, *a space-complexity upper bound of*

$$\text{space}\left(\mathcal{S}_{F_{\infty,1,1}}^{n \geq m}\right) \leq d \cdot m \cdot \left(1 + \left\lceil \frac{\log_2(\frac{n}{m})}{\log_2(2^d - 1)} \right\rceil\right) - d.$$

Proof. For any delimiter size $d \geq 2$, we define basic bit-strings of length d. d-times a 1 is the delimiter. All other basic bit-strings of length d are required for the frequency counting representing the numbers 0 to $2^d - 2$. Similar to the algorithm in Theorem 5.5, the first update algorithm computation stores the $(m - 1)$ delimiters in the cache and the frequency per item is counted afterwards. As the basic bit-string can represent the numbers 0 to $2^d - 2$, we are not counting with a binary base, but have a base of $(2^d - 1)$. The output algorithm transforms the highest frequency from the basis $(2^d - 1)$ to a binary base and outputs it.

Of course, this streaming algorithm solves the most frequent item problem, as it is a simple transformation of the algorithm in Theorem 5.5. The described streaming algorithm requires $d \cdot (m-1)$ bits for the delimiters. Analogously to Theorem 5.5, the worst space-efficient input stream has a uniform distribution over all items. Then, we have to represent the value $\lceil \frac{n}{m} \rceil$ in the numeral system of basis $(2^d - 1)$, which requires $\lceil \log_{2^d-1}(\frac{n}{m}) \rceil$ basic bit strings. Therefore, we have in total

$$d \cdot (m-1) + d \cdot m \cdot \left\lceil \log_{2^d-1}\left(\frac{n}{m}\right) \right\rceil = d \cdot m \cdot \left(1 + \left\lceil \frac{\log_2(\frac{n}{m})}{\log_2(2^d - 1)} \right\rceil\right) - d$$

bits. □

While this formula can give an improved upper bound, it might also be useless if one chooses a bad d. For any fixed n, m, one can identify the best d to decrease the space complexity upper bound. This space complexity function is, dependent on d, similar to a parable: There is a lowest point and, for all delimiter sizes above or below, the space complexity function will output a higher result. Therefore, one can simply evaluate the space complexity function from above with some $d \in \{2, 3, \dots\}$ until the lowest space complexity has been located.

But to illustrate the usage of Theorem 5.6, we can show that, for any $n \geq m$ and with $d = 2$, the space complexity upper bound is generally below the one from Theorem 5.5. One can see this with the following inequality:

$$\text{space}\left(\mathcal{S}_{F_\infty,1,1}\right) \leq d \cdot m \cdot \left(1 + \left\lceil \frac{\log_2(\frac{n}{m})}{\log_2(2^d - 1)} \right\rceil\right) - d \qquad \text{Theorem 5.6}$$

$$= 2m \cdot \left(1 + \left\lceil \frac{\log_2(\frac{n}{m})}{\log_2(3)} \right\rceil\right) - 2 \qquad \text{replace } d = 2$$

$$\leq 2m \cdot \left(1 + \left\lceil \log_2\left(\frac{n}{m}\right) \right\rceil\right) - 2 \qquad \text{Theorem 5.5}$$

As an example, if we have $n = 10^{12}$ and $m = 10^6$, one can calculate upfront the space complexity of Theorem 5.6 with different $d \geq 2$, as illustrated in Figure 5.1. For these concrete n and m, we choose $d = 3$ as it leads to the most space-efficient approach. For the sake of comparison, the space complexity of Theorem 5.5 has been added to this figure.

In the following, we will see some lower bound proofs for the space complexity of the most frequent item problem. Some are used as basis for further, more complicated proofs in the setting of approximation and randomization. One proof will get a tight lower bound for the general one in Theorem 5.2, which is only given in Ω-notation. This exact lower bound is then better comparable with the exact upper bounds of Theorem 5.5 and Theorem 5.6.

Enhanced Lower Bounds

In this part, we will prove a tight lower bound for the exact deterministic most frequent item streaming problem. Furthermore, it is an exact bound for the one in Theorem 5.1, which is only given in Ω-notation. Additionally, it is more general, as there are no conditions on n and m. The first one illustrates the usage of the

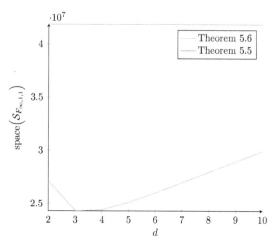

Figure 5.1. Illustration of the space complexity of the exact deterministic most frequent item problem

fooling set in detail, which was introduced in Chapter 4. This analysis and proof idea is later used to extend this lower bound to an approximative and probabilistic setting. The second lower bound proof will deliver an exact bound of Theorem 5.2.

First, we will start with a simple and intuitively comprehensible lower bound of $\Omega(\min\{m, n\})$.

Theorem 5.7. *The streaming problem* $\mathcal{S}_{F_{\infty,1,1}}$ *has, for any* $n, m \in \mathbb{N}^+$, *a space complexity lower bound of*

$$\text{space}\left(\mathcal{S}_{F_{\infty,1,1}}\right) \geq \min\{n, m\} - \frac{1}{2} \cdot \log_2(\min\{n, m\}) - \frac{1}{2}$$
$$\geq \min\{n, m\} - \log_2(\min\{n, m\}) \in \Omega(\min\{n, m\}).$$

Proof. To show this lower bound, we will distinguish between two different cases: The first one for $n \leq m$ and the second one for $m > n$. For both cases, we will *i)* introduce a fooling set, *ii)* show, that it is a fooling set for the most frequent item problem, and *iii)* calculate the space complexity lower bound with the fooling set size.

Case 1: If $n \leq m$, we define a fooling set of size $\binom{n}{n/2}$ consisting of sequences of $\frac{n}{2}$ different elements as representatives, which are associated with the left computer for the two-computer model or stand for the first input stream parts, respectively. The right side contains some test entries, each with $\frac{n}{2}$ occurrences of the same item. Then, for any two representatives, we can choose one test with some item that is present in only one representative. As a consequence, the highest frequency is always different, which is the condition of a fooling set. We now describe the three steps *i)*, *ii)*, and *iii)* in detail.

i) We define the fooling set $\mathcal{F}^{n\leq m} = (\mathcal{F}_L^{n\leq m}, \mathcal{F}_R^{n\leq m})$ with the cut in the middle ($l := \frac{n}{2}$) by the following approach: A *set half* contains $\frac{n}{2}$ different values from $\{1, \ldots, n\} \subseteq \{1, \ldots, m\}$. $\mathcal{F}_L^{n\leq m}$ contains all possible, different *set halves*. This way, there are no two representatives that are equal. This implies that all representatives have a length of $\frac{n}{2}$, a frequency of exactly 1, and consequently, $\frac{n}{2}$ distinct items. Obviously, there exist $\binom{n}{n/2}$ distinct set halves. The test simply contains n different $I_R^i \in \mathcal{F}_R^{n\leq m}$ of $\frac{n}{2}$ times the same value, namely $\mathcal{F}_R^{n\leq m} = \{\{1, \ldots, 1\}, \ldots, \{n, \ldots, n\}\}$.

ii) Now we have to verify that $\mathcal{F}_R^{n\leq m}$ is a test for the representatives $\mathcal{F}_L^{n\leq m}$. The definition of the representatives states that no two representatives are equal. Therefore, for any two representatives, there exists an item v that is present in only one of the representatives, i.e.,

$$\forall I_L^i, I_L^j \in \mathcal{F}_L^{n\leq m}, I_L^i \neq I_L^j, \exists v \in \{1, \ldots, n\} \text{ such that } v \in I_L^i \text{ and } v \notin I_L^j.$$

For these two representatives I_L^i, I_L^j, we choose $I_R^v = \{v, \ldots, v\}$ as a test, then the highest frequency is either $\frac{n}{2}$ (if v is not present in the representative) or $\frac{n}{2} + 1$ (if v is present). Formally, the inequality is

$$f(I_L^i, I_R^v) = \frac{n}{2} + 1 \neq \frac{n}{2} = f(I_L^j, I_R^v).$$

Therefore, $\mathcal{F}^{n\leq m} = (\mathcal{F}_L^{n\leq m}, \mathcal{F}_R^{n\leq m})$ has a test for any two representatives, so that the highest frequency is different and the cache states have to be different. Hence, it is a fooling set for $\mathcal{S}_{F_\infty}$.

iii) At last, we can calculate the space-complexity lower bound. Based on Theorem 4.1 and the approximation in Lemma 3.2, we can prove the space complexity lower bound for $\mathcal{S}_{F_{\infty,1,1}}$ and $n \leq m$ of

$$
\begin{aligned}
\text{space}(\mathcal{S}_{F_{\infty,1,1}}^{n\leq m}) &\geq \log_2(|\mathcal{F}_L^{n\leq m}|) = \log_2\left(\binom{n}{n/2}\right) && \text{fooling set size} \\
&> \log_2\left(\frac{2^n}{\sqrt{2n}}\right) = n - \log_2(\sqrt{2n}) && \text{Lemma 3.2} \\
&= n - \frac{\log_2(2n)}{2} = n - \frac{\log_2(n)}{2} - \frac{1}{2} && \text{basic transformation} \\
&\geq n - \log_2(n) \in \Omega(n) && \text{basic transformation}
\end{aligned}
$$

This is the space complexity lower bound for the first case.

Case 2: If $m < n$, then we define the set of representatives similar to the first case, but now, for each element of the fooling set, we use only $\frac{m}{2}$ different elements from the set of all possible items. The testing set is also similar to above, but now we have to fill it up more repetitively, until the representative and test set contain n input values. The three steps *i*), *ii*), and *iii*) are now described in detail.

i) We define the fooling set $\mathcal{F}^{m<n} = (\mathcal{F}_L^{m<n}, \mathcal{F}_R^{m<n})$ as follows: The set of representatives contains, similarly to the first case, all different *set halves*, each with $\frac{m}{2}$ different items from $\{1, \ldots, m\}$. Then the representative set has a size of

$|\mathcal{F}_L^{m<n}| = \binom{m}{m/2}$. Now, the cut between representatives and test is not in the middle, but at $l := \frac{m}{2} < \frac{n}{2}$. The test simply contains m different I_R^v, each with $(n - \frac{m}{2})$ times the same value, namely

$$\mathcal{F}_R^{m<n} = \{\{1, \ldots, 1\}, \ldots, \{m, \ldots, m\}\}.$$

ii) Now, we verify that $\mathcal{F}^{m<n} = (\mathcal{F}_L^{m<n}, \mathcal{F}_R^{m<n})$ is a fooling set, because it contains an item v for every possible two representatives, such that v is represented in only one of the two. Then, the highest frequency is either $(n - \frac{m}{2})$ (if v is not present at the representative) or $(n - \frac{m}{2} + 1)$ (if v is present). More formally, this inequality can be shown as follows:

$$\forall I_L^i, I_L^j \in \mathcal{F}_L^{m<n}, I_L^i \neq I_L^j \; \exists v \in \{1, \ldots, m\} \text{ such that } v \in I_L^i \text{ and } v \notin I_L^j.$$

With $I_R^v = \{v, \ldots, v\}$, we have $|I_R^v| = n - \frac{m}{2}$ and the required inequality

$$f(I_L^i, I_R^v) = n - \frac{m}{2} + 1 \neq n - \frac{m}{2} = f(I_L^j, I_R^v).$$

Therefore $\mathcal{F}^{m<n}$ is a fooling set for $\mathcal{S}_{F_\infty}$.

iii) Based on Theorem 4.1 and the approximation in Lemma 3.2, we can similarly prove a space complexity lower bound for $\mathcal{S}_{F_{\infty,1,1}}$ and $m < n$ of

$$
\begin{aligned}
\text{space}(\mathcal{S}_{F_{\infty,1,1}}^{m<n}) &\geq \log_2(|\mathcal{F}_L^{m<n}|) = \log_2\left(\binom{m}{m/2}\right) && \text{fooling set size} \\
&> \log_2\left(\frac{2^m}{\sqrt{2m}}\right) = m - \log_2(\sqrt{2m}) && \text{Lemma 3.2} \\
&\geq m - \log_2(m) \in \Omega(m) && \text{basic transformation}
\end{aligned}
$$

With these two cases, we can summarize that, for any $m, n \in \mathbb{N}^+$, the space complexity lower bound is given by

$$\text{space}(\mathcal{S}_{F_{\infty,1,1}}) \geq \min\{n, m\} - \log_2(\min\{n, m\}) \in \Omega(\min\{n, m\}). \qquad \square$$

Now, we will prove a tight lower bound for the known space complexity of $\Omega(m \cdot \log(\frac{n}{m}))$ for any $n > 4m$, as stated in Theorem 5.2.

Theorem 5.8. *The streaming problem* $\mathcal{S}_{F_{\infty,1,1}}$ *has, for any* $n > 4m$, *a space-complexity lower bound of*

$$\text{space}\left(\mathcal{S}_{F_{\infty,1,1}}\right) \geq \frac{m}{2} \cdot \log_2\left(\frac{n}{m}\right) - 0.21m \in \Omega\left(m \cdot \log\left(\frac{n}{m}\right)\right).$$

Proof. To get a space complexity lower bound in the order of $\Omega(m \cdot \log(\frac{n}{m}))$, we are required to have an enormously larger fooling set, compared to the ones from Theorem 5.7 of size $\approx 2^n$ or $\approx 2^m$, respectively. Instead, we require a fooling set of the order of $\approx 2^{m \cdot \log_2(n/m)}$.

To build such a large set of representatives, we vary the frequency count within the representatives. The representatives of the fooling set in Theorem 5.7 have a frequency of one. If we now vary the frequency within the representatives, we are challenging the situation that, at the end, every input stream is required to have a length of n input values. Therefore, we will use the items $\{1, \ldots, \frac{m}{2}\}$ for the frequency influence and the second half of the items, namely $\{\frac{m}{2} + 1, \ldots, m\}$, as spacer with a frequency below a certain minimum. Then, we can fill up the rest of the space until we have the required n input values, but these spacer items are not affecting the overall streaming problem result, as their frequency is at most as high as that of the test entries. We will define this minimum as a fraction dependent on n and m. Once again, we will i) introduce the fooling set formally, ii) justify that it is a fooling set (namely, that any combination of representative and test have the required input stream size of n and that for any two representatives, there is a test element such that the highest frequency is different), and iii) calculate the space-complexity lower bound.

i) First, we define the frequency maximum for the spacer items as the frequency minimum for the testing set. This fraction is defined as follows,

$$\text{frac} := \left\lfloor \frac{n}{\frac{m}{2} + 1} \right\rfloor = \left\lfloor \frac{2n}{m + 2} \right\rfloor.$$

The fooling set $\mathcal{F} = (\mathcal{F}_L, \mathcal{F}_R)$ has a cut at $l := (n - \text{frac})$, we define a test set of size $\frac{m}{2}$, each test with frac times the same item from $\{1, \ldots, \frac{m}{2}\}$, namely $\mathcal{F}_R = \{\{1, \ldots, 1\}, \ldots, \{\frac{m}{2}, \ldots, \frac{m}{2}\}\}$. Consequently, the representatives are sets of size $l = (n - \text{frac})$. Each representative can logically be split into two parts, a content part and a spacer part. We construct a set of representatives with $\approx (\frac{\text{frac}}{2})^{\frac{m}{2}}$ different content parts. Each content item $j \in \{1, \ldots, \frac{m}{2}\}$ has a frequency from the range $\{\lceil \frac{\text{frac}}{2} \rceil, \ldots, \text{frac}\}$. Then, we can vary the frequency of every content item individually, and we will have in total

$$(\# \text{ frequency states})^{(\# \text{ content items})} = \left(\text{frac} - \left\lceil \frac{\text{frac}}{2} \right\rceil + 1\right)^{\frac{m}{2}} \tag{5.1}$$

$$\geq \left(\frac{\text{frac}}{2}\right)^{\frac{m}{2}} \tag{5.2}$$

different content parts, such that there exists, for any two representatives, a content item $v \in \{1, \ldots, \frac{m}{2}\}$ with different frequencies of v in the two representatives. These content parts have in total between $\lceil \frac{\text{frac}}{2} \rceil \cdot \frac{m}{2}$ and $\text{frac} \cdot \frac{m}{2}$ input values. The spacer part of every representative is filled up with spacer items $\{\frac{m}{2} + 1, \ldots, m\}$ with a frequency of at most frac.

ii) Second, we will verify that this spacing approach will lead to input streams of size n and afterwards, that $\mathcal{F} = (\mathcal{F}_L, \mathcal{F}_R)$ is a fooling set for the most frequent item streaming problem.

We further use the following approximation that, for any $n > 4m$,

$$\frac{2n}{m} > \text{frac} > \frac{3}{2} \cdot \frac{n}{m} \quad \text{with frac} = \left\lfloor \frac{n}{\frac{m}{2} + 1} \right\rfloor = \left\lfloor \frac{2n}{m + 2} \right\rfloor. \tag{5.3}$$

The first inequality is obvious. The second is also clear, using the condition that $n > 4m$.

As stated above, the content parts of the representatives have a size between $\lceil \frac{\text{frac}}{2} \rceil \cdot \frac{m}{2}$ and $\text{frac} \cdot \frac{m}{2}$. If the content part contains only $\lceil \frac{\text{frac}}{2} \rceil \cdot \frac{m}{2}$ items, we have to verify that the maximal amount of spacer items with limited frequency are sufficient to get a representative size of $l = (n - \text{frac})$. The spacer part has a maximal size of $\text{frac} \cdot \frac{m}{2}$. Therefore, we can validate that,

$$
\begin{aligned}
\left\lceil \frac{\text{frac}}{2} \right\rceil \cdot \frac{m}{2} + \text{frac} \cdot \frac{m}{2} &\geq \frac{\text{frac}}{2} \cdot \frac{m}{2} + \text{frac} \cdot \frac{m}{2} && \text{simple approximation} \\
&= \text{frac} \cdot \left(\frac{m}{4} + \frac{m}{2} \right) && \text{basic transformation} \\
&> \frac{3}{2} \cdot \frac{n}{m} \cdot \frac{3m}{4} = \frac{9n}{8} && \text{inequality from (5.3)} \\
&> n - \text{frac} = l.
\end{aligned}
$$

On the other side, we have to verify that, if the content part contains the maximum of $\text{frac} \cdot \frac{m}{2}$ entries, it does not exceed the size limit of the representatives, namely its size remains below $l = n - \text{frac}$. Or, in other words, the maximal content part plus the testing size is required to be at most n. Therefore,

$$
\begin{aligned}
\text{frac} \cdot \frac{m}{2} + \text{frac} &= \left\lfloor \frac{2n}{m+2} \right\rfloor \cdot \frac{m}{2} + \left\lfloor \frac{2n}{m+2} \right\rfloor && \text{using the definition} \\
&\leq \left\lfloor \frac{2n}{m+2} \cdot \frac{m}{2} + \frac{2n}{m+2} \right\rfloor && \text{simple approximation} \\
&= \left\lfloor \frac{2n \cdot m + 4n}{2 \cdot (m+2)} \right\rfloor = \left\lfloor \frac{2n \cdot (m+2)}{2 \cdot (m+2)} \right\rfloor && \text{basic transformation} \\
&= \lfloor n \rfloor = n.
\end{aligned}
$$

Now, we know that this approach will lead to a valid input stream length. Next, we need to verify that $\mathcal{F} = (\mathcal{F}_L, \mathcal{F}_R)$ is a fooling set for the most frequent item problem. By definition, every two representatives have a content item $v \in \{1, \ldots, \frac{m}{2}\}$ such that their frequency of this content item is different. With the corresponding representative $I_R^v \in \mathcal{F}_R$, the highest frequency is different. As a consequence, the cache states are required to be different and we have proven that $\mathcal{F}$ is a fooling set for the most frequent item problem.

iii) At last, we can calculate the tight space complexity lower bound for $\mathcal{S}_{F_{\infty,1,1}}$ and $n > 4m$, which is,

$$
\begin{aligned}
\text{space}(\mathcal{S}_{F_{\infty,1,1}}^{n>4m}) &\geq \log_2(|\mathcal{F}_L|) && \text{Theorem 4.1} \\
&= \log_2\left(\left(\text{frac} - \left\lceil \frac{\text{frac}}{2} \right\rceil + 1 \right)^{\frac{m}{2}} \right) && \text{fooling set size} \\
&\geq \log_2\left(\left(\frac{\text{frac}}{2} \right)^{\frac{m}{2}} \right) && \text{approx. from (5.1), (5.2)} \\
&= \frac{m}{2} \cdot \log_2\left(\frac{\text{frac}}{2} \right) && \text{basic transformation}
\end{aligned}
$$

$$> \frac{m}{2} \cdot \log_2\left(\frac{3}{4} \cdot \frac{n}{m}\right) \qquad \text{approx. from (5.3)}$$

$$= \frac{m}{2} \cdot \log_2\left(\frac{n}{m}\right) + m \cdot \left(\frac{\log_2(3)}{2} - 1\right) \qquad \text{basic transformation}$$

$$> \frac{m}{2} \cdot \log_2\left(\frac{n}{m}\right) - 0.21 \cdot m \qquad \text{simple approximation}$$

$$\in \Omega\left(m \cdot \log\left(\frac{n}{m}\right)\right). \qquad\qquad\qquad \Box$$

In the following, we will analyze the possible decreases of the upper bound and the validity of the lower bounds in a probabilistic setting.

Exact Probabilistic Most Frequent Item Problem

The exact probabilistic most frequent item problem with a success probability of $p < 1$ is analyzed. Once again, the output value has to be exact, namely the approximation ratio is $\alpha = 1$. We use the notation of $\mathcal{S}_{F_\infty,1,p}$ for the exact probabilistic most frequent item problem.

Known Bounds from the Literature

The known space complexity lower bound of $\Omega(m)$ for any $\frac{m}{2} \le n \le 2m$ from Theorem 5.1 stated by Alon et al. [AMS99] is also valid in the probabilistic setting, specifically if $p \ge \frac{1}{2}$. The lower bounds of Theorem 5.2 and Theorem 5.3 are not proven again for a probabilistic environment.

The upper bound of $\mathcal{O}(m \cdot \log(n))$ described by Indyk and Woodruff [IW05] is, of course, also valid in a probabilistic environment. However, so far, there are no known literature proposing streaming algorithms for the most frequent item problem with a lower complexity order for the probabilistic setting.

Enhanced Upper Bounds

In the following parts, we introduce a simple technique to decrease the deterministic upper bound by a multiplicative factor of the success probability p. Afterwards, the two lower bound proofs from Theorem 5.7 and Theorem 5.8 are extended for a probabilistic environment.

Above, we have seen three algorithms to solve the most frequent item problem exactly and have deterministically proven that,

- $\text{space}\left(\mathcal{S}_{F_\infty,1,1}\right) \le m \cdot \lceil \log_2(n) \rceil$ bits (Theorem 5.4),

- $\text{space}\left(\mathcal{S}_{F_\infty,1,1}\right) \le 2m \cdot \left(\lceil \log_2\left(\frac{n}{m}\right)\rceil + 1\right) - 2$ bits (Theorem 5.5), and

- $\text{space}\left(\mathcal{S}_{F_\infty,1,1}\right) \le d \cdot m \cdot \left(1 + \left\lceil \frac{\log_2\left(\frac{n}{m}\right)}{\log_2(2^d-1)}\right\rceil\right) - d$ bits (Theorem 5.6).

With a simple trick, we can show that the space complexity of these three algorithms can be decreased by a multiplicative factor of $p < 1$ for the corresponding success probability, namely,

$$\text{space}\left(\mathcal{S}_{F_\infty,1,p}\right) \le p \cdot \text{space}\left(\mathcal{S}_{F_\infty,1,1}\right).$$

The three deterministic algorithms are all storing a histogram of the frequencies of all individual items $j \in \{1, \ldots, m\}$ in a more or less space-efficient way. For a success probability of $p < 1$, we will just track $p \cdot m$ randomly chosen items and output the highest frequency of the tracked items. For example, for a required success probability of $p = \frac{1}{2}$, we will just analyze every second item. Namely, at the beginning, the algorithm flips a coin and decides whether the even or odd items are counted. With this approach, the probabilistic algorithm requires only half the space and gets the exact correct result with a success probability of at least $p = \frac{1}{2}$. For a required success probability of $p = \frac{3}{4}$, one can randomly choose one excluded number out of the four values $\{0, 1, 2, 3\}$, and then the algorithm just counts all items, where the item modulo 4 is not the excluded one. Then, once again, the success probability for an exact result is the probability that the modulo 4 value of the most frequent item is not the excluded one, which is at least $p = \frac{3}{4}$. If p is any rational number, i.e., $p \in \mathbb{Q}^+$ or $p = \frac{a}{b}$ for some $a, b, \in \mathbb{N}^+$, then we can randomly choose a numbers out of the set $\{0, \ldots, b-1\}$ and count only the items with a result of modulo b within this chosen items.

We could describe these algorithms in detail and more formally, but we observe the following: This approach may reduce the space complexity, but the effect is only minor, and, therefore, it is not interesting for a concrete implementation. But the study of probabilistic algorithms for the most frequent item problem shows that it is possible to decrease the space complexity slightly. Furthermore, it seems to be very hard, if not impossible, to decrease the space complexity using random bits in a really effective way.

Therefore, we will now analyze what order the space complexity lower bounds have in a probabilistic environment.

Enhanced Lower Bounds

We will prove, for any $m, n \in \mathbb{N}^+$ and some fixed success probability $p > \frac{1}{2}$, an exact space complexity lower bound for the probabilistic most frequent item problem of $\Omega(\min(m, n))$, which is of the same order as the deterministic lower bound given in Theorem 5.1 and Theorem 5.7. For the lower bound proof, we use a similar fooling set as in the proven theorem above. With Theorem 4.3, we can show an exact space complexity lower bound, completing the already known lower bound, which is given in the Ω-notation.

Theorem 5.9. *The streaming problem $\mathcal{S}_{F_{\infty,1,p}}$ has, for any $n, m \in \mathbb{N}^+$ and a success probability of $p = 1 - \varepsilon$ with $\varepsilon < \frac{1}{2}$, a space complexity lower bound of,*

$$\text{space}(\mathcal{S}_{F_{\infty,1,p}}) \geq (\min\{n, m\} - \log_2(\min\{n, m\})) \cdot$$
$$(1 + 1.01p \cdot \log_2(p) + 1.01\varepsilon \cdot \log_2(\varepsilon)) - 1.$$

Proof. Similarly to the proof for the deterministic lower bound, we distinguish the two cases $n \leq m$ and $m > n$. To use Theorem 4.3, we have to verify that the test set is minimal. As stated in (4.1) to (4.5), we can verify the following term to ensure the minimality of the test set:

$$\forall I_R^v \in \mathcal{F}_R,$$

For all elements of the test set,

$$\exists I_L^i, I_L^j \in \mathcal{F}_L, I_L^i \neq I_L^j$$

there are two different representatives,

$$\text{s.t. } \left(\mathcal{S}(I_L^i, I_R^v) \neq \mathcal{S}(I_L^j, I_R^v)\right.$$

such that the cache states have to be different.

$$\text{and } \forall I_R^{v'} \in (\mathcal{F}_R \setminus I_R^v):$$

And for all other tests,

$$\left.\mathcal{S}(I_L^i, I_R^{v'}) = \mathcal{S}(I_L^j, I_R^{v'})\right)$$

they are not required to be different.

With a small modification of the test set from the fooling set in Theorem 5.7, we have a valid fooling set with a minimal test set so that we can use Theorem 4.3 to have a space complexity lower bound for a probabilistic environment.

Case 1: $n \leq m$. We will i) define the fooling set, ii) show that it is a fooling set and has a minimal test set, and iii) calculate the probabilistic space complexity lower bound.

i) We define the fooling set $\mathcal{F}^{n \leq m} = (\mathcal{F}_L^{n \leq m}, \mathcal{F}_R^{n \leq m})$ with the same set of representatives from Theorem 5.7, namely the $\binom{n}{n/2}$ different *set halves* from $\{1, \ldots, n\} \subseteq \{1, \ldots, m\}$, which are all of length $\frac{n}{2}$. The test set contains $n-1$ different $I_R^v \in \mathcal{F}_R^{n \leq m}$ of $\frac{n}{2}$ times the same value, namely $\mathcal{F}_R^{n \leq m} = \{\{1, \ldots, 1\}, \ldots, \{n-1, \ldots, n-1\}\}$.

ii) First, it is verified, that $\mathcal{F}^{n \leq m}$ is still a fooling set, even though the test set is missing one test (i.e., $\{n, \ldots, n\}$) and, in advance, that $\mathcal{F}_R^{n \leq m}$ is minimal. In Theorem 5.7, we justified the fooling set with the argument that for any two representatives there is at least one item $v \in \{1, \ldots, n\}$ such that v is only present in one representative, and as a consequence, the highest frequency will be different for the corresponding test I_R^v. The new test set is missing one test. Nevertheless, $\mathcal{F}^{n \leq m}$ is still a fooling set because in any pair of representatives not only one but at least two different items occur at only one representative, say $v, v' \in \{1, \ldots, n\}$, because all representatives have the same length and are all distinct. From these two items that are only present in one of the two representatives, we will take the smaller one (w.l.o.g., assume $v < v' \leq n$). With the test I_R^v, which is definitely present in the test set, we can show the inequality of the highest frequency. Therefore, $\mathcal{F}^{n \leq m}$ is a fooling set for the most frequent item problem.

As introduced above, we have to verify (4.1) to (4.5) to prove the minimality of the test set. Therefore, for all $v \in \{1, \ldots, n-1\}$, or their corresponding test entries $I_R^v \in \mathcal{F}_R^{n \leq m}$ respectively, we choose two different representatives $I_L^i, I_L^j \in \mathcal{F}_L^{n \leq m}$ that have $(\frac{n}{2} - 1)$ times the same items from $(\{1, \ldots, n\} \setminus \{v, n\})$ and the $\frac{n}{2}$-th item is v for I_L^i and n for I_L^j. Then, these two representatives have exactly $(\frac{n}{2} - 1)$ items in common and there are only two items, i.e., v and n, that are only present in one of the two representatives. Now, $f(I_L^i, I_R^v) = \frac{n}{2} + 1 \neq \frac{n}{2} = f(I_L^j, I_R^v)$, because the most frequent item of (I_L^i, I_R^v) is v with a frequency of 1 at the representative and $\frac{n}{2}$ at the test. The other pair only gets a highest frequency of $\frac{n}{2}$. Next, we want to verify that the cache states are not forced to be different for all other tests. We check this for each $v' \in (\{1, \ldots, n-1\} \setminus \{v\})$, or its corresponding test entry $I_R^{v'} \in \mathcal{F}_R^{n \leq m}$. The item v' is either present in both or in none of the two representatives, because the only distinguished items are v, n and $v' \notin \{v, n\}$. If v' is present in both, the highest frequency for both representatives $\frac{n}{2} + 1$; if not, then the most frequent item is still v' with a frequency of $\frac{n}{2}$. Therefore, we have verified (4.1) to (4.5) for the fooling set $\mathcal{F}^{n \leq m}$ and shown, that the test set is minimal. As a consequence, we may apply the referenced theorem.

iii) Finally, we can calculate the space complexity lower bound for the most frequent item problem having a success probability of $p > \frac{1}{2}$. Using Theorem 4.3 and the approximation from Lemma 3.2, the space complexity lower bound for the streaming problem $\mathcal{S}^{n \leq m}_{F_{\infty,1,p}}$ with $p > \frac{1}{2}$ is given by

$$\text{space}(\mathcal{S}^{n \leq m}_{F_{\infty,1,p}}) \geq \log_2(|\mathcal{F}^{n \leq m}_L|) \cdot \left(1 - \frac{|\mathcal{F}^{n \leq m}_R| \cdot h(p)}{\log_2(|\mathcal{F}^{n \leq m}_L|)}\right) - 1 \qquad \text{Theorem 4.3}$$

$$= \log_2\left(\binom{n}{n/2}\right) \cdot \left(1 - \frac{(n-1) \cdot h(p)}{\log_2(\binom{n}{n/2})}\right) - 1 \qquad \text{fooling set size}$$

$$> (n - \log_2(\sqrt{2n})) \cdot \left(1 - \frac{(n-1) \cdot h(p)}{n - \log_2(\sqrt{2n})}\right) - 1 \quad \text{Lemma 3.2}$$

$$> (n - \log_2(n)) \cdot (1 - 1.01 \cdot h(p)) - 1, \qquad \text{apx. for large } n$$

where $h(p) = -p \cdot \log_2(p) - (1 - p) \cdot \log_2(1 - p)$, as defined in Theorem 4.3.

We have shown the probabilistic space complexity lower bound for the case $n \leq m$.

Case 2: If $m < n$, we can similarly prove a probabilistic space complexity lower bound. We define the fooling set $\mathcal{F}^{m < n} = (\mathcal{F}^{m < n}_L, \mathcal{F}^{m < n}_R)$ that is almost the same one as in the second case of Theorem 5.7, but similarly to above, exclude the last element of the test set such that $\mathcal{F}^{m < n}_R = \{\{1, \dots, 1\}, \dots, \{m-1, \dots, m-1\}\}$. With the same argument as above, it is evident that $\mathcal{F}^{m < n}$ is still a fooling set and that the test set is minimal. If one wants to repeat the detailed proof of ii), one can simply replace in the proof above the letters n with m and the possible streaming problem result of $\frac{n}{2}$ and $\frac{n}{2} + 1$ respectively, with $n - \frac{m}{2}$ and $n - \frac{m}{2} + 1$ respectively. At last, the probabilistic space complexity lower bound can be approximated analogously as,

$$\text{space}(\mathcal{S}^{m < n}_{F_{\infty,1,p}}) \geq \log_2(|\mathcal{F}^{m < n}_L|) \qquad \text{Theorem 4.3}$$

$$\cdot \left(1 - \frac{|\mathcal{F}^{m < n}_R|}{\log_2(|\mathcal{F}^{m < n}_L|)} \cdot h(p)\right) - 1$$

$$= \log_2\left(\binom{m}{m/2}\right) \qquad \text{fooling set size}$$

$$\cdot \left(1 - \frac{(m-1)}{\log_2(\binom{m}{m/2})} \cdot h(p)\right) - 1$$

$$> (m - \log_2(m)) \cdot (1 - 1.01 \cdot h(p)) - 1. \quad \text{approx. as in Case 1}$$

Therefore, we can conclude that for any $n, m \in \mathbb{N}^+$, the space complexity lower bound for the probabilistic most frequent item streaming problem with a success

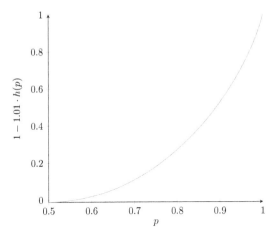

Figure 5.2. Illustration of the lower bound factor

probability of $p = 1 - \varepsilon$ with $\varepsilon < \frac{1}{2}$ is,

$$\text{space}(\mathcal{S}_{F_{\infty,1,p}}) \geq (\min\{n,m\} - \log_2(\min\{n,m\})) \cdot (1 - 1.01 \cdot h(p)) - 1$$
$$= (\min\{n,m\} - \log_2(\min\{n,m\})) \cdot$$
$$(1 + 1.01p \cdot \log_2(p) + 1.01\varepsilon \cdot \log_2(\varepsilon)) - 1.$$

With this analysis, we have proven the stated theorem.   □

This probabilistic space complexity lower bound is dependent on the success probability and as a result, difficult to compare to the deterministic one. Figure 5.2 illustrates the term $(1 - 1.01 \cdot h(p))$ for the success probability $p > \frac{1}{2}$.

This illustration shows that, with large success probabilities close to $p = 1$, we have the same space complexity lower bound as the deterministic one. For small success probabilities of $p \leq 0.558$, we have a meaningless lower bound, because it is negative. However, on the other side, for any $p \geq 0.559$, we have a lower bound of the space complexity order $\Omega(\min\{n,m\})$.

As two concrete examples, we have the following space complexity lower bounds for the success probabilities $p = 0.75$ and $p = 0.95$.

Corollary 5.1. *The streaming problem* $\mathcal{S}_{F_{\infty,1,p}}$ *has, for any* $n, m \in \mathbb{N}^+$ *and a success probability of* $p = 0.75$ *or* $p = 0.95$, *a space complexity lower bound of ,*

$$\text{space}(\mathcal{S}_{F_{\infty,1,0.75}}) \geq 0.181 \cdot (\min\{n,m\} - \log_2(\min\{n,m\})) - 1 \ and$$

$$\text{space}(\mathcal{S}_{F_{\infty,1,0.95}}) \geq 0.711 \cdot (\min\{n,m\} - \log_2(\min\{n,m\})) - 1.$$

This result can be achieved by just evaluating the theorem above with $p = 0.75$ or $p = 0.95$. This analysis shows that the space complexity lower bound is of the same order as the deterministic one. With the next theorem, we prove that the probabilistic space complexity lower bound is of the same order of $\Omega(m \cdot \log(\frac{n}{m}))$ as the deterministic ones in Theorem 5.2 and Theorem 5.8. This tight lower bound will allow a more interesting analysis and conclusion.

Theorem 5.10. *The streaming problem $\mathcal{S}_{F_{\infty,1,p}}$ has, for any $n \geq m$ and a success probability of $p = 1 - \varepsilon$ with $\varepsilon < \frac{1}{2}$, a space complexity lower bound of,*

$$\text{space}(\mathcal{S}_{F_{\infty,1,p}}^{n \geq m}) \geq \frac{m}{2} \cdot \log_2\left(\frac{n}{m}\right) - 0.21m - \frac{m \cdot h(p)}{2} - 1$$

$$\geq \frac{m}{2} \cdot \log_2\left(\frac{n}{m}\right) - 0.71m - 1.$$

Proof. Fortunately, the introduced fooling set of the deterministic proof has an already minimal test set. Therefore, *i)* we can simply use exactly the same fooling set as in Theorem 5.8, *ii)* which is also proven to be a fooling set. We just have to verify that the test set is minimal. And then, *iii)* we can calculate the space complexity lower bound.

ii) All representatives have different frequencies of the content items $j \in \{1, \ldots, \frac{m}{2}\}$. With this fact, for any test $I_R^v = \{v, \ldots, v\} \in \mathcal{F}_R$, we can simply choose two representatives that have equal frequencies of the content items except the item v. Then, I_R^v is a test, as the highest frequency is different between these two representatives, but all other tests $I_R^{v'}$ for $v' \in (\{1, \ldots, \frac{m}{2}\} \setminus \{v\})$ are not forcing different cache states, as the most frequent item will always be v' with a frequency of frac. Therefore, the test set is minimal.

iii) Now, we can use Theorem 4.3 to prove a probabilistic space complexity lower bound.

$$\text{space}(\mathcal{S}_{F_{\infty,1,p}}^{n \geq m}) \geq \log_2(|\mathcal{F}_L^{n \geq m}|) \cdot \left(1 - \frac{|\mathcal{F}_R^{n \geq m}| \cdot h(p)}{\log_2(|\mathcal{F}_L^{n \geq m}|)}\right) - 1 \quad \text{Theorem 4.3}$$

$$> \left(\frac{m}{2} \cdot \log_2\left(\frac{n}{m}\right) - 0.21m\right) \cdot \qquad\qquad \text{Theorem 5.8}$$

$$\left(1 - \frac{\frac{m}{2} \cdot h(p)}{\frac{m}{2} \cdot \log_2(\frac{n}{m}) - 0.21m}\right) - 1$$

$$= \frac{m}{2} \cdot \left(\log_2\left(\frac{n}{m}\right) - 0.42\right) \qquad\qquad \text{basic transformation}$$

$$\cdot \left(1 - \frac{h(p)}{\log_2(\frac{n}{m}) - 0.42}\right) - 1$$

$$= \frac{m}{2} \cdot \left(\log_2\left(\frac{n}{m}\right) - h(p) - 0.42\right) - 1 \qquad \text{basic transformation}$$

$$= \frac{m}{2} \cdot \log_2\left(\frac{n}{m}\right) - 0.21m - \frac{m \cdot h(p)}{2} - 1 \qquad \text{basic transformation}$$

$$\geq \frac{m}{2} \cdot \log_2\left(\frac{n}{m}\right) - 0.71m - 1 \qquad\qquad \text{as } h(p) \leq 1$$

With this calculation, we have finished the proof of this space complexity lower bound. □

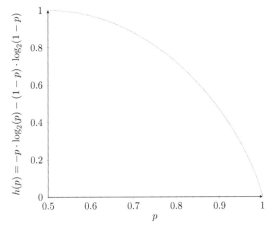

Figure 5.3. Illustration of $h(p)$

Corollary 5.2. *The streaming problem $\mathcal{S}_{F_\infty,1,p}$ has, for any $n \geq m \in \mathbb{N}^+$ and a success probability of $p = 0.75$ or $p = 0.95$, a space complexity lower bound of*

$$\text{space}(\mathcal{S}_{F_\infty,1,0.75}^{n \geq m}) \geq \frac{m}{2} \cdot \log_2\left(\frac{n}{m}\right) - 0.616m - 1 \ and$$

$$\text{space}(\mathcal{S}_{F_\infty,1,0.95}^{n \geq m}) \geq \frac{m}{2} \cdot \log_2\left(\frac{n}{m}\right) - 0.353m - 1.$$

This result can be achieved by just evaluating the theorem above with $p = 0.75$ or $p = 0.95$.

Similarly to Figure 5.2, we will illustrate the relevant part of the factor of the minor term $\frac{m \cdot h(p)}{2}$, namely $h(p)$ for the success probabilities $p > \frac{1}{2}$, in Figure 5.3.

We observe that the dominant part, i.e., $\frac{m}{2} \cdot \log_2(\frac{n}{m})$, is not affected by the success probability. This implies that for a large factor between n and m, the usage of randomization does not significantly decrease the proven space complexity lower bound. Furthermore, with the algorithm of Theorem 5.6 and cleverly chosen n, m, and d, we may get a space complexity that is very close to $m \cdot (1 + \log_2(\frac{n}{m}))$. Therefore, the dominant part of this space complexity is, for a large fraction $\frac{n}{m}$, only twice the given space complexity lower bound. If we additionally decrease the space complexity using the randomization approach from Section 5.1, we have a space complexity dominant part that is close to $p \cdot m \cdot \log_2(\frac{n}{m})$. For the validity of the probabilistic lower bound, with a success probability of $p > \frac{1}{2}$, this is very close to the above lower bound. Now, we can conclude that these upper and lower bounds are almost tight. As a consequence, it is impossible to significantly improve the probabilistic algorithm from above for the exact most frequent item problem. Or in other words, the above described algorithm is almost optimal.

In the following, we will analyze the effect of allowing solution approximations on the upper and lower bound of the space complexity.

Approximative Deterministic Most Frequent Item Problem

Once again, we first introduce the known space complexities from the literature and then explain some techniques and proofs to enhance the space complexity bounds. We use the notation of $\mathcal{S}_{F_{\infty,\alpha,1}}$ for the approximative deterministic most frequent item problem.

Known Bounds from the Literature

The only space complexity bound we are aware of for an approximation rate of $\alpha > 1$ for the most frequent item streaming problem is the following one:

Theorem 5.11 (Alon et al. [AMS99]). *The streaming problem $\mathcal{S}_{F_{\infty,\alpha,1}}$ with a 2-sided approximation ratio of $\alpha = \frac{4}{3} \approx 1.333$, has, for any $\frac{m}{2} \leq n \leq 2m$, a space complexity lower bound of,*

$$\mathrm{space}\left(\mathcal{S}_{F_{\infty,\frac{4}{3},1}}^{\frac{m}{2} \leq n \leq 2m}\right) \in \Omega(m).$$

Probably, because of the same complexity order of this lower bound, there are no further, well-known results. The stated algorithm by Indyk and Woodruff [IW05] is for sure also valid for an approximative environment, as it solves the task exactly, but it is not further optimized.

We show in the following how we can cut the space size in half if we allow approximations of the ratio $\alpha = \sqrt{2}$. Or more generally, how to divide the space size with factor d if we allow an approximation of $\alpha = \sqrt{d}$. Afterwards, we show an exact space complexity lower bound of the same order as the one above, but with an approximation ratio of $\alpha < \sqrt{2}$ for a 2-sided approximation. Finally, we show a technique to prove a space complexity lower bound for $\alpha \geq \sqrt{2}$ and explain why it is difficult to find a better one.

Enhanced Upper Bounds

Similar to the approach in the probabilistic environment, we can reduce the space complexity of the algorithms in Theorem 5.4, Theorem 5.5, and Theorem 5.6 by allowing approximative results.

If a 2-sided approximation ratio of $\alpha = \sqrt{2}$ is allowed, we modify the histogram-counting of the individual algorithms. We do not count the frequencies of every individual item, but count the item pairs $\{1, 2\}$, $\{3, 4\}$, and so on. After processing the entire input stream and counting the frequency pairs, the algorithms simply outputs the highest frequency of any such pair divided by $\sqrt{2}$. With this approach, the algorithm will output a result that has an approximation ratio of at most $\alpha = \sqrt{2}$. We observe, that the highest pair-frequency is at most twice the optimal result and at the other extrema, the highest pair-frequency is exactly the optimal result. At one first extreme, an item-pair has a frequency of twice the optimal, namely $2 \cdot f(x)$.

Then the algorithm will output $\frac{2 \cdot f(x)}{\sqrt{2}}$ and the approximation value is at most $\sqrt{2}$ because,

$$\frac{\frac{2 \cdot f(x)}{\sqrt{2}}}{f(x)} = \frac{2}{\sqrt{2}} = \sqrt{2}.$$

In the second extreme, the highest pair-frequency is just $f(x)$. However, the approximation value between the delivered result of $\frac{f(x)}{\sqrt{2}}$ and the optimal value is still at most $\sqrt{2}$, since

$$\frac{f(x)}{\frac{f(x)}{\sqrt{2}}} = \frac{1}{\frac{1}{\sqrt{2}}} = \sqrt{2}.$$

For any result between these two extrema, the approximative value is even better. Therefore, this approach will deliver an approximation of the most frequent item with an approximation ratio of $\sqrt{2}$ with half the required space as in the algorithms of Theorem 5.4, Theorem 5.5, and Theorem 5.6.

Similarly, we can achieve a reduction of the required space size by the factor d if we allow an approximation ratio of $\sqrt{d}$. We get this, by counting frequency tuples of always d items, namely by counting the total frequency of $\{1, \ldots, d\}$, $\{d+1, \ldots, 2d\}$, and so on. At the end, the algorithm divides the tuple frequency by $\sqrt{d}$. Obviously, this algorithm requires d times less storage. The highest tuple frequency is between $f(x)$ and $d \cdot f(x)$. With the same argument as above, one can simply verify the claimed bound on the approximation ratio.

Of course, this approach is only valid if both approximation values above and below the optimal result are allowed. If only 1-sided approximations are allowed, we are not allowed to eventually overestimate the optimal value and therefore, cannot use this approach.

In the following, we will analyze two space-complexity lower bounds for the approximative deterministic most frequent item streaming problem.

Enhanced Lower Bounds

For a space complexity lower bound in an approximative environment, we have to identify an α-fooling set for the corresponding streaming problem. As introduced in Theorem 4.4, we have to verify that the cache states for any two representatives have to be different. This implies that the streaming problem result between any two representatives and their test entry is required to be different by a factor of more than α. With such an α-fooling set, we can prove a space complexity lower bound of $\log_2(|\mathcal{F}_L|)$, if an approximation ratio of α is allowed for 1-sided approximations. If 2-sided approximations are allowed, then we have the same lower bound, if an approximation ratio of $\sqrt{\alpha}$ is allowed.

Theorem 5.12. *The streaming problem* $\mathcal{S}_{F_\infty, \alpha, 1}$ *has, for any* $n, m \in \mathbb{N}^+$ *and a 1-sided approximation ratio of* $\alpha < 2$, *a space complexity lower bound of*

$$\mathrm{space}\left(\mathcal{S}_{F_\infty, \alpha < 2, 1}\right) \geq \min\left\{n - \log_2(n), \frac{m}{2} - \frac{\log_2(m)}{2}\right\} \in \Omega(\min\{n, m\}).$$

Proof. To prove this theorem, we use a case distinction between $n \leq m$ and $m < n$ and, for both cases, *i*) introduce the α-fooling set, *ii*) verify the α-fooling set, and *iii*) calculate the space complexity lower bound. For ease of presentation, we assume, that m is not only even, but a multiple of 4, i.e., $m = 4 \cdot d$ for some $d \in \mathbb{N}^+$.

First, one may realize, that the fooling sets of the two cases from Theorem 5.7 from above are not usable to verify any fixed approximation ratio $\alpha < 2$, because the streaming problem will produce the following output values for any possible representative $I_L^i \in \mathcal{F}_L$ and test entry $I_R^v \in \mathcal{F}_R$:

$$f(I_L^i, I_R^v) \in \left\{ \frac{n}{2}, \frac{n}{2}+1 \right\} \cup \left\{ n - \frac{m}{2}, n - \frac{m}{2}+1 \right\}.$$

The fraction between the streaming problem output of two different representatives is very low, namely below $\frac{1}{\min\{n,m\}}$. With this fooling set, we calculate the space complexity lower bound for an approximation ratio of $\alpha < \frac{1}{\min\{n,m\}}$. As we want to show an approximation ratio of $\alpha < 2$, we are looking for a fooling set whose entries will lead to highest frequencies of two different values that are apart by a factor of at least 2. In the following, we will describe and justify such an α-fooling set.

Case 1: If $n \leq m$, we will define and analyze the fooling set as follows:

i) We define the α-fooling set $\mathcal{F}_{F_{\infty,\alpha<2,1}}^{n \leq m} = (\mathcal{F}_L^{n \leq m}, \mathcal{F}_R^{n \leq m})$ with a cut at $l := n-2$. This means, that the representatives contain $n-2$ items and the test set only two input values. Each representative has $(\frac{n}{2}-1)$ different items from the set $\{1, \ldots, n\} \subseteq \{1, \ldots, m\}$, but each item occurs twice. Therefore, every representative has $2 \cdot (\frac{n}{2}-1) = n-2$ input values. In total, there are $\binom{n}{n/2-1}$ different representatives. As test set, we choose $n-1$ entries each containing one value from $\{1, \ldots, n-1\}$ twice, namely $\mathcal{F}_R^{n \leq m} = \{\{1,1\}, \{2,2\}, \ldots, \{n-1, n-1\}\}$. Intentionally, the test set does not contain the logical completing element $\{n, n\}$ such that the test set is minimal (to be proven later), and the entire fooling set can be used for the probabilistic analysis in the later parts as well.

ii) Then, we have to verify, that $\mathcal{F}_{F_{\infty,\alpha<2,1}}^{n \leq m}$ is an α-fooling set for the most frequent item problem. As stated and explained in Definition 4.3, we have to verify that,

$$\forall I_L^i, I_L^j \in \mathcal{F}_L \text{ with } I_L^i \neq I_L^j \colon \exists I_R^v \in \mathcal{F}_R \text{ s.t. } \frac{f(I_L^i, I_R^v)}{f(I_L^j, I_R^v)} < \frac{1}{\alpha} \text{ or } \frac{f(I_L^i, I_R^v)}{f(I_L^j, I_R^v)} > \alpha.$$

Similarly to the proof in Theorem 5.9, any two representatives will lead to at least two items $v, v' \in \{1, \ldots, n\}$, such that v and v' are only present in one of the two representatives. W.l.o.g, we assume $v < v' \leq n$. With the test $I_R^v = \{v, v\}$, we have a highest frequency of 4, if v is present in the representative, or 2 if not. Finally, one of the following two conditions is satisfied:

$$\frac{f(I_L^i, I_R^v)}{f(I_L^j, I_R^v)} = \frac{2}{4} = \frac{1}{2} < \frac{1}{\alpha} \quad \text{or} \quad \frac{f(I_L^i, I_R^v)}{f(I_L^j, I_R^v)} = \frac{4}{2} = 2 > \alpha.$$

Therefore, $\mathcal{F}_{F_{\infty,\alpha<2,1}}^{n \leq m}$ is an α-fooling set for the most frequent item problem for any $\alpha < 2$.

iii) At last, we can calculate the space complexity lower bound:

$$\text{space}(\mathcal{S}_{F_{\infty,\alpha<2,1}}^{n\leq m}) \geq \log_2(|\mathcal{F}_L^{n\leq m}|) = \log_2\left(\binom{n}{n/2-1}\right) \quad \text{fooling set size}$$

$$> \log_2\left(\frac{2^n\cdot\sqrt{2n}}{2n+4}\right) \qquad\qquad\qquad \text{Lemma 3.3}$$

$$= n + \log_2(\sqrt{2n}) - \log_2(2n+4) \qquad\quad \text{basic transformation}$$

$$= n + \frac{\log_2(n)}{2} + \frac{1}{2} - \log_2(n+2) - 1 \quad \text{basic transformation}$$

$$> n + \frac{\log_2(n)}{2} + \frac{1}{2} - \log_2(n) - 1 - 1 \quad \text{simple approximation}$$

$$= n - \frac{1}{2}\cdot\log_2(n) - 1.5 \qquad\qquad\quad \text{basic transformation}$$

$$> n - \log_2(n) \qquad\qquad\qquad\qquad\quad \text{simple approximation}$$

This is the space complexity lower bound for the first case.

Case 2: If $m < n$, it is a little bit more complicated to ensure an α-fooling set, because we cannot simply encode frequencies of 2 and 4, as we did in the first case, because the highest frequency will be at least $\lceil\frac{n}{m}\rceil$, which is larger than 4 for some $m \ll n$. We will therefore define a basic value replication dependent on the fraction between n and m. Similarly to Theorem 5.8, we will implement this basic value replication using content items and fill up the stream with spacer items.

i) Before we define the α-fooling set, we define the basic value replication as

$$r := \left\lfloor\frac{n}{\frac{m}{2}}\right\rfloor = \left\lfloor\frac{2n}{m}\right\rfloor \geq 2. \tag{5.4}$$

With this basic value replication r, we define the α-fooling set $\mathcal{F}^{m<n}$ with $\mathcal{F}^{m<n} = (\mathcal{F}_L^{m<n}, \mathcal{F}_R^{m<n})$, such that all possible input stream combinations of any representative and test entry will lead to a problem function value that is either r or $2r$, more formally,

$$\forall I_L^i \in \mathcal{F}_L^{m<n}, \forall I_R^v \in \mathcal{F}_R^{m<n}: f(I_L^i, I_R^v) \in \{r, 2r\}.$$

We define the α-fooling set $\mathcal{F}_{F_{\infty,\alpha<2,1}}^{m<n} = (\mathcal{F}_L^{m<n}, \mathcal{F}_R^{m<n})$ with a cut at $l = n - r = n - \lfloor\frac{2n}{m}\rfloor$. The test set contains $(\frac{m}{2}-1)$ different test entries, each with r times the same item $j \in \{1,\ldots,\frac{m}{2}-1\}$, namely,

$$\mathcal{F}_R^{m<n} = \left\{\{1,\ldots,1\},\ldots,\left\{\frac{m}{2}-1,\ldots,\frac{m}{2}-1\right\}\right\}.$$

The representatives are representing possible combinations of $\frac{m}{4}$ different elements from the content items $\{1,\ldots,\frac{m}{2}\} \subset \{1,\ldots,m\}$. Each content item occurs r times in the corresponding representative. Therefore, each representative has $r \cdot \frac{m}{4}$ input values with the content items. The rest of the representative stream is filled up with spacer items $j \in \{\frac{m}{2}+1,\ldots,m\}$ with a maximal frequency of r. Therefore, there are in total $(l - r \cdot \frac{m}{4})$ such spacer values within every representative, as l is the size of the input stream of the representatives and $r \cdot \frac{m}{4}$ stands for the ones filled with the content items. As at most $r \cdot \frac{m}{2}$ spacer items are allowed to ensure the highest frequency of r of every spacer item, we have to verify that

$$0 \leq l - r \cdot \frac{m}{4} \leq r \cdot \frac{m}{2}. \tag{5.5}$$

The left inequality of (5.5) states that the number of required spacer items is not negative. It can be easily shown with the following calculation:

$$
\begin{aligned}
l - r \cdot \frac{m}{4} &= n - r - r \cdot \frac{m}{4} = n - r \cdot \left(1 + \frac{m}{4}\right) && \text{basic transformation} \\
&= n - \left\lfloor \frac{2n}{m} \right\rfloor \cdot \left(1 + \frac{m}{4}\right) && \text{definition of } r, \text{ (5.4)} \\
&\geq n - \frac{2n}{m} \cdot \left(1 + \frac{m}{4}\right) && \text{simple approximation} \\
&= n - \frac{2n}{m} - \frac{n}{2} && \text{basic transformation} \\
&= n \cdot \left(\frac{1}{2} - \frac{2}{m}\right) && \text{basic transformation} \\
&\geq 0
\end{aligned}
$$

Next, the right inequality of (5.5) states that the frequency limit of r for the spacer item does not have to be exceeded to fill the representatives with $l = n - r$ input values. As $\lfloor \frac{2n}{m} \rfloor \geq 2$, the effect of rounding down the replication value r is at most a factor of $\frac{1}{3}$, namely from $2.\bar{9}$ to 2, therefore

$$\lfloor \frac{2n}{m} \rfloor \geq \frac{2n}{m} \cdot \frac{2}{3} = \frac{4n}{3m}. \tag{5.6}$$

Using this approximation, we can verify the right inequality as follows:

$$
\begin{aligned}
l - r \cdot \frac{m}{4} &= n - r - r \cdot \frac{m}{4} = n - r \cdot \left(1 + \frac{m}{4}\right) && \text{basic transformation} \\
&= n - \left\lfloor \frac{2n}{m} \right\rfloor \cdot \left(1 + \frac{m}{4}\right) && \text{use definition of } r, \text{ (5.4)} \\
&\leq n - \frac{4n}{3m} \cdot \left(1 + \frac{m}{4}\right) && \text{approximation of (5.6)} \\
&= n - \frac{4n}{3m} - \frac{n}{3} = \frac{2n}{3} - \frac{4n}{3m} && \text{basic transformation} \\
&< \frac{2n}{3} && \text{simple approximation} \\
&= \frac{4n}{3m} \cdot \frac{m}{2} && \text{basic transformation} \\
&\leq \left\lfloor \frac{2n}{m} \right\rfloor \cdot \frac{m}{2} && \text{approximation of (5.6)} \\
&= r \cdot \frac{m}{2}
\end{aligned}
$$

Therefore, the set of representatives is valid, which means that it has input streams of length l, whose frequencies are additionally at most r. Now, we have to verify that $\mathcal{F}^{m<n}_{F_\infty,\alpha<2,1}$ is an α-fooling set for $\alpha < 2$.

$ii)$ Similarly to the proof of the first case, any two representatives $I^i_L, I^j_L \in \mathcal{F}^{m<n}_L$ will lead to at least two content items $v, v' \in \{1, \ldots, \frac{m}{2}\}$, such that v and v' are only present in one of the two representatives. W.l.o.g., we assume $v < v' \leq \frac{m}{2}$. With the test $I^v_R = \{v, \ldots, v\}$, we have a highest frequency of exactly $2r$, if v is present in the representative, or r if not. Therefore, we have one of the two conditions,

$$\frac{f(I^i_L, I^v_R)}{f(I^j_L, I^v_R)} = \frac{r}{2r} = \frac{1}{2} < \frac{1}{\alpha} \quad \text{or} \quad \frac{f(I^i_L, I^v_R)}{f(I^j_L, I^v_R)} = \frac{2r}{r} = 2 > \alpha.$$

That is why $\mathcal{F}^{m<n}_{F_\infty,\alpha<2,1}$ is an α-fooling set for the most frequent item problem for any $\alpha < 2$.

$iii)$ At last, we can calculate the space complexity lower bound, which is,

$$\begin{aligned}
\text{space}(\mathcal{S}^{m<n}_{F_\infty,\alpha<2,1}) &\geq \log_2(|\mathcal{F}^{m<n}_L|) = \log_2\left(\binom{m/2}{m/4}\right) && \text{fooling set size} \\
&> \log_2\left(\frac{2^{m/2}}{\sqrt{m}}\right) && \text{Lemma 3.2} \\
&= \frac{m}{2} - \log_2(\sqrt{m}) && \text{basic transformation} \\
&= \frac{m}{2} - \frac{\log_2(m)}{2}. && \text{basic transformation}
\end{aligned}$$

Therefore, we can conclude a space complexity lower bound for any approximation ratio $\alpha < 2$ and for any m, n, as follows,

$$\text{space}\left(\mathcal{S}_{F_\infty,\alpha<2,1}\right) \geq \min\left\{n - \log_2(n), \frac{m}{2} - \frac{\log_2(m)}{2}\right\} \in \Omega(\min\{n, m\}). \qquad \square$$

Corollary 5.3. *The streaming problem $\mathcal{S}_{F_\infty,\alpha,1}$ has, for any $n, m \in \mathbb{N}^+$ and a 2-sided approximation ratio of $\alpha < \sqrt{2}$, a space complexity lower bound of*

$$\text{space}\left(\mathcal{S}_{F_\infty,\alpha<\sqrt{2},1}\right) \geq \min\left\{n - \log_2(n), \frac{m}{2} - \frac{\log_2(m)}{2}\right\} \in \Omega(\min\{n, m\}).$$

This corollary follows directly from the proven α-fooling set from Theorem 5.12 with Theorem 4.5 on space complexity lower bounds for 2-sided approximations.

When we compare the two space complexity lower bounds for the exact and approximative setting, one can observe that, for the first case, which is $n \leq m$, both lower bounds are exactly the same. This does not necessarily imply that it is not possible to decrease the space complexity of streaming algorithms with approximative results, as we have seen in Section 5.1. But the equality is an indicator that it might be hard to decrease the space complexity significantly. For the other case, which is $m < n$, the space complexity lower bound for the approximative setting is half the one from the exact environment. But with a smaller approximation ratio of $\alpha = 1.19$, instead of $\alpha < 2$, we can show a space complexity lower bound that is closer to the one of the non-approximative setting.

Theorem 5.13. *The streaming problem* $\mathcal{S}_{F_\infty, \alpha=1.19,1}$ *has, for any* $n > m \geq 100$ *with* $n, m \in \mathbb{N}^+$ *and for a* 1*-sided approximation ratio of* $\alpha = 1.19$, *a space complexity lower bound of*

$$\text{space}\left(\mathcal{S}_{F_\infty,1.19,1}^{m<n}\right) \geq 0.915m - \frac{\log_2(m)}{2} - 1 \in \Omega(m).$$

Proof. To prove this theorem, the fooling set will, once again, use the idea of content and spacer items. However, they are no longer strictly separated but individually distributed per representative. As a consequence, the α-fooling set will allow a lower approximation ratio than in the case above, but we are able to have a fooling set with more representatives and as a consequence, a higher space complexity lower bound is proven. Once again, we will *i*) define the fooling set, *ii*) verify it and *iii*) calculate the space complexity lower bound. For ease of presentation, we also assume, that m is a multiple of 4, i.e., $m = 4 \cdot d$ for some $d \in \mathbb{N}^+$.

i) Similarly to Theorem 5.12, we first define a basic value replication, which is

$$r := \left\lfloor \frac{n}{\frac{m}{4} + 1} \right\rfloor = \left\lfloor \frac{4n}{m + 4} \right\rfloor. \tag{5.7}$$

With this basic value replication, we define an α-fooling set $\mathcal{F}_{F_\infty,\alpha=1.19,1} = (\mathcal{F}_L, \mathcal{F}_R)$ with a cut at $l = n - r$. The test set contains $(m - 1)$ entries with r times the same item $j \in \{1, \ldots, m-1\}$, namely $\mathcal{F}_R = \{\{1, \ldots, 1\}, \ldots, \{m-1, \ldots, m-1\}\}$. The set of representatives contains an entry for every possible *set quarter*, that contains $\frac{m}{4}$ different content items from $\{1, \ldots, m\}$. As a consequence, we have in total $\binom{m}{m/4}$ different representatives. Each representative contains these $\frac{m}{4}$ different content items with a frequency of r. Then, we have to fill up each representative with spacer items until they have an input stream length of l, which means we require $l - r \cdot \frac{m}{4} = n - r \cdot (1 + \frac{m}{4})$ spacer item values. They are chosen from the other $m - \frac{m}{4}$ spacer items (more precisely: the items that are not chosen as set quarter) with a uniform distribution, such that the highest frequency of these spacer items is minimal. As a consequence, the highest frequency of these spacer items is

$$\left\lceil \frac{\# \text{ spacer values}}{\# \text{ spacer items}} \right\rceil = \left\lceil \frac{l - r \cdot \frac{m}{4}}{m - \frac{m}{4}} \right\rceil = \left\lceil \frac{n - r \cdot (1 + \frac{m}{4})}{m - \frac{m}{4}} \right\rceil. \tag{5.8}$$

Similarly to Theorem 5.12, we have to verify that the amount of spacer values is not negative, namely $l - r \cdot \frac{m}{4} \geq 0$. For this, we require the following approximation of the basic replication value r, i.e.,

$$\frac{3n}{m+4} \leq r \leq \frac{4n}{m+4}. \tag{5.9}$$

The right approximation of (5.9) is trivial, as the removal of the floor operator on the definition of r, see (5.7), always leads to an equal or a greater value. The left inequality of (5.9) can be verified by analyzing the highest possible impact of the floor operators. As we assume $m \geq 100$ in this theorem, $r \geq 3$, because $\frac{4n}{m} \geq 4$ for any $m < n$, and the addition of 4 impacts the non-rounded result by at most 1.04

for any $m \geq 100$. Therefore, the highest impact of the decrease is from $3.\bar{9}$ down to 3, which is a factor of at most $\frac{3}{4}$. Therefore,

$$r = \left\lfloor \frac{4n}{m+4} \right\rfloor \geq \frac{3}{4} \cdot \frac{4n}{m+4} = \frac{3n}{m+4}. \tag{5.10}$$

Now, the positiveness of the amount of spacer items can be shown with following approximation:

$$
\begin{aligned}
\text{\# spacer values} &= l - r \cdot \frac{m}{4} && \text{definition of spacer values} \\
&= n - r \cdot \left(1 + \frac{m}{4}\right) && \text{definition of cut } l \\
&= n - \left\lfloor \frac{4n}{m+4} \right\rfloor \cdot \left(1 + \frac{m}{4}\right) && \text{definition of } r, \text{ (5.7)} \\
&\geq n - \frac{4n}{m+4} \cdot \frac{m+4}{4} && \text{approx. of } r, \text{ (5.10)} \\
&= n - n \geq 0
\end{aligned}
$$

As a consequence, this approach leads to a set of representatives and tests with the required amount of input values.

$ii)$ To verify, that $\mathcal{F}_{F_{\infty,\alpha=1.19,1}}$ is an α-fooling set with $\alpha = 1.19$, we approximate the highest frequency of the spacer items as intermediate result. We use the formula from above and approximate it, namely,

$$
\begin{aligned}
\left\lceil \frac{\text{\# spacer values}}{\text{\# spacer items}} \right\rceil &= \left\lceil \frac{l - r \cdot \frac{m}{4}}{m - \frac{m}{4}} \right\rceil && \text{definition from (5.8)} \\
&= \left\lceil \frac{n - r \cdot \left(1 + \frac{m}{4}\right)}{m - \frac{m}{4}} \right\rceil && \text{definition of cut } l \\
&\leq \left\lceil \frac{n - \frac{3n}{m+4} \cdot \frac{m+4}{4}}{m - \frac{m}{4}} \right\rceil && \text{approx. of } r, \text{ (5.10)} \\
&= \left\lceil \frac{\frac{n}{4}}{\frac{3m}{4}} \right\rceil && \text{basic transformation} \\
&= \left\lceil \frac{n}{3m} \right\rceil && \text{basic transforamtion} \\
&\leq \frac{n}{m} && \text{simple approx. for } m < n
\end{aligned}
$$

Therefore, the highest frequency of any spacer item is at most $\frac{n}{m}$. Finally, we can verify the α-fooling set. For any two representatives $I_R^i, I_R^j \in \mathcal{F}_R$, there are at least two items $v, v' \in \{1, \ldots, m\}$, such that both v and v' are content items in only one of the representatives, which means, that these two items are present with a frequency of exactly r in only one of the two representatives. W.l.o.g., we assume that $v < v' \leq m$ and I_R^i contains v with a frequency of r, namely v is a content item of I_R^i. With the test entry $I_R^v = \{v, \ldots, v\}$, we have a highest frequency of either $2r = f(I_L^i, I_R^v)$, if v is present with a frequency of r in the representative, or a highest frequency of $r + \left\lceil \frac{\text{\# spacer values}}{\text{\# spacer items}} \right\rceil = f(I_L^j, I_R^v)$, if v is not a content item of the representative. Therefore, for any two representatives, there is a test entry such that the fraction between the two highest frequency counts is more than $\alpha = 1.19$:

$$
\begin{aligned}
\frac{f(I_L^i, I_R^v)}{f(I_L^j, I_R^v)} &= \frac{2r}{r + \left\lceil \frac{\# \text{ spacer values}}{\# \text{ spacer items}} \right\rceil} && \text{definition from above} \\[2mm]
&\geq \frac{2 \cdot \frac{3n}{m+4}}{\frac{4n}{4+m} + \frac{n}{m}} && \text{approx. from above} \\[2mm]
&= \frac{6n}{m+4} \cdot \frac{(m+4) \cdot m}{4nm + n \cdot (m+4)} && \text{basic transformation} \\[2mm]
&= \frac{6m}{5m+4} && \text{basic transformation} \\[2mm]
&\geq \frac{6m}{5.04m} = \frac{6}{5.04} > 1.19 && \text{for } m \geq 100
\end{aligned}
$$

Therefore, $\mathcal{F}_{F_\infty, \alpha = 1.19, 1} = (\mathcal{F}_L, \mathcal{F}_R)$ is an α-fooling set for $\alpha = 1.19$ for the most frequent item problem.

iii) Now, we can calculate the space complexity lower bound:

$$
\begin{aligned}
\text{space}(\mathcal{S}_{F_\infty, \alpha = 1.19, 1}^{m < n}) &\geq \log_2(|\mathcal{F}_L|) = \log_2\left(\binom{m}{m/4} \right) && \text{fooling set size} \\[2mm]
&> \log_2\left(\frac{0.916}{\sqrt{m}} \cdot 2^{0.915m} \right) && \text{Lemma 3.4} \\[2mm]
&= 0.915m + \log_2(0.916) - \log_2(\sqrt{m}) && \text{basic transformation} \\[2mm]
&> 0.915m - \frac{\log_2(m)}{2} - 1 && \text{simple approximation}
\end{aligned}
$$

With this calculation, we have finished the proof of this space complexity lower bound.   □

Corollary 5.4. *The streaming problem $\mathcal{S}_{F_\infty, \alpha = 1.09, 1}$ has, for any $n > m \geq 100$ with $n, m \in \mathbb{N}^+$ and for a 2-sided approximation ratio of $\alpha = 1.09$, a space complexity lower bound of*

$$
\text{space}\left(\mathcal{S}_{F_\infty, \alpha = 1.09, 1}^{m < n} \right) \geq 0.915m - \frac{\log_2(m)}{2} - 1 \in \Omega(m).
$$

This corollary follows directly from the proven α-fooling set from Theorem 5.13 and Theorem 4.5.

In Theorem 5.8 and Theorem 5.10, we have proven a space complexity lower bound of $\Omega(m \cdot \log(\frac{n}{m}))$ for the exact (approximation ratio is $\alpha = 1$), deterministic and probabilistic setting. The introduced fooling set leads, for any representative $I_L^i \in \mathcal{F}_L$ and test $I_R^v \in \mathcal{F}_R$, to a highest frequency of

$$
f\left(I_L^i, I_R^v\right) \in \left\{ \left\lceil \frac{\text{frac}}{2} \right\rceil + \text{frac}, \dots, 2 \cdot \text{frac} \right\}.
$$

With these optimal output values, it is complicated to find a space complexity lower bound of the same order for any approximation ratio $\alpha > 1$, because the differences between these highest frequencies are, for any pair of representatives $I_L^i, I_L^j \in \mathcal{F}_L$ and a test entry $I_R^v \in \mathcal{F}_R$, bounded by,

$$1 \leq \max\left\{ \frac{f(I_L^i, I_R^v)}{f(I_L^j, I_R^v)}, \frac{f(I_L^j, I_R^v)}{f(I_L^i, I_R^v)} \right\} \leq \frac{2 \cdot \text{frac}}{\left\lceil \frac{\text{frac}}{2} \right\rceil + \text{frac}} \leq \frac{4}{3}.$$

The left side of the inequality is still very close to 1 for differing frequencies. This small gap between the highest frequencies makes it hard to define an α-fooling set with the same fooling set concept. Therefore, we will now focus on another aspect. So far, we have analyzed the space complexity lower bound of approximation ratios $\alpha < 2$ for 1-sided approximations. When we want to prove such a lower bound for approximation ratios of $\alpha \geq 2$, we have the following challenge: For all representatives $I_L^i \in \mathcal{F}_L$ and tests $I_R^v \in \mathcal{F}_R$, the highest frequency of the combination of representative and test is at most the addition of the individual ones, namely,

$$\max\left\{ f(I_L^i), f(I_R^v) \right\} \leq f\left(I_L^i, I_R^v \right) \leq f(I_L^i) + f(I_R^v) \leq 2 \cdot \max\left\{ f(I_L^i), f(I_R^v) \right\}.$$

The left inequality is trivial, because $f(I_L^i), f(I_R^v) \geq 0$ for all representatives and tests. The middle inequality reaches equality if and only if the most frequent items of both representative and test are the same. Otherwise, if the most frequent items are not the same, then the highest frequency of the combination is lower. The right inequality is likewise trivial.

From these estimations, we can conclude: To ensure, that $\mathcal{F}^\alpha$ is an α-fooling set with an $\alpha \geq 2$, we cannot combine representatives and tests cleverly as in the theorems above, but we have to encode different frequency values in either the representative or test entries.

We will now introduce a possible way to prove a space complexity lower bound for an approximation ratio of $\alpha \geq 2$. This lower bound is very small, but unfortunately, we are not able to design a better approximative algorithm that may benefit from this small space complexity lower bound significantly, as we have seen in the previous section.

Theorem 5.14. *The streaming problem $\mathcal{S}_{F_{\infty,\alpha\geq 2,1}}$ has, for any $n, m \in \mathbb{N}^+$ and for a 1-sided approximation ratio of $\alpha \geq 2$, a space complexity lower bound of*

$$\text{space}\left(\mathcal{S}_{F_{\infty,\alpha\geq 2,1}} \right) \geq \log_2\left(\log_2\left(\min\left\{ n, \frac{m-1}{2} \right\} \right) \right) - \log_2\left(\log_2\left(\frac{3}{2} \cdot \alpha \right) \right).$$

Proof. Once again, we do a case distinction between $n \leq m$ and $m < n$.

Case 1: If $n \leq m$: We define the α-fooling set $\mathcal{F}_{F_{\infty,\alpha\geq 2,1}}^{n\leq m} = (\mathcal{F}_L^{n\leq m}, \mathcal{F}_R^{n\leq m})$ that has a cut at $l = n - 1$. The set of tests contains only one entry that covers the item m, namely, $\mathcal{F}_R^{n\leq m} = \{\{m\}\}$. The set of representatives contains different entries $\mathcal{F}_L^{n\leq m} = \{I_L^1, \ldots, I_L^d\}$ such that, for any $i \in \{1, \ldots, d\}$, the representative I_L^i contains $k(i)$ times the item 1 and $l - k(i) = n - 1 - k(i)$ different items from $\{2, \ldots, m-1\}$. Next, we will define this function $k(i)$ that encodes different frequencies. But first, we observe, that $f(I_L^i, I_R^v) = k(i)$ for any representative and test.

To define the frequency function $k(i)$, we will use the definition of

$$\alpha^+ := \alpha + \varepsilon \text{ for an arbitrarily small } \varepsilon > 0. \tag{5.11}$$

The frequency function $k(i)$ assigns the first representative I_L^1 a frequency of 1, namely, $k(1) = 1$. The second representative is required to have a fraction to $f(I_L^1) = 1$ of more than α. Therefore, $k(2) = \lceil \alpha^+ \rceil$. The third representative is defined as $k(3) = \lceil \alpha^+ \cdot k(2) \rceil$. Consequently, we define the frequency function $k(i)$ recursively:

$$k(1) = 1 \text{ and } k(i) = \lceil \alpha^+ \cdot k(i-1) \rceil \text{ for all } i \geq 2.$$

We use d representatives, with the highest possible d, such that $k(d) < n$. If $k(d) \geq n$, the representative cannot contain only $l = n - 1$ items with $k(d) \geq n$ times the item 1. One may observe that the effect of rounding up by the evaluation of the recursive $k(i)$ is always below $\frac{3}{2}$. This value is reached for $k(2)$ with $\alpha = 2$, then $\lceil \alpha^+ \rceil = 3$. Therefore, we can conclude, for a sufficiently small $\varepsilon > 0$, that,

$$k(i) = \lceil \alpha^+ \cdot k(i-1) \rceil \leq \frac{3}{2} \cdot \alpha \cdot k(i-1),$$

with α^+ as defined in (5.12).

With this insight, we can approximate the size of the set of representatives with the following idea:

We presume $k(d) < n$, which is true when $\left(\frac{3}{2} \cdot \alpha \right)^{(d-1)} < n,$

therefore, we have a $d = \log_{\frac{3}{2} \cdot \alpha}(n) = \dfrac{\log_2(n)}{\log_2\left(\frac{3}{2} \cdot \alpha \right)}.$

Obviously, this definition of $\mathcal{F}_{F_{\infty, \alpha \geq 2, 1}}^{n \leq m} = (\mathcal{F}_L^{n \leq m}, \mathcal{F}_R^{n \leq m})$ results in an α-fooling set for $\alpha \geq 2$, because any two representatives $I_L^i, I_L^j \in \mathcal{F}_L^{n \leq m}$ will lead to fractions of their highest frequency value of at least $(\alpha^+)^{|i-j|} \geq (\alpha^+)^1 > \alpha$. Therefore, we can show a space complexity lower bound of,

$$\text{space}(\mathcal{S}_{F_{\infty, \alpha \geq 2, 1}}^{n \leq m}) \geq \log_2(|\mathcal{F}_L^{n \leq m}|) = \log_2 \left(\dfrac{\log_2(n)}{\log_2\left(\frac{3}{2} \cdot \alpha \right)} \right) \quad \text{fooling set size}$$

$$= \log_2(\log_2(n)) - \log_2\left(\log_2\left(\frac{3}{2} \cdot \alpha \right) \right). \quad \text{basic transformation}$$

This is the space complexity lower bound for the first case. For the second case, we will use almost the same approach.

Case 2: If $m < n$, we cannot implement a highest frequency of only 1 as for I_L^1 from the first case. We will always have at least a highest frequency of $f(I_L^i, I_R^v) \geq \lceil \frac{n}{m} \rceil$, which is the case when the input values are uniformly distributed on the items. Therefore, we define this basic replication of $r := \lceil \frac{n}{m} \rceil$. With a cut of $l = n - r$, the set of representatives from the α-fooling set $\mathcal{F}_{F_{\infty, \alpha \geq 2, 1}}^{m < n} = (\mathcal{F}_L^{m < n}, \mathcal{F}_R^{m < n})$ contains r times the item m, namely $\mathcal{F}_R^{m < n} = \{\{m, \ldots, m\}\}$. The set of representatives simulates the frequency values $r, \lceil r \cdot \alpha^+ \rceil, \lceil \lceil r \cdot \alpha^+ \rceil \cdot \alpha^+ \rceil, \ldots$ as in the first case. More formally, the frequency function $k(i)$ is now defined recursively as

$$k(1) = r = \left\lceil \frac{n}{m} \right\rceil \text{ and } k(i) = \lceil \alpha^+ \cdot k(i-1) \rceil, \text{ for all } i \geq 2,$$

with α^+ as defined in (5.12).

The representatives are filled up with further items from $\{2, \ldots, m-1\}$ with a maximal frequency of up to r. Obviously, this leads to a valid definition of a fooling set because

$$k(i) + r \cdot (m-2) + r \geq r \cdot (m-1) + r = \left\lceil \frac{n}{m} \right\rceil \cdot m \geq n.$$

Once again, we have to ensure that $k(d) \leq l = n - r$, therefore,

$$\left\lceil \frac{n}{m} \right\rceil \cdot \left(\frac{3}{2} \cdot \alpha \right)^{d-1} \leq n - r = n - \left\lceil \frac{n}{m} \right\rceil,$$

which is true with,

$$d = \log_{\frac{3}{2} \cdot \alpha} \left(\frac{n - \left\lceil \frac{n}{m} \right\rceil}{\left\lceil \frac{n}{m} \right\rceil} \right) \geq \log_{\frac{3}{2} \cdot \alpha} \left(\frac{m-1}{2} \right) = \frac{\log_2(\frac{m-1}{2})}{\log_2(\frac{3}{2} \cdot \alpha)}. \tag{5.12}$$

The left inequality from (5.12) is a simple approximation using the fact that $\frac{n}{m} \leq \left\lceil \frac{n}{m} \right\rceil \leq 2 \cdot \frac{n}{m}$ for any $n > m$. Of course, with this definition of $\mathcal{F}_{F_{\infty,\alpha \geq 2,1}}^{m<n} = (\mathcal{F}_L^{m<n}, \mathcal{F}_R^{m<n})$, we still have an α-fooling set for any $\alpha \geq 2$ because the frequency count fraction between any two representatives is at least $\alpha^+ > \alpha$. That is why we can calculate the space complexity as,

$$\text{space}(\mathcal{S}_{F_{\infty,\alpha \geq 2,1}}^{m<n}) \geq \log_2(|\mathcal{F}^{m<n}|) = \log_2 \left(\frac{\log_2(\frac{m-1}{2})}{\log_2(\frac{3}{2} \cdot \alpha)} \right) \qquad \text{fooling set size}$$

$$= \log_2 \left(\log_2 \left(\frac{m-1}{2} \right) \right) - \log_2 \left(\log_2 \left(\frac{3}{2} \cdot \alpha \right) \right). \quad \text{basic transf.}$$

With both cases, we can conclude the finale space complexity lower bound:

$$\text{space}\left(\mathcal{S}_{F_{\infty,\alpha \geq 2,1}} \right) \geq \log_2 \left(\log_2 \left(\min\left\{ n, \frac{m-1}{2} \right\} \right) \right) - \log_2 \left(\log_2 \left(\frac{3}{2} \cdot \alpha \right) \right). \qquad \square$$

Corollary 5.5. *The streaming problem* $\mathcal{S}_{F_{\infty,\alpha \geq \sqrt{2},1}}$ *has, for any* $n, m \in \mathbb{N}^+$ *and for a 2-sided approximation ratio of* $\alpha \geq \sqrt{2}$, *a space complexity lower bound of*

$$\text{space}\left(\mathcal{S}_{F_{\infty,\alpha \geq \sqrt{2},1}} \right) \geq \log_2 \left(\log_2 \left(\min\left\{ n, \frac{m-1}{2} \right\} \right) \right) - \log_2 \left(\log_2 \left(\frac{3}{2} \cdot \alpha \right) \right).$$

This corollary follows directly from the proven α-fooling set from Theorem 5.14 and Theorem 4.5.

This space complexity lower bound is very low, because the term $\log_2(\log_2(i))$ increases very slowly for higher i. For example, for one million, this value is only $\log_2(\log_2(10^6)) \approx 4.3$. As another example, $\log_2(\log_2(10^{12})) \approx 5.3$, for an input stream with a trillion numbers. Nevertheless, this analysis shows on the other side that it is possible to prove a lower bound above a constant value.

Unfortunately, it is impossible to prove a space complexity lower bound of a higher order than $\Theta(\log(n))$ using the technique of communication complexity.

Theorem 5.15. *For any 2-sided approximation ratio $\alpha \geq \sqrt{2}$, it is impossible to prove a higher space complexity lower bound than $\lceil \log_2(n) \rceil$ using the proof technique of communication complexity.*

Proof. Communication complexity assumes to have two computers C_L and C_R that have infinite resources but a limited communication between each other. We can show that, for any input stream distribution among the two computers (x_l for the left and x_r for the right computer, such that $(x_l, x_r) \in \mathcal{X}$) with a communication complexity of $\lceil \log_2(n) \rceil$, the two computers can solve the most frequent item problem with a 2-sided approximation ratio of $\alpha = \sqrt{2}$, using the following algorithm:

The left computer calculates the highest frequency of its input part, namely $f(x_l)$ and communicates this value to the right computer. This requires at most $\lceil \log_2(n) \rceil$ communication bits. The right computer calculates its own highest frequency $f(x_r)$, sums up the two values and outputs $(f(x_l) + f(x_r))/\sqrt{2}$. Of course, this output value is a $\sqrt{2}$-approximation of $f(x)$, as proven in Section 5.1.

Therefore, with only $\lceil \log_2(n) \rceil$ communication bits, the two-computer model of the communication complexity theory solves the most frequent item streaming problem with a 2-sided approximation ratio of $\alpha = \sqrt{2}$. Therefore, it is impossible to prove a lower bound that is higher than this one using the technique of communication complexity.   □

With this theorem, we have shown that we cannot increase the proven lower bound to the known upper bound for this setting using the technique of communication complexity. We will now focus on the last setting that allows both approximative and probabilistic output values.

Approximative Probabilistic Most Frequent Item Problem

In the following, we will mainly transform the three approximative space complexity lower bounds to a probabilistic setting. As in the previous section, we will first introduce the known bounds from the literature and briefly discuss enhanced upper bounds. We use the notation of $\mathcal{S}_{F_\infty, \alpha, p}$ for the approximative probabilistic most frequent item problem.

Known Bounds from the Literature

The proven space complexity lower bound of $\Omega(m)$ for any $\frac{m}{2} \leq n \leq 2m$ by Alon et al. [AMS99] is valid for any success probability $p > \frac{1}{2}$ and approximation ratio $\alpha \leq \frac{4}{3}$.

The known upper bounds are not further improved for a probabilistic setting. As we will see in the following lower bound analysis, it seems to be impossible to benefit significantly from the randomization.

Enhanced Upper Bounds

We have seen in the analysis of the exact, probabilistic most frequent item streaming problem that the space complexity can be reduced by a multiplicative factor of the success probability $p < 1$. In the analysis of the approximative, deterministic most frequent item problem, we have seen that if 2-sided approximations are allowed, we can further decrease the space by a factor of $d \in \mathbb{N}^+$ if we allow an approximative error of $\alpha = \sqrt{d}$.

Obviously, these two concepts are independent of each other and can therefore be combined. Which means that it is possible to create an algorithm that produces an α-approximation for any $\alpha^2 \in \mathbb{N}^+$ with success probability $p < 1$, such that it only requires $\frac{p}{\alpha^2}$ times the space complexity of the algorithms from Theorem 5.4, Theorem 5.5, or Theorem 5.6.

The space complexity decrease with the approach above is not significant. Therefore, we do not introduce the procedure to generate such an algorithm in detail or formally, but we will now verify, that the space complexity lower bounds for the deterministic approximation are also valid for the probabilistic environment.

Enhanced Lower Bounds

As we are interested in using Theorem 4.3 to prove a probabilistic lower bound, we have to verify the minimality of the test set of the α-fooling set. As introduced in (4.6) to (4.11), we can verify this by showing that:

$$\forall I_R^v \in \mathcal{F}_R, \qquad \text{For all elements of the test set,}$$

$$\exists I_L^i, I_L^j \in \mathcal{F}_L, I_L^i \neq I_L^j \qquad \text{there are two different representatives,}$$

$$\text{s.t. } \left(\left(\frac{f(I_L^i, I_R^v)}{f(I_L^j, I_R^v)} < \frac{1}{\alpha} \right. \right. \qquad \begin{array}{l} \text{such that the cache states} \\ \text{have to be different} \end{array}$$

$$\left. \text{or } \frac{f(I_L^i, I_R^v)}{f(I_L^j, I_R^v)} > \alpha \right) \qquad \text{as stated above in Definition 4.3.}$$

$$\text{and } \left(\forall I_R^{v'} \in (\mathcal{F}_R \setminus I_R^v) : \qquad \text{And for all other tests,} \right.$$

$$\left. \left. \frac{1}{\alpha} \leq \frac{f(I_L^i, I_R^{v'})}{f(I_L^j, I_R^{v'})} \leq \alpha \right) \right) \qquad \text{they are not required to be different.}$$

Now, we will analyze the space complexity lower bound for the probabilistic and approximative most frequent item problem. The first proof is a probabilistic version of Theorem 5.12.

Theorem 5.16. *The streaming problem* $\mathcal{S}_{F_\infty, \alpha, p}$ *has, for any* $n, m \in \mathbb{N}^+$, *a success probability of* $p > \frac{1}{2}$, *and a* 1-*sided approximation ratio of* $\alpha < 2$, *a space complexity lower bound of*

$$\text{space}\left(\mathcal{S}_{F_\infty, \alpha < 2, p} \right) \geq \min\left\{ n, \frac{m}{2} \right\} \cdot (1 - h(p)) - \min\left\{ \log_2(n), \frac{\log_2(m)}{2} \right\} - 1.$$

Proof. Both fooling set definitions $\mathcal{F}_{F_\infty, \alpha < 2, 1}^{n \leq m} = (\mathcal{F}_L^{n \leq m}, \mathcal{F}_R^{n \leq m})$ and $\mathcal{F}_{F_\infty, \alpha < 2, 1}^{m < n} = (\mathcal{F}_L^{<n}, \mathcal{F}_R^{<n})$ from Theorem 5.12 already contain minimal test sets. Therefore we will use exactly these α-fooling sets. We just have to *i*) verify the minimality of the test sets and *ii*) calculate the probabilistic space complexity lower bound for both cases.

Case 1: Suppose $n \leq m$:

i) We have to verify (4.6) to (4.11) to show the minimality of the test set. For every item $v \in \{1, \ldots, n-1\}$, or its corresponding test entry $I_R^v = \{v, v\}$, respectively, we choose two representatives that are only different in two items, namely v and n. More formally, these two representatives I_L^i and I_L^j contain $\frac{n}{2} - 2$ equal items out of $\{1, \ldots, n\} \subseteq \{1, \ldots, m\}$, each twice, and I_L^i covers additionally $\{v, v\}$ whereas I_L^j covers $\{n, n\}$. Of course, (4.8) and (4.9) are true because

$$\frac{f(I_L^i, I_R^v)}{f(I_L^j, I_R^v)} = \frac{4}{2} = 2 > \alpha.$$

Now, for all other $I_R^{v'} = \{v', v'\}$ with $v' \in (\{1, \ldots, n\} \setminus \{v, n\})$, this fraction is either

$$\frac{f(I_L^i, I_R^{v'})}{f(I_L^j, I_R^{v'})} = \frac{4}{4} = 1, \text{ and then } \frac{1}{\alpha} \leq 1 \leq \alpha,$$

if v' is present in I_L^i and I_L^j. If v' is not present in both representatives, we have:

$$\frac{f(I_L^i, I_R^{v'})}{f(I_L^j, I_R^{v'})} = \frac{2}{2} = 1, \text{ and then } \frac{1}{\alpha} \leq 1 \leq \alpha.$$

Therefore, we have shown (4.6) to (4.11) and proven the minimality of the test set.

ii) Using Theorem 4.3, we have the following space complexity lower bound:

$$\begin{aligned}
\text{space}(\mathcal{S}_{F_{\infty, \alpha \leq 2, p}}^{n \leq m}) &\geq \log_2(|\mathcal{F}_L^{n \leq m}|) \cdot \left(1 - \frac{|\mathcal{F}_R^{n \leq m}| \cdot h(p)}{\log_2(|\mathcal{F}_L^{n \leq m}|)}\right) - 1 && \text{Theorem 4.3} \\
&= \log_2\left(\binom{n}{\frac{n}{2} - 1}\right) \cdot \left(1 - \frac{(n-1) \cdot h(p)}{\log_2(\binom{n}{\frac{n}{2} - 1})}\right) - 1 && \text{fooling set size} \\
&> \log_2\left(\frac{2^n \cdot \sqrt{2n}}{2n + 4}\right) \cdot \left(1 - \frac{(n-1) \cdot h(p)}{\log_2\left(\frac{2^n \cdot \sqrt{2n}}{2n+4}\right)}\right) - 1 && \text{Lemma 3.3} \\
&> (n - \log_2(n)) \cdot \left(1 - \frac{(n-1) \cdot h(p)}{(n - \log_2(n))}\right) - 1 && \text{Theorem 5.12} \\
&= n - \log_2(n) - (n-1) \cdot h(p)) - 1 && \text{basic transf.} \\
&> n \cdot (1 - h(p)) - \log_2(n) - 1, && \text{simple approx.}
\end{aligned}$$

with $h(p) = -p \cdot \log_2(p) - (1 - p) \cdot \log_2(1 - p)$. Then, we have proven the space complexity lower bound for the first case.

Case 2: Suppose $m < n$:

i) We similarly verify the minimality of the test set $\mathcal{F}_R^{m < n}$ with (4.6) to (4.11). For every item $v \in \{1, \ldots, \frac{m}{2} - 1\}$ or its test entries $I_R^v = \{v, \ldots, v\} \in \mathcal{F}_R^{m < n}$, we choose two representatives $I_L^i, I_L^j \in \mathcal{F}_L^{m < n}$ that have the same $\frac{m}{4} - 1$ content items $\{1, \ldots, \frac{m}{2}\} \subset \{1, \ldots, m\}$, each with a frequency of r. Additionally, I_L^i contains r times the content item v and I_L^j contains r times the content item $\frac{m}{2}$. Then, the cache states for these two representatives have to be different because,

$$\frac{f(I_L^i, I_R^v)}{f(I_L^j, I_R^v)} = \frac{2r}{r} = 2 > \alpha.$$

And for all other items $v' \in (\{1, \dots, \frac{m}{2}\} \setminus \{v, \frac{m}{2}\})$, or the test entries $I_R^{v'} = \{v', \dots, v'\}$, respectively, the highest frequency is either $f(I_L^i, I_R^{v'}) = 2r = f(I_L^j, I_R^{v'})$ or $f(I_L^i, I_R^{v'}) = r = f(I_L^j, I_R^{v'})$. Therefore, the test set is minimal.

$ii)$ Similarly to the first case, we can calculate the space complexity lower bound:

$$
\begin{aligned}
\text{space}(\mathcal{S}_{F_\infty, \alpha \leq 2, p}^{m<n}) &\geq \log_2(|\mathcal{F}_L^{m<n}|) \cdot \left(1 - \frac{|\mathcal{F}_R^{m<n}| \cdot h(p)}{\log_2(|\mathcal{F}_L^{m<n}|)}\right) - 1 && \text{Theorem 4.3} \\
&= \log_2\left(\binom{m/2}{m/4}\right) \cdot \left(1 - \frac{(\frac{m}{2} - 1) \cdot h(p)}{\log_2(\binom{m/2}{m/4})}\right) - 1 && \text{fooling set size} \\
&> \log_2\left(\frac{2^{m/2}}{\sqrt{m}}\right) \cdot \left(1 - \frac{(\frac{m}{2} - 1) \cdot h(p)}{\log_2(\frac{2^{m/2}}{\sqrt{m}})}\right) - 1 && \text{Lemma 3.2} \\
&> \left(\frac{m}{2} - \frac{\log_2(m)}{2}\right)\left(1 - \frac{(\frac{m}{2} - 1) \cdot h(p)}{\frac{m}{2} - \frac{\log_2(m)}{2}}\right) - 1 && \text{Theorem 5.12} \\
&= \frac{m}{2} - \frac{\log_2(m)}{2} - \left(\frac{m}{2} - 1\right) \cdot h(p) - 1 && \text{basic transf.} \\
&> \frac{m}{2} \cdot (1 - h(p)) - \frac{\log_2(m)}{2} - 1, && \text{simple approx.}
\end{aligned}
$$

with $h(p) = -p \cdot \log_2(p) - (1 - p) \cdot \log_2(1 - p)$.

Therefore, we have a space complexity lower bound for both cases, which is,

$$
\text{space}\left(\mathcal{S}_{F_\infty, \alpha < 2, p}\right) \geq \min\left\{n, \frac{m}{2}\right\} \cdot (1 - h(p)) - \min\left\{\log_2(n), \frac{\log_2(m)}{2}\right\} - 1 \quad \square
$$

Corollary 5.6. *The streaming problem $\mathcal{S}_{F_\infty, \alpha, p}$ has, for any $n, m \in \mathbb{N}^+$, a success probability of $p > \frac{1}{2}$, and a 2-sided approximation ratio of $\alpha < \sqrt{2}$, a space complexity lower bound of*

$$
\text{space}\left(\mathcal{S}_{F_\infty, \alpha < \sqrt{2}, p}\right) \geq \min\left\{n, \frac{m}{2}\right\} \cdot (1 - h(p)) - \min\left\{\log_2(n), \frac{\log_2(m)}{2}\right\} - 1.
$$

This corollary follows directly from the proven α-fooling set from Theorem 5.16 and Theorem 4.5.

The second space complexity lower bound proof corresponds to Theorem 5.13, but now in a randomized setting.

Theorem 5.17. *The streaming problem $\mathcal{S}_{F_\infty, 1.19, 1}$ has, for any $n > m \geq 100$ with $n, m \in \mathbb{N}^+$, a success probability of $p > \frac{1}{2}$ and a 1-sided approximation ratio of $\alpha = 1.19$, a space complexity lower bound of*

$$
\text{space}\left(\mathcal{S}_{F_\infty, 1.19, p}^{m<n}\right) \geq m \cdot (0.915 - h(p)) - \frac{\log_2(m)}{2} - 3.
$$

Proof. As in the theorem above, we can use the definition of the α-fooling set $\mathcal{F}_{F_\infty, \alpha=1.19, 1} = (\mathcal{F}_L, \mathcal{F}_R)$ from the deterministic proof, namely Theorem 5.13. Now, we are only required to verify the minimality of the test set and then, we can calculate the space complexity lower bound.

For every item $v \in \{1, \ldots, m-1\}$, or its corresponding test entry $I_R^v = \{v, \ldots, v\} \in \mathcal{F}_R$, respectively, we choose two representatives $I_L^i, I_L^j \in \mathcal{F}_L$ such that they have $\frac{m}{4} - 1$ content items in common. This means that there are $\frac{m}{4} - 1$ content items $j \in (\{1, \ldots, m\} \setminus \{v, m\})$ that have a frequency of $r = \left\lfloor \frac{4n}{m+4} \right\rfloor$ for both representatives. By definition, both representatives have an additional, but different item with the same frequency of r. For I_L^i, we choose this last content item as v, and for I_L^j, this content item is m. Then, we have,

$$f(I_L^i, I_R^v) = 2r \text{ and } f(I_L^j, I_R^v) = r + \left\lceil \frac{\text{\# spacer values}}{\text{\# spacer items}} \right\rceil = r + \left\lceil \frac{n - r \cdot (1 + \frac{m}{4})}{m - \frac{m}{4}} \right\rceil.$$

In Theorem 5.13, we have proven that the fraction between $f(I_L^i, I_R^v) = 2r$ and $f(I_L^j, I_R^v)$ is more than 1.19. Therefore, (4.8) and (4.9) of the test set minimality verification are satisfied. For every other item $v' \in (\{1, \ldots, m\} \setminus \{v, m\})$, we can show that

$$\frac{1}{\alpha} \leq \frac{f(I_L^i, I_R^v)}{f(I_L^j, I_R^v)} \leq \alpha.$$

If v' is one of the content items for the two representatives, namely v' has a frequency of r in both I_L^i and I_L^j, then this fraction is $\frac{2r}{2r} = 1$ and we have the required condition. Otherwise, if v' is a spacer item for the two representatives, then v' has a frequency of either $\left\lceil \frac{\text{\# spacer values}}{\text{\# spacer items}} \right\rceil$ or $\left\lfloor \frac{\text{\# spacer values}}{\text{\# spacer items}} \right\rfloor$. By definition of the α-fooling set, the required spacer values are distributed uniformly over all available $\frac{3m}{4}$ spacer items. Therefore, the frequency of v' in the representatives is one of the two.

$$\frac{1}{\alpha} = \frac{1}{1.19} \leq \frac{r + \left\lfloor \frac{\text{\# spacer values}}{\text{\# spacer items}} \right\rfloor}{r + \left\lceil \frac{\text{\# spacer values}}{\text{\# spacer items}} \right\rceil} \leq \frac{f(I_L^i, I_R^{v'})}{f(I_L^j, I_R^{v'})} \leq \frac{r + \left\lceil \frac{\text{\# spacer values}}{\text{\# spacer items}} \right\rceil}{r + \left\lfloor \frac{\text{\# spacer values}}{\text{\# spacer items}} \right\rfloor} \leq 1.19 = \alpha$$

This implies that (4.10) and (4.11) are true and the test set is minimal. Now, we will calculate the space complexity lower bound:

$$\text{space}(\mathcal{S}_{F_{\infty,1.19,p}}) \geq \log_2(|\mathcal{F}_L|) \cdot \left(1 - \frac{|\mathcal{F}_R|}{\log_2(|\mathcal{F}_L|)} \cdot h(p) \right) - 1 \qquad \text{Theorem 4.3}$$

$$= \log_2\left(\binom{m}{m/4} \right) \cdot \left(1 - \frac{(m-1) \cdot h(p)}{\log_2(\binom{m}{m/4})} \right) - 1 \qquad \text{fooling set size}$$

$$= \log_2\left(\binom{m}{m/4} \right) - (m-1) \cdot h(p) - 1 \qquad \text{basic transf.}$$

$$> \left(0.915m - \frac{\log_2(m)}{2} - 1 \right) - \qquad \text{Theorem 5.13}$$
$$(m-1) \cdot h(p) - 1$$

$$= m \cdot (0.915 - h(p)) - \frac{\log_2(m)}{2} - h(p) - 2 \qquad \text{basic transf.}$$

$$> m \cdot (0.915 - h(p)) - \frac{\log_2(m)}{2} - 3, \qquad \text{simple approx.}$$

with $h(p) = -p \cdot \log_2(p) - (1 - p) \cdot \log_2(1 - p)$. $\square$

As usual, the lower bound can also be transformed to the setting where 2-sided approximations are allowed.

Corollary 5.7. *The streaming problem* $\mathcal{S}_{F_{\infty,\alpha,p}}$ *has, for any* $n > m \geq 100$ *with* $n, m \in \mathbb{N}^+$, *with a success probability of* $p > \frac{1}{2}$ *and a 2-sided approximation ratio of* $\alpha = 1.09$, *a space complexity lower bound of*

$$\text{space}\left(\mathcal{S}_{F_{\infty,1.09,p}}^{m<n}\right) \geq m \cdot (0.915 - h(p)) - \frac{\log_2(m)}{2} - 3.$$

This corollary follows directly from the proven α-fooling set from Theorem 5.17 and Theorem 4.5.

The next theorem refers to Theorem 5.14.

Theorem 5.18. *The streaming problem* $\mathcal{S}_{F_{\infty,\alpha \geq 2,p}}$ *has, for any* $n, m \in \mathbb{N}^+$, *with a success probability of* $p > \frac{1}{2}$, *and a 1-sided approximation ratio of* $\alpha \geq 2$, *a space complexity lower bound of*

$$\text{space}\left(\mathcal{S}_{F_{\infty,\alpha \geq 2,p}}\right) \geq \log_2\left(\log_2\left(\min\left\{n, \frac{m}{2}\right\}\right)\right) - \log_2\left(\log_2\left(\frac{3}{2} \cdot \alpha\right)\right) - 2.$$

Proof. We will use the α-fooling sets from Theorem 5.14 for this proof, $\mathcal{F}_{F_{\infty,\alpha \geq 2,1}}^{n \leq m} = (\mathcal{F}_L^{n \leq m}, \mathcal{F}_R^{n \leq m})$ for the first case and $\mathcal{F}_{F_{\infty,\alpha \geq 2,1}}^{m<n} = (\mathcal{F}_L^{m<n}, \mathcal{F}_R^{m<n})$ for the second case. Obviously, both test sets are minimal as they contain only one test entry. Therefore, we can just calculate the probabilistic space complexity lower bound:

$$\text{space}(\mathcal{S}_{F_{\infty,\alpha,p}}) \geq \log_2(|\mathcal{F}_L|) \cdot \left(1 - \frac{|\mathcal{F}_R| \cdot h(p)}{\log_2(|\mathcal{F}_L|)}\right) - 1 \qquad \text{Theorem 4.3}$$

$$\geq \log_2(|\mathcal{F}_L|) - |\mathcal{F}_R| \cdot h(p) - 1 \qquad \text{basic transf.}$$

$$\geq \log_2\left(\log_2\left(\min\left\{n, \frac{m}{2}\right\}\right)\right) - \qquad \text{Theorem 5.14}$$
$$\log_2\left(\log_2\left(\frac{3}{2} \cdot \alpha\right)\right) - h(p) - 1$$

$$\geq \log_2\left(\log_2\left(\min\left\{n, \frac{m}{2}\right\}\right)\right) - \qquad \text{simple approx.}$$
$$\log_2\left(\log_2\left(\frac{3}{2} \cdot \alpha\right)\right) - 2 \qquad\qquad \square$$

This theorem implies that the space complexity lower bound for the probabilistic setting is only 2 bits lower than the deterministic one. Of course, we can transform this theorem to a 2-sided approximative setting, too.

Corollary 5.8. *The streaming problem* $\mathcal{S}_{F_{\infty,\alpha \geq \sqrt{2},p}}$ *has, for any* $n, m \in \mathbb{N}^+$, *a success probability of* $p > \frac{1}{2}$, *and a 2-sided approximation ratio of* $\alpha \geq \sqrt{2}$, *a space complexity lower bound of*

$$\text{space}\left(\mathcal{S}_{F_{\infty,\alpha \geq \sqrt{2},p}}\right) \geq \log_2\left(\log_2\left(\min\left\{n, \frac{m}{2}\right\}\right)\right) - \log_2\left(\log_2\left(\frac{3}{2} \cdot \alpha\right)\right) - 2.$$

This corollary follows directly from the proven α-fooling set from Theorem 5.18 and Theorem 4.5.

Summary of the General Most Frequent Item Problem

With the proven theorems, we can create an overview of all space complexity upper and lower bounds for the general most frequent item problem, which are listed in table 5.1. For a probabilistic setting, we assume that the success probability is at least $p > \frac{1}{2}$. Any results on the approximative setting cover the analysis of the 2-sided approximation.

In the deterministic setting, the known space complexity lower bound order from Theorem 5.1 and Theorem 5.2 is proven as an exact lower bound in Theorem 5.7 and Theorem 5.8. With the described algorithm of Theorem 5.5 and Theorem 5.6, we have an almost tight lower bound for the case $n \geq m$. As the space complexity lower bounds for a probabilistic setting are of the same order as the deterministic one, we can conclude that randomization does not help to improve the algorithmic complexity significantly. The known lower bound complexity of $\Omega(m)$ described in Theorem 5.11 is also valid for an approximation ratio of $\alpha = \frac{4}{3} \approx 1.333$. With Corollary 5.3 and Corollary 5.6, the same complexity order could be extended to an approximation ratio of $\alpha < \sqrt{2} \approx 1.414 > 1.333$ and to a probabilistic setting. Unfortunately, it was not possible to extend the lower bound order of $\Omega(m \cdot \log(\frac{n}{m}))$ for the case $n \geq m$ from Theorem 5.2, Theorem 5.8, or Theorem 5.10 in a randomized environment using the same fooling set concept. For an approximation ratio $\alpha \geq \sqrt{2}$, we have a large gap between the upper bound, which is $\mathcal{O}(m \cdot \log(\frac{n}{m}) \cdot \frac{p}{\alpha^2})$, that is informally described in Section 5.1 and the proven lower bound of $\Omega(\log(\log(\min\{n, m\})) - \log(\log(\alpha)))$ from Corollary 5.5 and Corollary 5.8. The difference between these two space complexity orders is very large, but it could not be closed with the analysis of this thesis. Possibly, one can find an approach to decrease the upper bound or increase the lower bound to the described limitation of communication complexity (Theorem 5.15).

Approx. ratio	Succ. prob.	Space bound	Condition	Reference
1	1	$\Omega(m)$	$\frac{m}{2} \leq n \leq 2m$	[AMS99]
1	1	$\Omega(m \cdot \log(\frac{n}{m}))$	$n > 4m$	[KSP03]
1	1	$\Omega(n \cdot \log(m))$	$m > n^2$	[TW12]
1	1	$\leq m \cdot \lceil \log_2(n) \rceil$	—	Theorem 5.4
1	1	$\leq 2m \cdot (\lceil \log_2(\frac{n}{m}) \rceil + 1) - 2$	$n \geq m$	Theorem 5.5
1	1	$\leq d \cdot m \cdot \left(1 + \left\lceil \frac{\log_2(\frac{n}{m})}{\log_2(2^d-1)} \right\rceil\right) - d$	$n \geq m, d \geq 2$	Theorem 5.6
1	1	$\geq \min\{n, m\} - \log_2(\min\{n, m\})$	—	Theorem 5.7
1	1	$\geq \frac{m}{2} \cdot \log_2(\frac{n}{m}) - 0.21m$	$n > 4m$	Theorem 5.8
1	p	$\geq (\min\{n, m\} - \log_2(\min\{n, m\})) \cdot (1 - 1.01 \cdot h(p) - 1$	—	Theorem 5.9
1	p	$\geq \frac{m}{2} \cdot \log_2(\frac{n}{m}) - 0.71m - 1$	—	Theorem 5.10
$\alpha = \frac{4}{3}$	1	$\Omega(m)$	$\frac{m}{2} \leq n \leq 2m$	[AMS99]
$\alpha < \sqrt{2}$	1	$\geq \min\{n - \log_2(n), \frac{m}{2} - \frac{\log_2(m)}{2}\}$	—	Corollary 5.3
$\alpha = 1.09$	1	$\geq 0.915m - \frac{\log_2(m)}{2} - 1$	$n > m \geq 100$	Corollary 5.4
$\alpha \geq \sqrt{2}$	1	$\geq \log_2(\log_2(\min\{n, \frac{m}{2}\})) - \log_2(\log_2(\frac{3}{2} \cdot \alpha))$	—	Corollary 5.5
$\alpha < \sqrt{2}$	p	$\geq \min\{n, \frac{m}{2}\} \cdot (1 - h(p)) - \min\{\log_2(n), \frac{\log_2(m)}{2}\} - 1$	—	Corollary 5.6
$\alpha = 1.09$	p	$\geq m \cdot (0.915 - h(p)) - \frac{\log_2(m)}{2} - 3$	$n > m \geq 100$	Corollary 5.7
$\alpha \geq \sqrt{2}$	p	$\geq \log_2(\log_2(\min\{n, \frac{m}{2}\})) - \log_2(\log_2(\frac{3}{2} \cdot \alpha)) - 2$	—	Corollary 5.8

Table 5.1. Summary of general most frequent item problem

5.2   Hypothesis Verification Analysis

In this section, we analyze the impact of additional information on the most frequent item problem. We identify some upper and lower bounds if we want to verify any possible hypothesis.

For the hypothesis verification, there is no known literature about this kind of problem configuration. That is why we will directly introduce the identified complexities.

We are able to reproduce the proof from Corollary 5.3 and Corollary 5.6 in the setting of hypothesis verification. These two corollaries and their corresponding theorems state a space complexity lower bound of $\Omega(\min(n,m))$ in the setting of approximation and randomization with any approximation ratio $\alpha < \sqrt{2}$ for a 2-sided approximation and a success probability $p > \frac{1}{2}$. Now, we will show that these fooling and α-fooling sets can be transformed to *hypothesis fooling* and *hypothesis α-fooling sets* of the same size. These two types of fooling sets are defined in Definition 4.4 and Definition 4.5.

We use the notation of $\mathcal{S}_{F_{\infty,1,1}}^{HYP}$, $\mathcal{S}_{F_{\infty,1,p}}^{HYP}$, $\mathcal{S}_{F_{\infty,\alpha,1}}^{HYP}$, or $\mathcal{S}_{F_{\infty,\alpha,p}}^{HYP}$ for the different settings of the verification of any possible solution hypothesis for the most frequent item problem.

Theorem 5.19. *The streaming problem* $\mathcal{S}_{F_{\infty,\alpha,p}}^{HYP}$, *that has any* $n,m \in \mathbb{N}^+$, *a success probability of* $p > \frac{1}{2}$, *and a 1-sided approximation ratio of* $\alpha < 2$, *requires a space complexity of at least*

$$\text{space}\Big(\mathcal{S}_{F_{\infty,\alpha<2,p}}^{HYP}\Big) \geq \min\Big\{n, \frac{m}{2}\Big\} \cdot (1 - h(p)) - \min\Big\{\log_2(n), \frac{\log_2(m)}{2}\Big\} - 1.$$

Proof. We introduce a hypothesis α-fooling set as defined in Definition 4.5, that uses the same concept as the α-fooling set from Theorem 5.12. In the following, *i*) this fooling set is defined, *ii*) verified and *iii*) the space complexity is calculated. We make a case distinction between $n \leq m$ and $m < n$.

Case 1: Suppose $n \leq m$.
i) We define the hypothesis α-fooling set $\mathcal{F}_{F_{\infty,\alpha<2,1}}^{HYP,n\leq m} = (\mathcal{F}_L^{HYP,n\leq m}, \mathcal{F}_R^{HYP,n\leq m})$ with a cut at $l := n-2$. All representatives $I_L^i = (y^i, \tilde{x}^i) \in \mathcal{F}_L^{HYP,n\leq m}$ contain as solution hypothesis the frequency number $4 = y^i \in \mathcal{Y}_x = \{1, \ldots, m\}$. The second part of the representatives contains $(\frac{n}{2}-1)$ different items from $\{1, \ldots, n\} \subseteq \{1, \ldots, m\}$, each with a frequency of 2 as the representatives from Theorem 5.12. Therefore, each representative input part has $2 \cdot (\frac{n}{2}-1) = n-2$ items in total, and there are $\binom{n}{n/2-1}$ different representatives. The test set contains $n-1$ different entries with twice the same item from $\{1, \ldots, n-1\} \subset \{1, \ldots, m\}$, namely, $\mathcal{F}_R^{HYP,n\leq m} = \{\{1,1\}, \ldots, \{n-1, n-1\}\}$.

ii) Now, we verify, that $\mathcal{F}_{F_{\infty,\alpha<2,1}}^{HYP,n\leq m}$ is a hypothesis α-fooling set and that the test set is minimal. As stated in Definition 4.5, we can show that we have a hypothesis α-fooling set, with this term:

$$\forall I_L^i = (y^i, \tilde{x}^i), I_L^j = (y^j, \tilde{x}^j) \in \mathcal{F}_L^\alpha \text{ with } I_L^i \neq I_L^j: \ \exists I_R^v \in \mathcal{F}_R^\alpha \text{ s.t.}$$
$$\left(\frac{1}{\alpha} \leq \frac{f(\tilde{x}^i, I_R^v)}{y^i} \leq \alpha\right) \iff\!\!\!\!\!/ \ \left(\frac{1}{\alpha} \leq \frac{f(\tilde{x}^j, I_R^v)}{y^j} \leq \alpha\right)$$

For every pair of representatives $I_L^i = (4, \tilde{x}^i), I_L^j = (4, \tilde{x}^j) \in \mathcal{F}_L^{HYP,n\leq m}$, we choose an item $v \in \{1, \ldots, n-1\}$, or the corresponding test entry $I_R^v = \{v, v\} \in \mathcal{F}_R^{HYP,n\leq m}$ such that this v is only present in one of the two representatives, or their input stream parts. In previous theorems, as e.g., in Theorem 5.12, we have verified the existence of such an item. W.l.o.g., we assume that $v \in \tilde{x}^i \in I_L^i$. Then, we have

$$\frac{f(\tilde{x}^i, I_R^v)}{y^i} = \frac{4}{2} = 2 \quad \text{and} \quad \frac{f(\tilde{x}^j, I_R^v)}{y^j} = \frac{2}{2} = 1.$$

Therefore, for any $1 \leq \alpha < 2$, the left term from the desired inequality of the boolean values above will be false, because $2 \not\leq \alpha$ and the right boolean value will be true, because $\frac{1}{\alpha} \leq 1 \leq \alpha$. Then, we have the required inequality.

For the verification of the minimality of the test set, we have to prove (4.20) to (4.27): For every item $v \in \{1, \ldots, n-1\}$, or its corresponding test entry $I_R^v = \{v, v\} \in \mathcal{F}_R^{HYP,n\leq m}$, we choose two representatives that have as input stream part $\frac{n}{2} - 2$ times the same items from $(\{1, \ldots, n\} \setminus \{v, n\})$. I_L^i additionally contains the item v, and I_L^j the item n. Then, we have, with exactly the same argument as above, the required inequality for the two representatives I_L^i, I_L^j and the test entry I_R^v, that is:

$$\left(\frac{1}{\alpha} \leq \frac{f(\tilde{x}^i, I_R^v)}{y^i} = \frac{4}{4} = 1 \leq \alpha \right) \iff \text{true}$$

$$\not\iff \text{false} \iff \left(\frac{1}{\alpha} \leq \frac{1}{2} = \frac{2}{4} = \frac{f(\tilde{x}^j, I_R^v)}{y^j} \leq \alpha \right)$$

And we have, for all other representatives $I_R^{v'} \in \mathcal{F}_R^{HYP,n\leq m}$ with $v' \in (\{1, \ldots, n\} \setminus \{v, n\})$, either an item v' that is represented in both representative's input stream part or one that is in none of the two. In the first case, if v' is an item of the input stream part of the two representatives, both fractions $\frac{f(\tilde{x}^i, I_R^v)}{y^i}$ and $\frac{f(\tilde{x}^j, I_R^v)}{y^j}$ are $\frac{4}{4} = 1$, both Boolean terms are true, and the required equality is given. In the other case, if v' is not present in both representatives, then this fraction is $\frac{2}{4} = \frac{1}{2}$. As a consequence, both boolean terms are false, because $\frac{1}{\alpha} \not\leq \frac{1}{2}$ for any $\alpha < 2$, and as a consequence, both Boolean terms outputs are equal. Therefore, the minimality of the test set is proven and we may apply Theorem 4.3.

iii) Now, we calculate the space complexity lower bound for the probabilistic, approximative verification of a hypothesis on the most frequent item problem. We have an approximation ratio of $\alpha < 2$ and a success probability of $p > \frac{1}{2}$. Then,

$$\text{space}(\mathcal{S}_{F_\infty, \alpha < 2, p}^{HYP,n\leq m}) \geq \log_2(|\mathcal{F}_L^{HYP,n\leq m}|) \cdot \qquad \text{Theorem 4.3}$$

$$\left(1 - \frac{|\mathcal{F}_R^{HYP,n\leq m}|}{\log_2(|\mathcal{F}_L^{HYP,n\leq m}|)} \cdot h(p) \right) - 1$$

$$= \log_2\left(\binom{n}{\frac{n}{2}-1} \right) \cdot \qquad \text{fooling set size}$$

$$\left(1 - \frac{n-1}{\log_2(\binom{n}{\frac{n}{2}-1})} \cdot h(p) \right) - 1$$

$$> n \cdot (1 - h(p)) - \log_2(n) - 1 \qquad\qquad \text{Theorem 5.16}$$

with $h(p) = -p \cdot \log_2(p) - (1 - p) \cdot \log_2(1 - p)$.

Then, we have proven the space complexity lower bound for the first case.

Case 2: Suppose $m < n$.

i) We define the hypothesis α-fooling set $\mathcal{F}_{F_\infty, \alpha < 2, 1}^{HYP, m < n} = (\mathcal{F}_L^{HYP, m < n}, \mathcal{F}_R^{HYP, m < n})$ that is similar to the second case of Theorem 5.12. We define the basic value replication as $r := \lfloor \frac{2n}{m} \rfloor \geq 2$. The hypothesis α-fooling set has a cut at $l := n - r$. The test set contains $(\frac{m}{2} - 1)$ different test entries, each with r times the same item $j \in \{1, \ldots, \frac{m}{2} - 1\}$, namely,

$$\mathcal{F}_R^{HYP, m < n} = \left\{ \{1, \ldots, 1\}, \ldots, \left\{ \frac{m}{2} - 1, \ldots, \frac{m}{2} - 1 \right\} \right\}$$

The representatives $I_L^i = (y^i, \tilde{x}^i)$ contain, as input stream part $\tilde{x}^i$, $\frac{m}{4}$ different content items from $\{1, \ldots, \frac{m}{2}\} \subset \{1, \ldots, m\}$, each with a frequency of r. The rest of the input stream part, namely $l - r \cdot \frac{m}{4} = n - r \cdot (1 + \frac{m}{4})$ input values, is filled up with spacer items $\{\frac{m}{2} + 1, \ldots, m\} \subset \{1, \ldots, m\}$ with a maximal frequency of r. Theorem 5.12 states, why this filling of spacer items still leads to a valid fooling set. All representatives have a solution hypothesis $y^i := 2r$.

ii) Now, we will verify similarly to the first case that we have a hypothesis α-fooling set and show the minimality of the test set.

For every pair of representatives $I_L^i = (2r, \tilde{x}^i), I_L^j = (2r, \tilde{x}^j) \in \mathcal{F}_L^{HYP, m < n}$, we choose an item $v \in \{1, \ldots, m - 1\}$, or its corresponding test entry $I_R^v = \{v, \ldots, v\} \in \mathcal{F}_R^{HYPm < n}$, that is only present in one of the two representatives. In the second case of Theorem 5.12, we have proven the existence of such an item v. W.l.o.g., we assume that v is in the representative I_L^i, namely $v \in \tilde{x}^i$. Then, we have the two Boolean terms:

$$\left(\frac{1}{\alpha} \leq \frac{f(\tilde{x}^i, I_R^v)}{y^i} \leq \alpha \right) \iff \left(\frac{1}{\alpha} \leq \frac{2r}{2r} \leq \alpha \right) \iff \left(\frac{1}{\alpha} \leq 1 \leq \alpha \right) \iff \text{true}$$

$$\left(\frac{1}{\alpha} \leq \frac{f(\tilde{x}^j, I_R^v)}{y^j} \leq \alpha \right) \iff \left(\frac{1}{\alpha} \leq \frac{r}{2r} \leq \alpha \right) \iff \left(\frac{1}{\alpha} \leq \frac{1}{2} \leq \alpha \right) \iff \text{false}$$

Therefore, we have verified, that we have a hypothesis α-fooling set. Now, we verify the minimality of the test set. For every item $j \in \{1, \ldots, \frac{m}{2} - 1\}$, or its corresponding test entry $I_R^v = \{v, \ldots, v\}$ respectively, we choose two representatives $I_L^i, I_L^j \in \mathcal{F}_L^{HYP, m < n}$, such that they have $(\frac{m}{4} - 1)$ content items from $(\{1, \ldots, \frac{m}{2}\} \setminus \{v, \frac{m}{2}\})$ in common, each with a frequency of r. I_L^i additionally has v as content item and I_L^j has $\frac{m}{2}$ as last content item. Then, obviously, we have,

$$\left(\frac{1}{\alpha} \leq \frac{f(\tilde{x}^i, I_R^v)}{y^i} \leq \alpha \right) \iff \left(\frac{1}{\alpha} \leq \frac{2r}{2r} \leq \alpha \right) \iff \text{true}$$

$$\iff\!\!\!/\ \text{false} \iff \left(\frac{1}{\alpha} \leq \frac{r}{2r} \leq \alpha \right) \iff \left(\frac{1}{\alpha} \leq \frac{f(\tilde{x}^j, I_R^v)}{y^j} \leq \alpha \right).$$

And, for all other items $v' \in (\{1, \ldots, \frac{m}{2}\} \setminus \{v, \frac{m}{2}\})$, or their representatives $I_R^{v'} = \{v', \ldots, v'\}$ respectively, the fraction in between the α-inequality is either

$$\frac{f(\tilde{x}^i, I_R^{v'})}{y^i} = \frac{2r}{2r} = 1 = \frac{2r}{2r} = \frac{f(\tilde{x}^j, I_R^{v'})}{y^j} \text{ or} \tag{5.13}$$

$$\frac{f(\tilde{x}^i, I_R^{v'})}{y^i} = \frac{r}{2r} = \frac{1}{2} = \frac{r}{2r} = \frac{f(\tilde{x}^j, I_R^{v'})}{y^j}, \tag{5.14}$$

because v' is either present in both representatives (5.13) or in none (5.14). Therefore, in both cases, we have verified the two Boolean term to be equal and as a consequence, the term to prove the minimality of the test set is verified.

iii) Because of the verification above, we can calculate the space complexity lower bound for the second case as,

$$\text{space}(\mathcal{S}_{F_{\infty, \alpha < 2, p}}^{HYP, m < n}) \geq \log_2(|\mathcal{F}_L^{HYP, m < n}|). \qquad \text{Theorem 4.3}$$

$$\left(1 - \frac{|\mathcal{F}_R^{HYP, m < n}|}{\log_2(|\mathcal{F}_L^{HYP, m < n}|)} \cdot h(p)\right) - 1$$

$$= \log_2\left(\binom{m/2}{m/4}\right) \cdot \qquad \text{fooling set size}$$

$$\left(1 - \frac{\frac{m}{2} - 1}{\log_2(\binom{m/2}{m/4})} \cdot h(p)\right) - 1$$

$$> \frac{m}{2} \cdot (1 - h(p)) - \frac{\log_2(m)}{2} - 1 \qquad \text{Theorem 5.16,}$$

with $h(p) = -p \cdot \log_2(p) - (1 - p) \cdot \log_2(1 - p)$.

Then, we have also proven the space complexity lower bound for the second case. Finally, we can conclude the space complexity on both cases:

$$\text{space}\left(\mathcal{S}_{F_{\infty, \alpha < 2, p}}^{HYP}\right) \geq \min\left\{n, \frac{m}{2}\right\} \cdot (1 - h(p)) - \min\left\{\log_2(n), \frac{\log_2(m)}{2}\right\} - 1. \quad \square$$

Corollary 5.9. *The streaming problem $\mathcal{S}_{F_{\infty, \alpha, p}}^{HYP}$, that has any $n, m \in \mathbb{N}^+$, a success probability of $p > \frac{1}{2}$, and a 2-sided approximation ratio of $\alpha < \sqrt{2}$, requires a space complexity of at least*

$$\text{space}\left(\mathcal{S}_{F_{\infty, \alpha < \sqrt{2}, p}}^{HYP}\right) \geq \min\left\{n, \frac{m}{2}\right\} \cdot (1 - h(p)) - \min\left\{\log_2(n), \frac{\log_2(m)}{2}\right\} - 1.$$

This corollary follows directly from the proven hypothesis α-fooling set from Theorem 5.19 and Theorem 4.5.

Corollary 5.10. *The streaming problem $\mathcal{S}_{F_{\infty, \alpha, 1}}^{HYP}$, that has any $n, m \in \mathbb{N}^+$ and a 1-sided approximation ratio of $\alpha < 2$, requires a space complexity of at least*

$$\text{space}\left(\mathcal{S}_{F_{\infty, \alpha < 2, 1}}^{HYP}\right) \geq \min\left\{n - \log_2(n), \frac{m}{2} - \frac{\log_2(m)}{2}\right\} \in \Omega(\min\{n, m\}).$$

Proof. For this corollary, we can use the verified hypothesis α-fooling set from Theorem 5.19. This theorem defines the hypothesis α-fooling set and justifies it. The fooling set sizes of this hypothesis α-fooling set is exactly the same as the fooling set size in Theorem 5.12. Therefore, we have the same space complexity lower bound. $\square$

Corollary 5.11. *The streaming problem* $\mathcal{S}_{F_{\infty,\alpha,1}}^{HYP}$, *that has any* $n, m \in \mathbb{N}^+$ *and a 2-sided approximation ratio of* $\alpha < \sqrt{2}$, *requires a space complexity of at least*

$$\text{space}\left(\mathcal{S}_{F_{\infty,\alpha<\sqrt{2},1}}^{HYP}\right) \geq \min\left\{n - \log_2(n), \frac{m}{2} - \frac{\log_2(m)}{2}\right\} \in \Omega(\min\{n, m\}).$$

This corollary follows directly from Corollary 5.10 and Theorem 4.5.

When we compare the space complexity lower bounds of these theorems and corollaries (Theorem 5.19, Corollary 5.9, Corollary 5.10, Corollary 5.11) with the lower bounds from the general most frequent item problem, we observe that they are equal. This implies that it is impossible that the verification of a hypothesis is *efficiently solvable* as defined in Definition 3.16, as the space complexity is at least linear to m or n, but not poly-logarithmic. It is still possible that the hypothesis verification is slightly more space efficient, because there is still a small gap between the identified upper bound of the general streaming problem and the proven lower bounds for the hypothesis verification. This study of upper and lower bounds did not reveal such an algorithm, which implies, that there might exist an approach to verify the hypothesis with significantly less storage, but more likely, we cannot benefit anything from the additional information.

For the general most frequent item problem, we were able to prove a space complexity lower bound of $\Omega(m \cdot \log(\frac{n}{m}))$ for any $n > 4m$. If we want to transform this proof to the hypothesis verification, we will struggle to find a good hypothesis such that, for every pair of representatives, we can ensure that the cache states have to be different. This leads to the following conjecture that is supported afterwards.

Conjecture 5.1. *It is not possible to prove a space complexity lower bound for the streaming problem* $\mathcal{S}_{F_{\infty,1,1}}^{HYP}$ *of* $\Omega(m \cdot \log(\frac{n}{m}))$.

In Theorem 5.8, we defined a fooling set of size $\approx 2^{m \cdot \log_2(n/m)}$ that has, for $\frac{m}{2}$ content items, different frequencies between $\left(\left\lceil \frac{\text{frac}}{2} \right\rceil + \text{frac}\right)$ and $2 \cdot \text{frac}$ with frac $= \left\lfloor \frac{2n}{m+2} \right\rfloor$. If we want to prove a space complexity lower bound of $\Omega(m \cdot \log(\frac{n}{m}))$, we are required to have a fooling set with a similar size. If we study the fooling set from Theorem 5.8, we can observe that, for any representative $I_L^i \in \mathcal{F}_L$ and any cleverly chosen frequency value

$$y^i \in \left\{ \left\lceil \frac{\text{frac}}{2} \right\rceil + \text{frac}, \dots, 2 \cdot \text{frac} \right\},$$

we only have to simulate the same Boolean values ($y^i = f(\tilde{x}^i, I_R^v)$), which is either true or false, with any possible test entry $I_R^v \in \mathcal{F}_R$ for just a second representative I_L^j. Then, we cannot verify the required inequality of the Boolean term as the definition of the hypothesis fooling set states. As we have $\approx 2^{m \cdot \log_2(\frac{n}{m})}$ representatives, but only

$2^{m/2}$ different $0/1$ possibilities, there will always be one representative I_L^j, such that the required inequality from the hypothesis fooling set that is defined in Definition 4.4 is not given.

As a consequence of this conjecture, we can make the following statement on the approximative and randomized setting:

Corollary 5.12. *If it is not possible to prove a space complexity lower bound for the streaming problem* $\mathcal{S}_{F_{\infty,1,1}}^{HYP}$ *of* $\Omega(m{\cdot}\log(\frac{n}{m}))$, *as stated in Conjecture 5.1, it is impossible to prove a space complexity lower bound of the same order in an approximative or probabilistic setting.*

Proof. Any space complexity lower bound in an approximative or probabilistic setting is always given for an exact and/or deterministic setting. If we have a space complexity lower bound for an approximation ratio $\alpha > 1$ and a success probability $p < 1$, then this lower bound is also true for the exact and/or deterministic setting, because any (hypothesis) α-fooling set is also a (hypothesis) fooling set and any deterministic setting has a success probability of $p = 1$. With this proof of the contrary, the stated corollary is true.　　　□

5.3   Analysis Conclusion

In this chapter, we have seen several space complexity upper and lower bounds for the most frequent item problem in many different settings. First of all, the most frequent item problem is not *efficiently solvable*, because it requires linear space, even for approximation, randomization, or for hypothesis verification. The proven lower bound of $\Omega(m \cdot \log(\frac{n}{m}))$ for the most common case of $m \leq n$ can be achieved with an algorithm of the same complexity order. If approximative and probabilistic output values are allowed, we can improve the streaming algorithms and space complexity upper bound by a multiplicative factor of $\frac{p}{\alpha^2}$ for a success probability $p < 1$ and 2-sided approximation ratio $\alpha > 1$, with $\alpha^2 \in \mathbb{N}^+$. With a success probability of $p > \frac{1}{2}$ and a 2-sided approximation ratio of $\alpha < \sqrt{2}$, we proved a space complexity lower bound that is almost tight to the upper bound for the case $n \leq m$, which implies that we have identified almost the optimal streaming algorithm for this setting. For a 2-sided approximation ratio $\alpha \geq \sqrt{2}$, we only proved a space complexity lower bound of the order $\Omega(\log(\log(\min\{n, m\})) - \log\log(\alpha)))$. But, we were not able to design a streaming algorithm that solves the most frequent item problem with a lower complexity order than $\mathcal{O}(m \cdot \log(\frac{n}{m}) \cdot \frac{p}{\alpha^2})$.

The analysis of hypothesis verification showed that the verification of any hypothesis requires at least linear storage size. While the proof for a lower bound of $\Omega(m \cdot \log(\frac{n}{m}))$ could not be reproduced for the hypothesis verification, it was still not possible to design a verification algorithm that requires a space size of a lower complexity order.

Chapter 6

Number of Distinct Items Problem

The second studied streaming problem is the *number of distinct items streaming problem*. Some known upper and lower bound proofs from the literature are presented and enhanced with more exact bounds.

After the problem definition, the general streaming problem with several different approximation ratios and success probabilities is studied first. Then, the algorithmic complexities of the verification of hypotheses are analyzed. At the end, the results are summarized and our insights are described.

6.1   General Streaming Problem Analysis

The general streaming counting problem *number of distinct items problem* $\mathcal{S}_{F_0}$ is defined as follows:

Definition 6.1. *The counting problem* **number of distinct items** $\mathcal{S}_{F_0} = (\mathcal{X}, \mathcal{Y}, f, s)$ *has input streams* $x = (x_1, \ldots, x_n) \in \mathcal{X}$ *containing n numbers with $x_i \in \{1, \ldots, m\}$. The result size function is $s(n, m) = m$, which implies that the feasible output values are $\mathcal{Y}_x = \{0, \ldots, m\}$. The problem function f defines the number of distinct items, i.e.,*

$$f(x) = f((x_1, \ldots, x_n)) = \left| \left\{ j \mid j \in (x_1, \ldots, x_n) \text{ with } j \in \{1, \ldots, m\} \right\} \right|.$$

The number of distinct items problem $\mathcal{S}_{F_0}$ is therefore a frequency moment (Definition 3.3) with $k = 0$.

For the ease of presentation, we assume that n and m are even. Similarly to searching the most frequent item, if n or m would be odd, then the proofs would often lead to the exact same results and sometimes affect the space complexity by an additive constant (but not a factor). These effects are normally negligible but the proofs for even numbers are less complicated.

Exact Deterministic Number of Distinct Items Problem

First, we will analyze the exact deterministic streaming problem, which asks for an approximation ratio of $\alpha = 1$ and a success probability of $p = 1$. We use the notation of $\mathcal{S}_{F_{0,1,1}}$ for the exact deterministic number of distinct items problem. Alon et al. state the following space complexity lower bound:

Theorem 6.1 (Alon et al. [AMS99]). *The streaming problem* $\mathcal{S}_{F_{0,1,1}}$ *has, for* $2n = m$, *a space complexity lower bound of,*

$$\operatorname{space}\left(\mathcal{S}_{F_{0,1,1}}^{2n=m}\right) \in \Omega(m).$$

Alon et al. define as fooling set using *set quarters* that contain $\frac{m}{4}$ different items from the set of all items $\{1, \ldots, m\}$. Each of these set quarters has at most $\frac{m}{8}$ items in common with any other set quarter. The authors state, that there exist $2^{\Omega(m)}$ such set quarters, that have at most $\frac{m}{8}$ items in common with any other set quarter. With these set quarters, they prove the above lower bound of $\Omega(m)$.

With the same argumentation, one can generalize this proof by replacing the strict condition $2n = m$ with the more general $n \in \Theta(m)$. This means that, for any $n \in \Theta(m)$, we have a space complexity lower bound of $\Omega(m)$. Later, we will prove this statement formally.

Furthermore, the authors state, that this lower bound is, apart from a constant factor, tight. An upper bound of $\mathcal{O}(m)$ follows, if we simply track the existence of any possible item with a bit string. More formally, we obtain the following complementing theorem.

Theorem 6.2. *The streaming problem* $\mathcal{S}_{F_{0,1,1}}$ *has, for any* $n, m \in \mathbb{N}^+$, *a space complexity upper bound of*

$$\operatorname{space}\left(\mathcal{S}_{F_{0,1,1}}\right) \leq m + \lceil \log_2(m) \rceil \in \mathcal{O}(m).$$

Proof. We will describe a simple streaming algorithm $\mathcal{A} = (\mathcal{A}_{update}, \mathcal{A}_{output})$ that solves the streaming problem exactly and deterministically. The cache state represents a bit string of length m, where each item $j \in \{1, \ldots, m\}$ is associated with one entry in the bit string. At the first computation of the update algorithm, this bit string is generated with all bit-entries set to 0. Then, every update computation (including the first one) processes the corresponding input value x_i, and turns the bit entry $j := x_i$ to 1 if it is currently still 0. At the end, after all update computations, this bit string gives a mapping which items occurred in the input stream. The output algorithm counts all bit entries that are 1, and outputs this value.

Obviously, this algorithm computes the number of distinct items exactly and deterministically. It requires a storage size of m for the given bit string and, additionally, at most $\lceil \log_2(m) \rceil$ bits for counting the output value. $\square$

We will now prove a space complexity lower bound for the exact and deterministic setting, that is almost tight for any $n \geq m$. The following fooling set leads to a space complexity lower bound of $\min\{m, n\} - \log_2(\min\{m, n\})$. As we will show right after this theorem, it is possible to define a fooling set that yields a space complexity lower bound of $\min\{m, n\} - 1$. However, this better fooling set cannot be used for the probabilistic setting, because we cannot verify the minimality of the test set. That is why we will introduce it afterwards.

Theorem 6.3. *The streaming problem $\mathcal{S}_{F_{0,1,1}}$ has, for any $n, m \in \mathbb{N}^+$, a space complexity lower bound of*

$$\mathrm{space}\left(\mathcal{S}_{F_{0,1,1}}\right) \geq \min\{m, n\} - \log_2(\min\{m, n\}) \in \Omega(\min\{m, n\}).$$

Proof. To prove this space complexity lower bound, we will define two fooling sets for the two cases $n \leq m$ and $m < n$. For both cases, we will *i)* formally define a fooling set, *ii)* verify that it is a fooling set, and *iii)* calculate the space complexity lower bound.

Case 1: If $n \leq m$, we will define the fooling set with a set of representatives that contains $\binom{n}{n/2}$ different *set halves*.

i) We define the fooling set $\mathcal{F}^{n \leq m} = (\mathcal{F}_L^{n \leq m}, \mathcal{F}_R^{n \leq m})$ with a cut in the middle, i.e., at $l := \frac{n}{2}$. Recall, that we assume that n is even. The set of representatives contains all different *set halves* with $\frac{n}{2}$ different items from the set $\{1, \ldots, n\} \subseteq \{1, \ldots, m\}$. The test set contains $n - 1$ different entries, each with $\frac{n}{2}$ times the same item $j \in \{1, \ldots, n-1\}$, i.e.,

$$\mathcal{F}_R^{n \leq m} = \{\{1, \ldots, 1\}, \ldots, \{n-1, \ldots, n-1\}\}.$$

ii) $\mathcal{F}^{n \leq m}$ is a fooling set for $\mathcal{S}_{F_{0,1,1}}$, if, for any two representatives $I_L^i, I_L^j \in \mathcal{F}_L^{n \leq m}$, there is at least one test entry $I_R^v \in \mathcal{F}_R^{n \leq m}$, such that the cache states have to be different, i.e., $f(I_L^i, I_R^v) \neq f(I_L^j, I_R^v)$. For any two representatives, there are at least two items $v, v' \in \{1, \ldots, n\}$ that are only present in one of the two representatives, as verified e.g., in Theorem 5.9. W.l.o.g., we assume that $v < v' \leq n$ and $v \in I_L^i$. Then, we have $f(I_L^i, I_R^v) = \frac{n}{2}$, because we have $\frac{n}{2}$ different items with the set half of I_L^i, but I_R^v does not add another item. On the other side, we have $f(I_L^j, I_R^v) = \frac{n}{2} + 1$, because $v \in I_R^v$ is a further, distinct item for the representative I_L^j. Therefore, we have the required inequality and $\mathcal{F}^{n \leq m}$ is a fooling set for $\mathcal{S}_{F_{0,1,1}}$.

iii) Now we can calculate the space complexity lower bound for the first case, which is

$$\mathrm{space}(\mathcal{S}_{F_{0,1,1}}^{n \leq m}) \geq \log_2(|\mathcal{F}_L^{n \leq m}|) = \log_2\left(\binom{n}{n/2}\right) \quad \text{fooling set size}$$

$$> n - \log_2(n) \in \Omega(n). \qquad \text{approx. as in Theorem 5.7}$$

As a result, we have proven the claimed space complexity lower bound for the first case.

Case 2: If $m < n$, we can similarly define *set halves*, but as $m < n$, we choose the set halves from the set of all items, i.e., $\{1, \ldots, m\}$.

i) We define the fooling set $\mathcal{F}^{m < n} = (\mathcal{F}_L^{m < n}, \mathcal{F}_R^{m < n})$, this time with a cut at $l := \frac{m}{2}$. The set of representatives contains all different *set halves* containing $\frac{m}{2}$ different items from $\{1, \ldots, m\}$. The test set has $m - 1$ different entries. Each test $I_R^v \in \mathcal{F}_R^{m < n}$ with a $v \in \{1, \ldots, m-1\}$ contains the item v in total $n - \frac{m}{2}$ times.

ii) Similarly, we can verify the fooling set. For any two representatives $I_L^i, I_L^j \in \mathcal{F}_L^{m<n}$, there are at least two items $v, v' \in \{1, \ldots, m\}$ such that both v and v' are present in only one representative. W.l.o.g., we assume that $v < v' \leq m$. Then, with the test entry $I_R^v = \{v, \ldots, v\}$, we have a number of distinct items of either $\frac{m}{2}$ if v is present in the representative, or $\frac{m}{2} + 1$ if v is not present in the representative. Therefore, $\mathcal{F}^{m<n}$ is a fooling set for $\mathcal{S}_{F_{0,1,1}}$.

iii) As a consequence, the second case has a space complexity lower bound of,

$$\text{space}(\mathcal{S}_{F_{0,1,1}}^{m<n}) \geq \log_2(|\mathcal{F}_L^{m<n}|) = \log_2\left(\binom{m}{m/2}\right) \quad \text{fooling set size}$$

$$> m - \log_2(m) \in \Omega(m). \qquad \text{approx. as in Theorem 5.7}$$

Therefore, we can conclude that the space complexity lower bound of $\mathcal{S}_{F_{0,1,1}}$, for any $n, m \in \mathbb{N}^+$, is

$$\text{space}\left(\mathcal{S}_{F_{0,1,1}}\right) \geq \min\{m, n\} - \log_2(\min\{m, n\}) \in \Omega(\min\{m, n\}). \qquad \square$$

With this lower bound, we can conclude that, for any $n \geq m$, the upper and lower bound are almost tight. Even the constant factor of the leading term is the same. The only minor difference is $2 \cdot \log_2(m)$. With this, we can formally prove the statement from above.

Corollary 6.1. *The streaming problem* $\mathcal{S}_{F_{0,1,1}}$ *has, for any* $n \in \Omega(m)$, *a space complexity lower bound of* $\text{space}\left(\mathcal{S}_{F_{0,1,1}}^{n \in \Omega(m)}\right) \in \Omega(m)$.

Proof. If $n \in \Omega(m)$, then, by the definition of the Ω-notation, there are two positive numbers $a, b \in \mathbb{R}^+$, such that $n \geq a \cdot m - b$. Therefore, we have a space complexity lower bound of

$$\text{space}\left(\mathcal{S}_{F_{0,1,1}}^{n \in \Omega(m)}\right) \geq \min\{m, n\} - \log_2(\min\{m, n\}) \qquad \text{Theorem 6.3}$$

$$\geq \min\{m, am - b\} \qquad\qquad a, b \text{ such that}$$

$$- \log_2(\min\{m, am - b\}) \qquad n \geq a \cdot m - b$$

$$\in \Omega(m).$$

Thus, we have proven the stated corollary. $\qquad\qquad\qquad\qquad\qquad\qquad\qquad\square$

The above stated difference between the upper and the lower bound of $2 \cdot \log_2(m)$ bits can be decreased to $\log_2(m)$, when we use the following fooling set $\mathcal{F}^{n \leq m}$: The representatives of $\mathcal{F}^{n \leq m}$ for the first case contain $m - 1$ input values with different combinations of 1 to $n - 1$ different items from $\{1, \ldots, m\}$. The test set contains m entries, each with one item $v \in \{1, \ldots, m\}$. The set of representatives contains m different representatives with one item, $\binom{m}{2}$ different representatives with two items, and $\binom{m}{d}$ different representatives with d different items. We have, therefore, a fooling set size of $|\mathcal{F}_L^{n \leq m}| = \sum_{i=1}^{m-1} \binom{m}{i} = 2^m - 2$.

The validity of the fooling set can be seen with the following argument: For any two representatives $I_L^i, I_L^j \in \mathcal{F}_L^{n \leq m}$, we have either two representatives with the same number of distinct items, i.e., $f(I_L^i) = f(I_L^j)$ or not, i.e., $f(I_L^i) \neq f(I_L^j)$. In the first case, we have at least one item $v \in \{1, \ldots, m\}$ which is only present in one representative, as shown in previous theorems, and we get the required inequality of $f(I_L^i, I_R^v) \neq f(I_L^j, I_R^v)$. In the second case, we choose an item v that is present in the representative with the higher number of distinct items. Then, the inequality still holds. With this fooling set, we have a space complexity lower bound of at least

$$\text{space}\left(\mathcal{S}_{F_{0,1,1}}^{n \leq m}\right) \geq \log_2(|\mathcal{F}_L|) = \log_2(2^m - 2) > m - 1.$$

Similarly, one can show a space complexity lower bound of $\text{space}\left(\mathcal{S}_{F_{0,1,1}}^{m < n}\right) \geq n - 1$ for the second case. However, both fooling sets cannot be used for the probabilistic setting, because we were not able to verify the minimality of the test set with similar arguments as in previous theorems. The argumentation from below Theorem 4.3 is not strong enough, since for any test entry $I_R^v = v$, we do not have a pair of representatives $I_L^i, I_L^j \in \mathcal{F}_L$, such that $f(I_L^i, I_R^v) \neq f(I_L^j, I_R^v)$, and for all other items $v' \in \{1, \ldots, n\} \setminus \{v\}$, we have $f(I_L^i, I_R^{v'}) = f(I_L^j, I_R^{v'})$.

For the case $n \leq m$, it seems hard to find an algorithm that requires less storage than $m + \lceil \log_2(m) \rceil$, but with $n \ll m$, we can always just store the complete input stream, which has a size of $n \cdot \lceil \log_2(m) \rceil$. Nevertheless, the study of this case for space complexities between $\Omega(n)$ and $\mathcal{O}(m)$ is useless, as streaming problems are characterized by their enormous input stream length and to store "only" $\Omega(n)$ is not practical. Therefore, we will study the streaming problem in another setting.

Exact Probabilistic Number of Distinct Items Problem

For a probabilistic environment, we are able to reproduce a space complexity lower bound of the same complexity order as the deterministic one, namely $\Omega(\min\{m, n\})$. Depending on the success probability $p > \frac{1}{2}$, we have a space complexity that is only a constant factor smaller than in the deterministic environment, which still implies that a streaming algorithm cannot solve the problem *efficiently*, which is formally defined in Definition 3.16.

If we allow randomization and require any fixed success probability $p < 1$, we were unfortunately not able to significantly benefit from this randomization. In the most frequent item problem, we could reduce the space complexity by a multiplicative factor of p. This was the case, because we were storing a histogram of the individual item frequencies and by just ignoring $(1 - p) \cdot m$ items, we had a chance of at least p to have tracked the item with the highest frequency. If we want to transform this concept to the number of distinct item problem, i.e., we only track the existence of some, but not all items, we are likely to have an approximative but not an exact result. Therefore, this concept can only by applied to an approximative and probabilistic setting. As we will see later, there exists a significantly more space-efficient approach for this setting.

But first, we will verify that the identified space complexity lower bound for the deterministic setting is also valid for the probabilistic environment. We use the notation of $\mathcal{S}_{F_{0,1,p}}$ for the exact probabilistic number of distinct items problem.

Theorem 6.4. *The streaming problem* $\mathcal{S}_{F_{0,1,p}}$ *has, for any* $n, m \in \mathbb{N}^+$ *and success probability* $p > \frac{1}{2}$, *a space complexity lower bound of*

$$\text{space}(\mathcal{S}_{F_{0,1,p}}) \geq (\min\{n, m\} - \log_2(\min\{n, m\})) \cdot (1 - 1.01 \cdot h(p)) - 1$$
$$\text{with } h(p) = -p \cdot \log_2(p) - (1 - p) \cdot \log_2(1 - p).$$

Proof. To prove this probabilistic lower bound, we want to use Theorem 4.3, which requires a minimal test set. As both fooling sets from Theorem 6.3 have a minimal test set, we will use exactly the same definitions of the fooling sets. Therefore, we only have to *i*) verify the minimality of both test sets and *ii*) calculate the space complexity lower bound for both cases. Recall, that we can verify the minimality of the test set of the fooling set by showing (4.1) to (4.5), i.e.,

$\forall I_R^v \in \mathcal{F}_R,$	For all elements of the test set,
$\exists I_L^i, I_L^j \in \mathcal{F}_L, I_L^i \neq I_L^j$	there are two different representatives,
s.t. $\left(\mathcal{S}(I_L^i, I_R^v) \neq \mathcal{S}(I_L^j, I_R^v) \right)$	such that the cache states have to be different.
and $\forall I_R^{v'} \in (\mathcal{F}_R \setminus I_R^v):$	And for all other tests,
$\mathcal{S}(I_L^i, I_R^{v'}) = \mathcal{S}(I_L^j, I_R^{v'})\Big).$	they are not required to be different.

Case 1: Suppose $n \leq m$:

i) As described above, first, we will verify the minimality of the test set. We choose for every item $v \in \{1, \ldots, n-1\}$, or its corresponding test entry $I_R^v = \{v, \ldots, v\} \in \mathcal{F}_R^{n \leq m}$, two representatives $I_L^i, I_L^j \in \mathcal{F}_L^{n \leq m}$, which have $\frac{n}{2} - 1$ different items from $\{1, \ldots, n\} \setminus \{v, n\}$ in common. I_L^i additionally contains the item v and I_L^j the item n. Then, we have

$$f(I_L^i, I_R^v) = \frac{n}{2} \neq \frac{n}{2} + 1 = f(I_L^j, I_R^v), \text{ as shown in the proof of Theorem 6.3.}$$

And, for all other items $v' \in \{1, \ldots, n\} \setminus \{v, n\}$, we have either

$$f(I_L^i, I_R^{v'}) = \frac{n}{2} = f(I_L^j, I_R^{v'}) \text{ if } v' \text{ is present in both representatives, or}$$

$$f(I_L^i, I_R^{v'}) = \frac{n}{2} + 1 = f(I_L^j, I_R^{v'}) \text{ if } v' \text{ is not present in the representatives.}$$

Therefore, $\mathcal{F}_L^{n \leq m}$ from Theorem 6.3 has a minimal test set.

ii) We can calculate the space complexity lower bound for the first case. We assume a success probability of $p > \frac{1}{2}$. We get

$$\begin{aligned}
\text{space}(\mathcal{S}_{F_{0,1,p}}^{n \leq m}) &\geq \log_2(|\mathcal{F}_L^{n \leq m}|) \cdot \left(1 - \frac{|\mathcal{F}_R^{n \leq m}| \cdot h(p)}{\log_2(|\mathcal{F}_L^{n \leq m}|)} \right) - 1 & \text{Theorem 4.3} \\
&= \log_2\left(\binom{n}{n/2} \right) \cdot \left(1 - \frac{(n-1) \cdot h(p)}{\log_2(\binom{n}{n/2})} \right) - 1 & \text{fooling set size} \\
&> (n - \log_2(n)) \cdot (1 - 1.01 \cdot h(p)) - 1, & \begin{array}{l}\text{approximation as in}\\\text{Theorem 5.9}\end{array}
\end{aligned}$$

where $h(p) = -p \cdot \log_2(p) - (1-p) \cdot \log_2(1-p)$, as defined in Theorem 4.3. Consequently, we have shown the probabilistic space complexity lower bound for the case $n \leq m$.

Case 2: Suppose $m < n$:

i) We can verify the minimality of the test set from the fooling set $\mathcal{F}^{m<n}$ of Theorem 6.3 with the same argument as in the first case. For every item $v \in \{1, \ldots, m-1\}$, or its corresponding test entry $I_R^v = \{v, \ldots, v\} \in \mathcal{F}_R^{m<n}$, we choose two representatives $I_L^i, I_L^j \in \mathcal{F}_L^{m<n}$ that are equal in all but one item, such that I_L^i additionally contains the item v and I_L^j the item m. Then, we have

$$f(I_L^i, I_R^v) = \frac{m}{2} \neq \frac{m}{2} + 1 = f(I_L^j, I_R^v).$$

And, for all other items $v' \in \{1, \ldots, m\} \setminus \{v, m\}$, we have either

$$f(I_L^i, I_R^{v'}) = \frac{m}{2} = f(I_L^j, I_R^{v'}) \text{ or } f(I_L^i, I_R^{v'}) = \frac{m}{2} + 1 = f(I_L^j, I_R^{v'}).$$

That is why we have a minimal test set, too.

ii) Similarly, we can calculate the space complexity lower bound for a success probability of $p > \frac{1}{2}$. We obtain

$$\begin{aligned}
\text{space}(\mathcal{S}_{F_{0,1,p}}^{m<n}) &\geq \log_2(|\mathcal{F}_L^{m<n}|) \cdot \left(1 - \frac{|\mathcal{F}_R^{m<n}| \cdot h(p)}{\log_2(|\mathcal{F}_L^{m<n}|)}\right) - 1 \quad &\text{Theorem 4.3} \\
&= \log_2\left(\binom{m}{m/2}\right) \cdot \left(1 - \frac{(m-1) \cdot h(p)}{\log_2(\binom{m}{m/2})}\right) - 1. \quad &\text{fooling set size} \\
&> (m - \log_2(m)) \cdot (1 - 1.01 \cdot h(p)) - 1, \quad &\text{same apx. as above}
\end{aligned}$$

Therefore, we have proven a space complexity lower bound for the probabilistic setting in both cases, which is

$$\text{space}(\mathcal{S}_{F_{0,1,p}}) \geq (\min\{n, m\} - \log_2(\min\{n, m\})) \cdot (1 - 1.01 \cdot h(p)) - 1. \qquad \square$$

The factor $1 - 1.01 \cdot h(p)$ is the same as in Theorem 5.9 from the most frequent item streaming problem and therefore has the same shape as Figure 5.2.

With this theorem, we have proven that the relaxation on probabilistic results does not enable a significant space complexity reduction. At most, it might be reduced by the multiplicative factor of $1 - 1.01 \cdot h(p)$. However, as we showed above, it seems to be very complicated, if not impossible, to decrease the space complexity of a concrete streaming algorithm significantly for this setting. Therefore, we will now focus on the approximative, deterministic streaming problem in the next part.

Approximative Deterministic Number of Distinct Items Problem

For the approximative and deterministic setting, we will show a technique to decrease the space complexity by a factor of α^2 if a 2-sided approximation ratio of α with $\alpha^2 \in \mathbb{N}^+$ is allowed. Later, we will prove space complexity lower bounds for 2-sided approximation ratios $\alpha < \sqrt{\frac{3}{2}}$, $\alpha < \sqrt{2}$, and $\alpha \geq \sqrt{2}$. We use the notation of $\mathcal{S}_{F_{0,\alpha,1}}$ for the approximative deterministic number of distinct items problem.

Theorem 6.5. *The streaming problem* $\mathcal{S}_{F_{0,\alpha,1}}$ *has, for any* $n, m \in \mathbb{N}^+$ *and a 2-sided approximation ratio* α *with* $\alpha^2 \in \mathbb{N}^+$ *a space complexity upper bound of*

$$\text{space}\left(\mathcal{S}_{F_{0,\alpha,1}}\right) \leq \left\lceil \frac{m}{\alpha^2} \right\rceil + \lceil \log_2(m) \rceil \in \mathcal{O}\left(\frac{m}{\alpha^2} + \log(m)\right).$$

Proof. We adapt the streaming algorithm from Theorem 6.2 by limiting the bit string length. For the exact algorithm, we used a bit string of length m to track the presence of any item. Now, we only have one bit for all items $\{1, \ldots, \alpha^2\}$, a second bit is used for the items $\{\alpha^2 + 1, \ldots, 2 \cdot \alpha^2\}$, and so on. Therefore, we require only $\left\lceil \frac{m}{\alpha^2} \right\rceil$ bits for the entire bit string. At the beginning, this bit string is set to 0, as in the original algorithm (Theorem 6.2). Now, each update algorithm processes the input value x_i and sets the corresponding bit entry to 1, if it was 0 before. As illustrated above, the input value x_i corresponds to the $\left\lceil \frac{x_i}{\alpha^2} \right\rceil$-th bit of the bit string. As a consequence, at the end, the j-th bit of the bit string is set of 1, if at least one item of $\{\alpha^2 \cdot (j-1) + 1, \cdots, \alpha^2 \cdot j\}$ occurred in the input stream. The output algorithm counts the number of 1s in the bit strings and multiplies it by α. This is the output value.

With this approach, the algorithm will produce, for any input stream, an output value within a 2-sided approximation ratio of α. If we analyze a certain item set $\{d \cdot \alpha^2 + 1, \ldots, (d+1) \cdot \alpha^2\}$ that is represented by a single bit, we can observe the following fact: If none of these items occur in the input value, the output value will not be affected by these items, because the bit value will remain zero. If only one item occurs in the input stream, the output algorithm will falsely add α to the overall output value, even though only 1 would have been correct. However, the factor $\frac{\alpha}{1}$ is still within the tolerated approximation ratio. In the other extreme case, if all α^2 items from this item set occur in the input stream, then the output algorithm will only add α to the overall output value instead of α^2, which would have been correct. Once again, the approximative factor $\frac{\alpha^2}{\alpha} = \alpha$ is still acceptable. For all number of items between 1 and α^2, we have a better approximation value. Therefore, any item set will lead to a tolerated approximative output value and, as a logical consequence, the algorithm will produce, for any input stream, an output value within the accepted approximation ratio. $\qquad\square$

With this algorithm, we are able to reduce the space complexity, but only with a massive decrease of result accuracy.

In Theorem 6.1, we have introduced a space complexity lower bound of $\Omega(m)$ for $2n = m$ by Alon et al. [AMS99], and proved that this lower bound is also valid for all $n \in \Theta(m)$ (Corollary 6.1). The original theorem states this lower bound for a 2-sided approximation ratio of $\alpha = 1.1$. We will now enhance this approximation ratio to any $\alpha < \sqrt{\frac{3}{2}}$.

Theorem 6.6. *The streaming problem* $\mathcal{S}_{F_{0,\alpha < \frac{3}{2}, 1}}$ *has, for any* $n \in \Theta(m)$ *and a 1-sided approximation ratio of* $\alpha < \frac{3}{2}$, *a space complexity lower bound of*

$$\text{space}\left(\mathcal{S}_{F_{0,\alpha < \frac{3}{2}, 1}}\right) \in \Omega(m).$$

Proof. The proof of Theorem 6.1 uses a set of *set quarters* of $\frac{m}{4}$ different items, but any two set quarters have $\frac{m}{8}$ items in common. Alon et al. state that there exist $2^{\Omega(m)}$ such set quarters. If we choose all these set quarters as representatives and as tests, we have an α-fooling set for any $\alpha < \frac{3}{2}$. For any two representatives I_L^i, I_L^j, we can just choose a test that is equal to one of the representatives, i.e., $I_R^i := I_L^i$. Then, we have $f(I_L^i, I_R^i) = \frac{m}{4}$ and $f(I_L^j, I_R^i) = \frac{m}{4} + \frac{m}{8} = \frac{3}{2} \cdot \frac{m}{4}$, because I_L^j has $\frac{m}{8}$ items different to the test entry. Therefore, we have a factor between the two optimal output values of $\frac{3}{2}$ and, as a consequence, we have an α-fooling set for any $\alpha < \frac{3}{2}$. This implies that the 1-sided streaming problem $\mathcal{S}_{F_{0,\alpha,1}}$ has, for any approximation ratio $\alpha < \frac{3}{2}$, a space complexity lower bound of $\Omega(m)$. $\qquad\square$

With this argument, we have enhanced the originally stated approximation ratio of $\alpha = 1.1$ to $\alpha = \sqrt{\frac{3}{2}} - \varepsilon > 1.225 - \varepsilon$ for any arbitrarily small $\varepsilon > 0$.

Corollary 6.2. *The streaming problem* $\mathcal{S}_{F_{0,\alpha<\sqrt{\frac{3}{2}},1}}$ *has, for any* $n \in \Theta(m)$ *and a* 2-*sided approximation ratio of* $\alpha < \sqrt{\frac{3}{2}}$, *a space complexity lower bound of*

$$\mathrm{space}\left(\mathcal{S}_{F_{0,\alpha<\sqrt{\frac{3}{2}},1}}\right) \in \Omega(m).$$

This corollary follows directly from the α-fooling set from Theorem 6.6 and Theorem 4.5.

We have proven a space complexity lower bound of $\Omega(m)$ for any approximation ratio of $\alpha \leq 1.225$. In the following, we will analyze the possible space complexity lower bounds for larger 2-sided approximation ratios, namely for $\alpha < \sqrt{2}$ and $\alpha \geq \sqrt{2}$.

Theorem 6.7. *The streaming problem* $\mathcal{S}_{F_{0,\alpha<2,1}}$ *has, for any* $n,m \in \mathbb{N}^+$ *and a* 1-*sided approximation ratio of* $\alpha < 2$, *a space complexity lower bound of*

$$\mathrm{space}\left(\mathcal{S}_{F_{0,\alpha<2,1}}\right) \geq \frac{1}{\alpha - 1} \cdot \log_2(\min\{m,n\} \cdot (\alpha - 1)).$$

Proof. To prove the claimed space complexity lower bound, we will define two fooling sets $\mathcal{F}^{n\leq m} = (\mathcal{F}_L^{n\leq m}, \mathcal{F}_R^{n\leq m})$ and $\mathcal{F}^{m<n} = (\mathcal{F}_L^{m<n}, \mathcal{F}_R^{m<n})$ for the two cases $n \leq m$ and $m < n$. We will define and analyze these two sets in parallel, because they are very similar. We will *i)* define the fooling sets, *ii)* verify them, and *iii)* calculate the space complexity lower bounds.

i) For both fooling sets, we define a basic distinctness value d as

$$d := \left\lfloor \frac{1}{\alpha^+ - 1} \right\rfloor \text{ for an } \alpha^+ = \alpha + \varepsilon \text{ with an arbitrary small } \varepsilon > 0. \tag{6.1}$$

Both fooling sets have a cut at $l := d$, which implies that each representative has a length of d. The set of representatives $\mathcal{F}_L^{n\leq m}$ for the first case contains $\binom{n}{d}$ different entries, each with d different items from $\{1, \ldots, n\} \subseteq \{1, \ldots, m\}$. On the other side, there are $\binom{m}{d}$ representatives in $\mathcal{F}_L^{m<n}$, each with d different items from $\{1, \ldots, m\}$. The two test sets contain $n - 1$ entries in the first, and $m - 1$ entries in the second case respectively. Every test entry $I_R^v \in \mathcal{F}_R^{n\leq m} \cup \mathcal{F}_R^{m<n}$ contains

$n - d$ times the same item v, i.e., $\mathcal{F}_R^{n \leq m} = \{\{1, \ldots, 1\}, \ldots, \{n - 1, \ldots, n - 1\}\}$ and $\mathcal{F}_R^{m < n} = \{\{1, \ldots, 1\}, \ldots, \{m - 1, \ldots, m - 1\}\}$.

ii) With this definition of the two fooling sets, any combination of representative and test from a certain fooling set will have either d distinct items if the item from the test entries present in the representative, or $d + 1$ distinct items if the item from the test entry is not present in the representative. This implies that the fraction between $d + 1$ and d will definitely be interesting. Before we justify why we have indeed two fooling sets, we will first make the following, useful approximation:

$$\frac{d + 1}{d} = 1 + \frac{1}{d} = 1 + \frac{1}{\left\lfloor \frac{1}{\alpha^+ - 1} \right\rfloor} \geq 1 + \frac{1}{\frac{1}{\alpha^+ - 1}} = 1 + (\alpha^+ - 1) = \alpha^+ > \alpha. \quad (6.2)$$

For any two representatives $I_L^i, I_L^j \in \mathcal{F}_L^{n \leq m}$ from the first case, we have at least two items $v, v' \in \{1, \ldots, n\}$ that are only present in one of the two representatives. W.l.o.g., we assume that $v < v' \leq n$. With the test entry $I_R^v = \{v, \ldots, v\} \in \mathcal{F}_R^{n \leq m}$, we have either d or $d + 1$ distinct items, and therefore, using (6.2), $\mathcal{F}^{n \leq m}$ is an α-fooling set for any $\alpha < 2$. Similarly, one can prove that $\mathcal{F}^{m < n}$ is an α-fooling set for any $\alpha < 2$.

iii) Therefore, we can calculate the space complexity lower bounds by,

$$\text{space}(\mathcal{S}_{F_0, \alpha < 2, 1}^{n \leq m}) \geq \log_2(|\mathcal{F}_L^{n \leq m}|) = \log_2\left(\binom{n}{d}\right) \qquad \text{fooling set size}$$

$$> \log_2\left(\left(\frac{n}{d}\right)^d\right) = d \cdot \log_2\left(\frac{n}{d}\right) \qquad \begin{array}{l} \text{Lemma 3.1 and} \\ \text{basic operation} \end{array}$$

$$= \left\lfloor \frac{1}{\alpha^+ - 1} \right\rfloor \cdot \log_2\left(\frac{n}{\left\lfloor \frac{1}{\alpha^+ - 1} \right\rfloor}\right) \qquad \text{definition of } d, \text{ (6.2)}$$

$$> \frac{1}{\alpha - 1} \cdot \log_2(n \cdot (\alpha - 1)). \qquad \text{simple approximation}$$

Similarly, we can calculate the lower bound for the second case by,

$$\text{space}(\mathcal{S}_{F_0, \alpha < 2, 1}^{m < n}) \geq \log_2(|\mathcal{F}_L^{m < n}|) = \log_2\left(\binom{m}{d}\right) \qquad \text{fooling set size}$$

$$> \frac{1}{\alpha - 1} \cdot \log_2(m \cdot (\alpha - 1)). \qquad \text{approximation as above}$$

Finally, we obtain the general space complexity lower bound of both cases:

$$\text{space}(\mathcal{S}_{F_0, \alpha < 2, 1}) \geq \frac{1}{\alpha - 1} \cdot \log_2(\min\{m, n\} \cdot (\alpha - 1)). \qquad \qquad \square$$

Observe that, for any $\alpha \geq 2$, the basic distinctness value d, as defined in (6.1), would be zero and as a consequence, we do not have a fooling set any more, because there would be zero representatives. This is why we have the restriction $\alpha < 2$.

Corollary 6.3. *The streaming problem* $\mathcal{S}_{F_{0,\alpha<\sqrt{2},1}}$ *has, for any* $n, m \in \mathbb{N}^+$ *and a 2-sided approximation ratio of* $\alpha < \sqrt{2}$, *a space complexity lower bound of*

$$\mathrm{space}\Big(\mathcal{S}_{F_{0,\alpha<\sqrt{2},1}}\Big) \geq \frac{1}{\alpha-1} \cdot \log_2(\min\{m,n\} \cdot (\alpha-1)).$$

This follows directly from the α-fooling set from the proof of Theorem 6.7 and Theorem 4.5. Next, we want to identify a space complexity lower bound for a 1-sided approximation ratio of $\alpha \geq 2$.

Theorem 6.8. *The streaming problem* $\mathcal{S}_{F_{0,\alpha\geq2,1}}$ *has, for any* $n, m \in \mathbb{N}^+$ *and a 1-sided approximation ratio of* $\alpha \geq 2$, *a space complexity lower bound of*

$$\mathrm{space}\Big(\mathcal{S}_{F_{0,\alpha\geq2,1}}\Big) \geq \log_2(\log_2(\min\{n,m\})) - \log_2\Big(\log_2\Big(\frac{3}{2}\cdot\alpha\Big)\Big).$$

Proof. As this theorem states a very low space complexity lower bound and the proof of this theorem is very close to the proof of Theorem 5.14, we will only give a proof sketch. One can easily repeat the detailed definitions and calculations with the original theorem as basis.

With exactly the same concept as in the proof of Theorem 5.14, we can create two fooling sets for both cases $n \leq m$ and $m < n$, such that the representatives I_L^i simulate a distinctness function $d(i)$ which is similarly defined as the frequency function $k(i)$ from the original theorem. This distinctness function is recursively defined as

$$d(1) = 1 \text{ and } d(i) = \lceil \alpha^+ \cdot d(i-1) \rceil \text{ for all } i \geq 2,$$

with the condition that $d(i) < \min\{n, m\}$. For the first case, we have exactly the same lower bound as in the most frequent item problem. For the second case, we had to define $k(1) = \lceil \frac{n}{m} \rceil$, because this is the highest frequency one gets at least for any $m < n$. For the number of distinct items problem, we do not have such a condition, because all input values could be the same item. Therefore, we have a space complexity lower bound that is analogue to the first case. $\square$

Corollary 6.4. *The streaming problem* $\mathcal{S}_{F_{0,\alpha\geq\sqrt{2},1}}$ *has, for any* $n, m \in \mathbb{N}^+$ *and a 2-sided approximation ratio of* $\alpha \geq \sqrt{2}$, *a space complexity lower bound of*

$$\mathrm{space}\Big(\mathcal{S}_{F_{0,\alpha\geq\sqrt{2},1}}\Big) \geq \log_2(\log_2(\min\{n,m\})) - \log_2\Big(\log_2\Big(\frac{3}{2}\cdot\alpha\Big)\Big).$$

This follows directly from the α-fooling set from the proof of Theorem 6.8 and Theorem 4.5.

Similarly to the argumentation in Theorem 5.15, one can observe that, for any 2-sided approximation ratio $\alpha \geq \sqrt{2}$, it is impossible to prove a higher space complexity lower bound than $\Theta(\log(m))$ using the proof technique of communication complexity.

Theorem 6.9. *For any 2-sided approximation ratio* $\alpha \geq \sqrt{2}$, *it is impossible to prove a higher space complexity lower bound than* $\lceil \log_2(m) \rceil$ *using the proof technique of communication complexity.*

Proof. Similarly to Theorem 5.15, we can prove this theorem. The communication complexity assumes to have two computers C_L and C_R and their corresponding input stream parts x_l and x_r. With a communication complexity of $\lceil \log_2(m) \rceil$, the two computers can solve the number of distinct items problem with an approximation ratio of $\alpha = \sqrt{2}$. This is the case with the following algorithm:

The left computer calculates the number of distinct items of its input stream part and communicates this value to the right computer, i.e., $f(x_l)$. This requires at most $\lceil \log_2(m) \rceil$ communication bits. The right computer calculates its own number of distinct items $f(x_r)$, sums up the two values and outputs $\frac{f(x_l)+f(x_r)}{\sqrt{2}}$. This output value is a $\sqrt{2}$-approximation of $f(x)$, as one can verify with the same argument as for Theorem 5.15.

Therefore, with only $\lceil \log_2(m) \rceil$ communication bits, the two-computer model of the communication complexity theory solves the number of distinct items problem with a 2-sided approximation ratio of $\alpha \geq \sqrt{2}$. Therefore, it is impossible, to prove a lower bound, that is higher than this one, using the technique of communication complexity. $\square$

What follows next is the analysis of the approximative and probabilistic setting. Surprisingly, we can reduce the space complexity significantly, such that the number of distinct items problem can be *solved efficiently*.

Approximative Probabilistic Number of Distinct Items Problem

Alon et al. state that the number of distinct items problem can be solved for certain approximation ratios and success probabilities with a logarithmic space complexity. We use the notation of $\mathcal{S}_{F_0,\alpha,p}$ for the approximative probabilistic number of distinct items problem.

Theorem 6.10 (Alon et al. [AMS99]). *The streaming problem $\mathcal{S}_{F_0,\alpha,p}$ has, for any $n, m \in \mathbb{N}^+$, a 2-sided approximation ratio of $\alpha > 2$, and a success probability of $p = 1 - \frac{2}{\alpha}$, a space complexity upper bound of*

$$\text{space}\left(\mathcal{S}_{F_0,\alpha>2,p}\right) \in \mathcal{O}(\log(m)).$$

Proof. We will only sketch the proof of Proposition 2.3 [AMS99] and use it as an introduction to this algorithmic concept, which is used in an enhanced approach later on.

The algorithm requires a *finite field* $\mathbb{F} = GF(2^d)$ with a smallest integer d with $2^d > m$, that is used as a linear hash function. Observe that all items $j \in \{1, \ldots, m\}$ can be interpreted as entries of this finite field $\mathbb{F}$. Upfront the algorithm chooses two random members $a, b \in \mathbb{F}$, which are represented by binary vectors of length d. For processing the first input value x_1, which can also be interpreted as a binary vector of length d, the update algorithm computes $z_1 = a \cdot x_1 + b$, with addition and multiplication in $\mathbb{F}$. Then, z_1 is once again a binary vector of length d. The first update computation analyzes this vector and counts, starting at its end, the number of successive zeros and stores this value $r_1 \in \{0, \ldots, d-1\}$. The second update algorithm computation calculates, with the input value x_2, the binary vector

$z_2 = a \cdot x_2 + b$ within $\mathbb{F}$ and counts the number of successive zeros at its end, which is stored as a value r_2. After that, the value $r_{\max}$ is cached as the maximum of r_1 and r_2. Any further update algorithm computation calculates, for the input value x_i, the binary vector z_i, the number of successive 0s r_i, and updates $r_{\max}$ if the current r_i is larger than $r_{\max}$. At the end, the algorithm outputs $2^{r_{\max}}$.

This algorithm requires only $\mathcal{O}(\log(m))$ storage bits for the three variables a, b, and $r_{\max}$, because the bit vector size d that determines the storage size of a and b is in $\Theta(\log(m))$. Furthermore, $r_{\max}$ requires only $\mathcal{O}(\log_2(d)) = \mathcal{O}(\log_2(\log_2(m)))$ storage bits. The intermediate results z_i and r_i are not required to be stored.

Now, we want to analyze the behaviour and probability distribution of any r_i. With the linear hash function $z_i = a \cdot x_i + b$ on the finite field $\mathbb{F}$, we have, for a certain input value x_i, the probability $\Pr[r_i = 0] = 0.5$ that r_i is zero. The probability that r_i is 1 is the probability that the binary vector z_i ends with "$\ldots 10$", which is $\Pr[r_i = 1] = 0.25 = \frac{1}{4}$. Likewise, r_i is 2 for a binary vector that ends with of "$\ldots 100$", which has a probability of $\Pr[r_i = 2] = \frac{1}{8} = \frac{1}{2^3}$. Therefore, we can derive the following probability distribution of r_i.

$$\Pr[r_i = k] = \left(\frac{1}{2}\right)^{k+1} \forall k \in \{0, \ldots, d-1\} \text{ and } \Pr[r_i = d] = \Pr[z_i = \text{``}0\ldots0\text{''}] = \left(\frac{1}{2}\right)^d.$$

With $f(x)$ distinct items, we have $f(x)$ random samples of r_i and it is very likely that the maximal r_i of these $f(x)$ random samples, $r_{\max}$, is roughly $\log_2(f(x))$. Therefore, the output value $2^{r_{\max}}$ is with a reasonable probability $2^{r_{\max}} \approx f(x)$. This informal analysis of the success probability and approximation ratio is proven mathematically for an approximation ratio of any $\alpha > 2$ and a corresponding success probability of $p = 1 - \frac{2}{\alpha}$ by Alon et al. [AMS99]. $\qquad\square$

Before we introduce an enhanced approach for solving $\mathcal{S}_{F_0, \alpha, p}$, we study the behaviour and the probability distribution of $r_{\max}$ in more detail. With a linear hash function in $\mathbb{F}$ as used in the proof of Theorem 6.10, we have an independent probability distribution of r_i on any individual input value. All input values with the same value will lead to the same z_i and r_i, therefore, we have exactly $f(x)$ different samples of r_i. Now, we can analyze the probability distribution of $r_{\max}$ for a certain input stream x with $f(x)$ distinct items. If we know the probability distribution of $r_{\max}$ explicitly, we can use this information to improve the concept of Theorem 6.10. For this purpose, we will now analyze the behaviour and probability distribution of $r_{\max} = 0$, $r_{\max} = 1$ and so on, until we can formulate an explicit probability function on any $r_{\max} \in \{0, \ldots, d-1\}$.

The probability that $r_{\max}$ is 0 is the probability that all $f(x)$ different samples of r_i are zero, i.e.,

$$\Pr[r_{\max} = 0] = (\Pr[r_i = 0])^{f(x)} = \left(\frac{1}{2}\right)^{f(x)}.$$

Next, the probability that $r_{\max}$ is 1, is the probability that at least one sample of r_i is 1, but none is larger. This is the probability that all different samples of r_i are at most 1, i.e., $(\Pr[r_i = 0] + \Pr[r_i = 1])^{f(x)}$, minus the probability that $r_{\max}$ is zero, which is,

$$\Pr[r_{\max} = 1] = (\Pr[r_i = 0] + \Pr[r_i = 1])^{f(x)} - (\Pr[r_i = 0])^{f(x)}$$

$$= \left(\frac{1}{2} + \frac{1}{4}\right)^{f(x)} - \left(\frac{1}{2}\right)^{f(x)} = \left(\frac{3}{4}\right)^{f(x)} - \left(\frac{1}{2}\right)^{f(x)}.$$

Likewise, the probability of $r_{\max}$ being 2 is the probability that none of the $f(x)$ samples of r_i are larger than 2, but at least one sample has $r_i = 2$, which is,

$$\Pr[r_{\max} = 2] = (\Pr[r_i = 0] + \Pr[r_i = 1] + \Pr[r_i = 2])^{f(x)}$$
$$- \Pr[r_{\max} = 1] - \Pr[r_{\max} = 0]$$
$$= \left(\frac{1}{2} + \frac{1}{4} + \frac{1}{8}\right)^{f(x)} - \left(\left(\frac{3}{4}\right)^{f(x)} - \left(\frac{1}{2}\right)^{f(x)}\right) - \left(\frac{1}{2}\right)^{f(x)}$$
$$= \left(\frac{7}{8}\right)^{f(x)} - \left(\frac{3}{4}\right)^{f(x)}.$$

Consequentially, we have, for $r_{\max} = 3$, a probability of,

$$\Pr[r_{\max} = 3] = (\Pr[r_i = 0] + \cdots + \Pr[r_i = 3])^{f(x)}$$
$$- (\Pr[r_{\max} = 2] + \cdots + \Pr[r_{\max} = 0])$$
$$= \left(\frac{1}{2} + \cdots + \frac{1}{16}\right)^{f(x)}$$
$$- \left(\left(\left(\frac{7}{8}\right)^{f(x)} - \left(\frac{3}{4}\right)^{f(x)}\right) + \cdots + \left(\frac{1}{2}\right)^{f(x)}\right)$$
$$= \left(\frac{15}{16}\right)^{f(x)} - \left(\frac{7}{8}\right)^{f(x)}.$$

With this analysis, we obtain the following probability distribution of $r_{\max} = k$ for a certain input stream x and its number of distinct items $f(x)$ for any $k < d$ with a simple induction argument:

$$\Pr[r_{\max} = k] = \left(\frac{2^{k+1} - 1}{2^{k+1}}\right)^{f(x)} - \left(\frac{2^k - 1}{2^k}\right)^{f(x)}$$
$$= \left(1 - \frac{1}{2^{k+1}}\right)^{f(x)} - \left(1 - \frac{1}{2^k}\right)^{f(x)} \text{ for all } k \in \{0, \ldots, d-1\}$$

This probability distribution is illustrated in Figure 6.1. For different numbers of distinct items $f(x) \in \{10, \ldots, 1\,000\}$ in the x-axis, this plot illustrates the probability distribution on the y-axis for some $r_{\max} = k \in \{4, \ldots, 8\}$. The dotted lines illustrate the further behavior of the probability function, but it might be possible that it is not defined, e.g., if $f(x) = m$. In this case, for, e.g., $f(x) = m = 100$, we have $d := 7$, because d is the smallest integer such that $2^d > m = 100$, and the probability distribution is only defined for $k < d = 7$. This is why the probability distribution for $f(x) = 100$ is only guaranteed to be defined for $k \leq 6$, but dotted for $k \geq 7$ (violet or blue line) in Figure 6.1.

Even though we do not know the number of distinct items $f(x)$, the algorithm that uses the linear hash function in the finite field $\mathbb{F} = GF(2^d)$ calculates $r_{\max}$ with

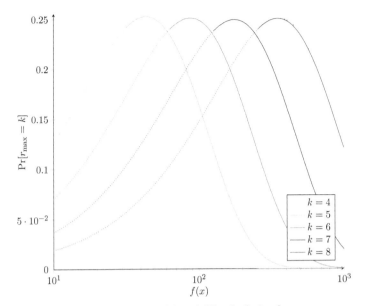

Figure 6.1. Illustration of the probability distribution of $r_{\max}$

the probability distribution from above as it has $f(x)$ independent samples of r_i. If we would execute the algorithm of Theorem 6.10 infinite times and stochastically learn the probability distribution of $\Pr[r_{\max} = k]$ for some different k, then we could determine the exact probability for $r_{\max} = k$, for any $k < d$. Furthermore, we could calculate the number of distinct items $f(x)$ from an input stream with the probability formula above, some $k < d$, and the corresponding, exactly determined probabilities $\Pr[r_{\max} = k]$. If we knew the probability of some event $\Pr[r_{\max} = k]$ for just one $k < d$ perfectly, we could determine one or two possible $f(x)$. As an example, for $\Pr[r_{\max} = 6] \approx 0.2$, we have $f(x) \in \{41, 165\}$. In other words, for the values $f(x) \in \{41, 165\}$ on the x-axis, we have a probability of 0.2 for $k = 6$ (the red line in Figure 6.1). With a second probability $\Pr[r_{\max} = k']$ for any $k \neq k' < d$, we can determine the exact $f(x)$. E.g., for the example above, with $\Pr[r_{\max} = 4] \approx 0.0053$ (the yellow line in Figure 6.1), we know that $f(x) = 165$, because $\left(1 - 1/2^5\right)^{165} - \left(1 - 1/2^4\right)^{165} \approx 0.0053$, but $\left(1 - 1/2^5\right)^{41} - \left(1 - 1/2^4\right)^{41} \approx 0.201$.

So far, we assumed that the algorithm is executed infinitely many times. If we learn the probability distribution with just a finite number of computations, we are able to approximate the number of distinct items $f(x)$ for a certain success probability. Unfortunately, the proof of this statement is not trivial. That is why we state this upper bound only as a conjecture, but not as a formally proven theorem. The detailed analysis in the proof sketch after the conjecture states why it is very probable to be true.

Conjecture 6.1. *The streaming problem* $\mathcal{S}_{F_{0,\alpha,p}}$ *has, for any* $n, m \in \mathbb{N}^+$, *a 2-sided approximation ratio of* $\alpha < 2$, *and a success probability of* $p > \frac{1}{2}$, *for any arbitrarily small* $\varepsilon, \delta > 0$ *with* $\alpha = 1 + \varepsilon$ *and* $p = 1 - \delta$, *a space complexity upper bound of,*

$$\text{space}\left(\mathcal{S}_{F_{0,\alpha,p}}\right) \leq \frac{3 \cdot \log_2(m) \cdot (46\,000)^2}{(\alpha - 1)^2 \cdot (1 - p)} \in \mathcal{O}\left(\frac{\log(m)}{(\alpha - 1)^2 \cdot (1 - p)}\right)$$

$$= \mathcal{O}\left(\frac{\log(m)}{\varepsilon^2 \cdot \delta}\right) \text{ with } \alpha = 1 + \varepsilon \text{ and } p = 1 - \delta.$$

As we stated above, if we knew the probability distribution of $r_{\max}$ perfectly, we could exactly calculate the number of distinct items $f(x)$. We will show in this proof sketch that, for a fixed approximation ratio $\alpha > 1$ and a success probability $p < 1$, with $g(\alpha, p)$ parallel executions of the algorithm described in Theorem 6.10, we have a success probability of p to indicate the number of distinct items within an approximation ratio of α. This function $g(\alpha, p)$ is defined as $g(\alpha, p) = \frac{(46\,000)^2}{(\alpha-1)^2 \cdot (p-1)}$.

The algorithm works as follows: It uses parallely $g(\alpha, p)$ different linear hashes in the finite field $\mathbb{F} = GF(2^d)$ with the smallest integer d such that $2^d > m$. This means, that the algorithm chooses $g(\alpha, p)$ different $a_j, b_j \in \mathbb{F}$ uniformly at random. For every input value x_i, the algorithm produces, similarly to the proof of Theorem 6.10, $z_{i,j} = a_j \cdot x_i + b_j$ and stores the current $r_{\max,j}$ for all $g(\alpha, p)$ different, parallel executions. The output algorithm creates a histogram for all different $r_{\max,j}$ and estimates the probability distribution with the $g(\alpha, p)$ samples of $r_{\max}$. Then, it identifies the most frequent $\hat{k}_{\max}$ of this histogram, such that $\Pr[r_{\max} = \hat{k}_{\max}]$ is the largest one. After that, it calculates the number of distinct items $f(x)$ with the formula $\Pr[r_{\max} = k] = \left(1 - \frac{1}{2^{k+1}}\right)^{f(x)} - \left(1 - \frac{1}{2^k}\right)^{f(x)}$ and $k := \hat{k}_{\max} - 2$ and the observed statistical probability of $\Pr[r_{\max} = k]$. As this formula is not stated explicitly to solve it for $f(x)$, we can simply approximate $f(x)$ optimally with few iteartion steps, as $f(x) \in \mathbb{N}^+$, using Newton's method (e.g., by Stoer et al. [SBB$^+$02], Deuflhard [Deu04] or Kelley [Kel03]) that identifies the root of $h(f(x)) = \left(1 - \frac{1}{2^{k+1}}\right)^{f(x)} - \left(1 - \frac{1}{2^k}\right)^{f(x)} - \Pr[r_{\max} = k]$ for the fixed $k = \hat{k}_{\max} - 2$ and the stochastically observed $\Pr[r_{\max} = k]$ with a starting point at $f(x) = 2^{\hat{k}_{\max}}$.

Now we want to analyze the correctness of this algorithm. Since we are considering 2-sided errors with approximation ratios of $\alpha > 1$, we are allowed to produce any output value between $\frac{f(x)}{\alpha}$ and $f(x) \cdot \alpha$. If we analyze the probability $\Pr[r_{\max} = \hat{k}_{\max} - 2]$, we observe that the function is continuously decreasing. E.g., for $f(x) = 100$, as Figure 6.1 demonstrates, it is very likely that with a sample size of $g(\alpha, p)$, we have $\hat{k}_{\max} = 6$, which corresponds to the red line. Even if $\hat{k}_{\max}$ were 5 or 7, the line corresponding to $\hat{k}_{\max} - 2$ is continuously decreasing between $\frac{f(x)}{\alpha}$ and $f(x) \cdot \alpha$ for any $1 < \alpha < 2$. Therefore, if the algorithm produces a sample frequency for $\hat{k}_{\max} - 2$ between

$$\left(\left(1 - \frac{1}{2^{\hat{k}_{\max}-1}}\right)^{f(x)\cdot\alpha} - \left(1 - \frac{1}{2^{\hat{k}_{\max}-2}}\right)^{f(x)\cdot\alpha}\right) \text{ and }$$

$$\left(\left(1 - \frac{1}{2^{\hat{k}_{\max}-1}}\right)^{\frac{f(x)}{\alpha}} - \left(1 - \frac{1}{2^{\hat{k}_{\max}-2}}\right)^{\frac{f(x)}{\alpha}}\right),$$

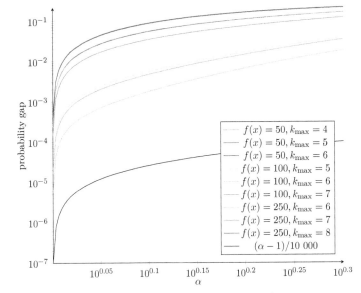

Figure 6.2. Illustration of the probability gap of r_{max}

our approach will produce a number of distinct items within the accepted approximation ratio. This implies that, if the observed frequency sample is within these two boundaries, which depend on α, we have an approximation ratio of α with a success probability of p. This probability gap is illustrated in Figure 6.2.

One can see that the probability gap is smaller if the measured $\hat{k}_{max}$ is not the theoretical one, but a lower one. With $g(\alpha, p) = \frac{(46\,000)^2}{(\alpha - 1)^2 \cdot (1-p)}$ samples, we can practically exclude the case that the observed most frequent $\hat{k}_{max}$ differs from the theoretical k_{max} by 2 or more, because k_{max} has a theoretical probability of more than 0.225, but $k_{max} \pm 2$ has a probability of less than 0.175, as one can easily verify by studying Figure 6.1. More formally, we can analyze the probability distribution of r_{max} and calculate the probability, that with $g(\alpha, p)$ samples, $k_{max} \pm 2$ gets a higher occurrence than k_{max}. For this purpose, we can analyze the probability of the binomial distribution $B = (n, p)$ with $n = g(\alpha, p)$ and $p \leq 0.175$ to get a frequency of more than $0.2 \cdot g(\alpha, p)$, which is only half the battle to have a higher occurrence of $k_{max} \pm 2$ than k_{max}. Now, this binomial distribution can be approximated using the normal distribution, which leads to the outcome, that we have a difference between the expected frequency of $0.175 \cdot g(\alpha, p)$ and the required occurrence of $0.2 \cdot g(\alpha, p)$ for $k_{max} \pm 2$ of a few hundred standard deviations, as $g(\alpha, p)$ is quite large. As an example, we have outliers of only 7 standard deviations with a probability of $p \approx 1.3 \cdot 10^{-12}$. Therefore, for any overall success probability $p < 1 - 10^{-100}$, we can ensure, that the described algorithm will lead to a $\hat{k}_{max} \in \{k_{max} - 1, k_{max}, k_{max} + 1\}$.

With a counting argument, we can verify that, for any $f(x) \in \mathbb{N}^+$, $\alpha > 1$ and

$\hat{k}_{\max} \in \{k_{\max} - 1, k_{\max}, k_{\max} + 1\}$, the probability gap is at least $\frac{\alpha - 1}{10\,000}$. For the purpose of this thesis, this counting argument has been verified for any $f(x) \in \{10, \ldots, 10\,000\}$ and plenty of different, small α-values. However, the mathematical proof of this statement is not trivial and is thus not given in this thesis. That is why this upper bound is 'only' a conjecture, but not a mathematically proven theorem.

Based on this assumption, one only has to verify that the measured frequency is within these gap boundaries with a probability of p. The frequency of $\hat{k}_{\max}$ has a theoretical probability of $0.3 > p > 0.2$. With $g(\alpha, p)$ samples, we can be positive that the measured probability of $k_{\max} \pm 1$ is $0.3 > \tilde{p} > 0.05$. The probability, that this is not the case, is almost insignificant for the largely chosen samples size of $g(\alpha, p)$. For a complete mathematical proof, one has to calculate the probability of this case and formulate a success probability upper bound or further increase the sample size. The binomial distribution of resulting a sample in $\hat{k}_{\max}$ or not, which defines the stochastical probability $\Pr[r_{\max} = \hat{k}_{\max}]$, has a confidence interval of

$$\frac{\sqrt{g(\alpha, p) \cdot \tilde{p} \cdot (1 - \tilde{p})}}{g(\alpha, p)} < \frac{\sqrt{0.3 \cdot 0.7}}{\sqrt{g(\alpha, p)}} < \frac{0.46}{\sqrt{g(\alpha, p))}},$$

which has to be smaller than $\frac{\alpha - 1}{10\,000}$.

Therefore, with $\frac{(46\,000)^2}{(\alpha - 1)^2}$ samples, we have the probability of one standard deviation, namely $p \approx 0.6827$ that the algorithm produces a result within the tolerated approximation ratio α. If we want to achieve a (fixed) success probability $p < 1$, we can calculate the number of standard deviations that are required to prove a success probability of p. One can easily verify that this number is below $\frac{1}{1-p}$. Therefore, with $g(\alpha, p) = \frac{(46'000)^2}{(\alpha - 1)^2} \cdot \frac{1}{1-p}$, we have a sample size such that the algorithm produces an output value within the approximation ratio α with a success probability of p.

For any of the $g(\alpha, p)$ samples this algorithm requires less than $3 \cdot \log_2(m)$ bits to store the linear hash values $a_j, b_j \in \mathbb{F}$ and the maximum for $r_{\max, j}$ as analyzed in Theorem 6.10. Therefore, it is reasonable that we have, for the streaming problem $\mathcal{S}_{F_0, \alpha, p}$ with any approximation ratio $1 < \alpha < 2$ and success probability $\frac{1}{2} < p < 1$ a space complexity of

$$\text{space}\Big(\mathcal{S}_{F_0, \alpha, p}\Big) \leq \frac{3 \cdot \log_2(m) \cdot (46\,000)^2}{(\alpha - 1)^2 \cdot (1 - p)} \in \mathcal{O}\Big(\frac{\log(m)}{(\alpha - 1)^2 \cdot (1 - p)}\Big).$$

With this algorithm, we can achieve an arbitrarily small approximation ratio $\alpha > 1$ for $\mathcal{S}_{F_0}$ with an arbitrarily high success probability $p < 1$, and require only a space complexity logarithmic in m for a fixed approximation ratio and success probability. This implies that the streaming problem $\mathcal{S}_{F_0, \alpha, p}$ is *efficiently solvable*. With a more exact analysis, one may prove a space complexity upper bound with a constant factor significantly smaller than $3 \cdot (46\,000)^2$. Furthermore, it is probably possible to decrease the factor $\frac{1}{1-p}$ to a lower order.

For a more mathematical analysis, one can transform the binomial distribution of reaching occurrences within the stated probability gap to an normal distribution, and then, calculate the probability, dependent on $g(\alpha, p)$ samples, that we reach a frequency of $\hat{k}_{\max}$ within the probability gap with a success probability of at least p. With this approach, the stated sample size factor of $\frac{1}{1-p}$ may be optimized.

We will now investigate if the identified lower bounds in the approximative setting are also valid if we allow randomization.

For space complexity lower bounds in a probabilistic setting, we generally try to apply Theorem 4.3. For this, we have to verify the minimality of the test set. The two fooling sets defined in Theorem 6.7 could be used for the probabilistic lower bound. Furthermore, one can similarly verify the minimality of the test sets. Nevertheless, applying Theorem 4.3 will lead to a useless lower bound, because this theorem states a probabilistic lower bound of

$$\text{space}(\mathcal{S}_{\alpha,p}) \geq \log_2(|\mathcal{F}_L|) \cdot \left(1 - \frac{|\mathcal{F}_R|}{\log_2(|\mathcal{F}_L|)} \cdot h(p)\right) - 1. \tag{6.3}$$

If we use the α-fooling sets from Theorem 6.7, we have a size of representatives of

$$|\mathcal{F}_L| = \binom{\min\{n,m\}}{d} > \frac{1}{\alpha - 1} \cdot \log_2(\min\{m,n\} \cdot (\alpha - 1)).$$

However, the test sets contain $n-1$ entries, or $m-1$ entries respectively. Therefore, for a fixed approximation ratio $\alpha > 1$ and large enough n, m, we can approximate the fraction of (6.3) with

$$\frac{|\mathcal{F}_R^{n \leq m}|}{\log_2(|\mathcal{F}_L^{n \leq m}|)} = \frac{n-1}{\binom{n}{d}} > \frac{n-1}{\frac{1}{\alpha-1} \cdot \log_2(n \cdot (\alpha - 1))} > 1, \text{ respectively,}$$

$$\frac{|\mathcal{F}_R^{m < n}|}{\log_2(|\mathcal{F}_L^{m < n}|)} = \frac{m-1}{\binom{m}{d}} > \frac{m-1}{\frac{1}{\alpha-1} \cdot \log_2(m \cdot (\alpha - 1))} > 1.$$

With this fact, (6.3) will result in a negative space complexity lower bound for most n, m, which is true yet useless. With Theorem 4.2, we can at least prove the following lower bound.

Theorem 6.11. *The streaming problem $\mathcal{S}_{F_0,\alpha<2,p}$ has, for any $n, m \in \mathbb{N}^+$, a 1-sided approximation ratio of $\alpha < 2$, and a success probability of $p > \frac{1}{2}$, a space complexity lower bound of*

$$\text{space}(\mathcal{S}_{F_0,\alpha<2,p}) \geq \log_2\left(\frac{\log_2(\min\{m,n\} \cdot (\alpha - 1))}{\alpha - 1}\right) - \log_2\left(\log_2\left(\frac{2p+1}{2p-1}\right)\right) - 1.$$

Proof. To prove this lower bound, we use the α-fooling set from the proof of Theorem 6.7 and Theorem 4.2. We do not have to verify it again as this was already done in the proof of Theorem 6.7. Therefore, we can directly calculate the space complexity lower bound. We start with the first case, where $n \leq m$. We obtain,

$$\text{space}(\mathcal{S}_{F_0,\alpha<2,p}^{n \leq m}) \geq \log_2(\log_2(|\mathcal{F}_L^{n \leq m}|)) \qquad \text{Theorem 4.2}$$

$$- \log_2\left(\log_2\left(\frac{2p+1}{2p-1}\right)\right) - 1$$

$$= \log_2\left(\log_2\left(\binom{n}{d}\right)\right) \qquad \text{fooling set size}$$

$$- \log_2\left(\log_2\left(\frac{2p+1}{2p-1}\right)\right) - 1$$

$$> \log_2\left(\frac{\log_2(n \cdot (\alpha - 1))}{\alpha - 1}\right) \qquad \text{Theorem 6.7}$$

$$- \log_2\left(\log_2\left(\frac{2p+1}{2p-1}\right)\right) - 1.$$

For the second case, where $m < n$, we get,

$$\text{space}(\mathcal{S}_{F_{0,\alpha<2,p}}^{m<n}) \geq \log_2(\log_2(|\mathcal{F}_L^{m<n}|)) \qquad \text{Theorem 4.2}$$

$$- \log_2\left(\log_2\left(\frac{2p+1}{2p-1}\right)\right) - 1$$

$$= \log_2\left(\log_2\left(\binom{m}{d}\right)\right) \qquad \text{fooling set size}$$

$$- \log_2\left(\log_2\left(\frac{2p+1}{2p-1}\right)\right) - 1$$

$$> \log_2\left(\frac{\log_2(m \cdot (\alpha - 1))}{\alpha - 1}\right) \qquad \text{Theorem 6.7}$$

$$- \log_2\left(\log_2\left(\frac{2p+1}{2p-1}\right)\right) - 1$$

Therefore, we have

$$\text{space}(\mathcal{S}_{F_{0,\alpha<2,p}}) \geq \log_2\left(\frac{\log_2(\min\{m,n\} \cdot (\alpha - 1))}{\alpha - 1}\right) - \log_2\left(\log_2\left(\frac{2p+1}{2p-1}\right)\right) - 1.$$

This completes the proof. □

As a consequence, we also have a space complexity lower bound for 2-sided approximations.

Corollary 6.5. *The streaming problem $\mathcal{S}_{F_{0,\alpha<\sqrt{2},p}}$ has, for any $n, m \in \mathbb{N}^+$, a 2-sided approximation ratio of $\alpha < \sqrt{2}$, and a success probability of $p > \frac{1}{2}$, a space complexity lower bound of*

$$\text{space}\left(\mathcal{S}_{F_{0,\alpha<\sqrt{2},p}}\right) \geq \log_2\left(\frac{\log_2(\min\{m,n\} \cdot (\alpha - 1))}{\alpha - 1}\right) - \log_2\left(\log_2\left(\frac{2p+1}{2p-1}\right)\right) - 1.$$

This corollary follows directly from the proven α-fooling set from the proof of Theorem 6.11 and Theorem 4.5. The idea is to approximate the space complexity from above using Corollary 4.1 for any success probability of $p \geq 0.505$.

Corollary 6.6. *The streaming problem $\mathcal{S}_{F_{0,\alpha<\sqrt{2},p}}$ has, for any $n, m \in \mathbb{N}^+$, a 2-sided approximation ratio of $\alpha < \sqrt{2}$, and a success probability of $p \geq 0.505$, a space complexity lower bound of*

$$\text{space}\left(\mathcal{S}_{F_{0,\alpha<\sqrt{2},p}}\right) \geq log_2\left(\frac{\log_2(\min\{m,n\} \cdot (\alpha - 1))}{\alpha - 1}\right) - 4.$$

Next, we want to prove a space complexity lower bound for a 1-sided approximation ratio of $\alpha \geq 2$ in the probabilistic setting.

Theorem 6.12. *The streaming problem* $\mathcal{S}_{F_{0,\alpha \geq 2,p}}$ *has, for any* $n, m \in \mathbb{N}^+$, *a 1-sided approximation ratio of* $\alpha \geq 2$, *and a success probability of* $p > \frac{1}{2}$, *a space complexity lower bound of*

$$\text{space}\Big(\mathcal{S}_{F_{0,\alpha \geq 2,p}}\Big) \geq \log_2(\log_2(\min\{n,m\})) - \log_2\left(\log_2\left(\frac{3}{2} \cdot \alpha\right)\right) - 2.$$

Proof. In the proof sketch of Theorem 6.8, we have described the two fooling sets for $n \leq m$ and $m < n$. Both test sets are obviously minimal, because they contain only one entry. Therefore, we have the following space complexity lower bound:

$$
\begin{aligned}
\text{space}\Big(\mathcal{S}_{F_{0,\alpha \geq 2,p}}\Big) &\geq \log_2(|\mathcal{F}_L|) \cdot \left(1 - \frac{|\mathcal{F}_R|}{\log_2(|\mathcal{F}_L|)} \cdot h(p)\right) - 1 && \text{Theorem 4.3} \\
&\geq \log_2(|\mathcal{F}_L|) \cdot \left(1 - \frac{|\mathcal{F}_R|}{\log_2(|\mathcal{F}_L|)}\right) - 1 && \text{as } h(p) \leq 1 \\
&= \log_2(|\mathcal{F}_L|) - |\mathcal{F}_R| - 1 && \text{basic trans.} \\
&> \log_2(\log_2(\min\{n,m\})) && \text{Theorem 6.8} \\
&\quad - \log_2\left(\log_2\left(\frac{3}{2} \cdot \alpha\right)\right) - 2 && \square
\end{aligned}
$$

This theorem leads to the conclusion that the effect of randomization for a 1-sided approximation ratio of $\alpha > 2$ only decreases the space complexity lower bound by 2 bits.

Corollary 6.7. *The streaming problem* $\mathcal{S}_{F_{0,\alpha \geq \sqrt{2},p}}$ *has, for any* $n, m \in \mathbb{N}^+$, *a 2-sided approximation ratio of* $\alpha \geq \sqrt{2}$, *and a success probability of* $p > \frac{1}{2}$, *a space complexity lower bound of*

$$\text{space}\Big(\mathcal{S}_{F_{0,\alpha \geq \sqrt{2},p}}\Big) \geq \log_2(\log_2(\min\{n,m\})) - \log_2\left(\log_2\left(\frac{3}{2} \cdot \alpha\right)\right) - 2.$$

This follows directly from Theorem 6.12 and Theorem 4.5.

In the approximative, deterministic setting we have seen a further lower bound: Corollary 6.2 states that, for any $n \in \Omega(m)$, the space complexity is at least $\text{space}(\mathcal{S}_{F_{0,\alpha < \sqrt{\frac{3}{2}},1}}) \in \Omega(m)$. This lower bound can be transformed to the probabilistic setting. Of course, we cannot apply Theorem 4.3, because the fooling set from Theorem 6.6, which addresses the 1-sided approximation and introduces the fooling set, has a test set size of $2^{\Omega(m)}$, which is obviously not minimal. However, we can still use Theorem 4.2 to identify a interesting space complexity lower bound.

Theorem 6.13. *The streaming problem* $\mathcal{S}_{F_{0,\alpha < \sqrt{\frac{3}{2}},p}}$ *has, for any* $n \in \Omega(m)$, *a 2-sided approximation ratio of* $\alpha < \sqrt{\frac{3}{2}}$, *and a success probability of* $p \geq 0.505$, *a space complexity lower bound of*

$$\text{space}\Big(\mathcal{S}_{F_{0,\alpha < \sqrt{3/2},p}}\Big) \geq \log_2(m) + \Omega(1).$$

Proof. Theorem 6.6 defines an α-fooling set of size $2^{\Omega(m)}$ for the streaming problem $\mathcal{S}_{F_{0,\alpha < \sqrt{3/2},p}}$. Using Theorem 4.2, we have a space complexity lower bound of,

$$\text{space}\left(\mathcal{S}_{F_{0,\alpha<\sqrt{3/2},p}}\right) \geq \log_2(\log_2(|\mathcal{F}_L|)) \qquad \text{Theorem 4.2}$$

$$- \log_2\left(\log_2\left(\frac{2p+1}{2p-1}\right)\right) - 1$$

$$= \log_2\left(\log_2\left(2^{\Omega(m)}\right)\right) \qquad \text{fooling set size}$$

$$- \log_2\left(\log_2\left(\frac{2p+1}{2p-1}\right)\right) - 1$$

$$= \log_2(\Omega(m)) - \log_2\left(\log_2\left(\frac{2p+1}{2p-1}\right)\right) - 1 \quad \text{basic trans.}$$

$$= \log_2(\Omega(m)) - 4 \qquad p \geq 0.505$$

$$= \log_2(m) + \Omega(1), \qquad \text{basic transf.}$$

which proves the claim. □

This theorem leads to the following conclusion. For a fixed approximation ratio $\alpha < \sqrt{3/2}$ and a fixed success probability $p < 1$, we have a space complexity lower and upper bound of the same complexity order. The upper bound increases with small approximation ratios and high success probabilities. Nevertheless, the gap between the proven upper and lower bound is small.

Summary of the General Number of Distinct Items Problem

With the proven theorems, we can create table 6.1 as an overview of all space complexity upper and lower bounds for the number of distinct items problem. For a probabilistic setting, we assume that the success probability is at least $p > \frac{1}{2}$. Any result on the approximative setting covers the analysis of the 2-sided approximation.

We have seen that with the relaxation of both result accuracy and success probability, the space complexity of $\mathcal{S}_{F_0}$ can be decreased from a linear to a logarithmic space complexity. For all three cases, exact deterministic (Theorem 6.3), exact probabilistic (Theorem 6.4) and approximative deterministic (with an approximation ratio $\alpha < \sqrt{3/2}$, Corollary 6.2), we proved a space complexity lower bound of $\Omega(m)$, which is of the same order as the exact deterministic algorithm described in Theorem 6.2 that requires $m + \lceil \log_2(m) \rceil$ storage bits. The approach by Alon et al. [AMS99], which solves $\mathcal{S}_{F_0,\alpha,p}$ with approximation ratio $\alpha > 2$ and success probability $p = 1 - \frac{1}{\alpha}$, and which has a space complexity of $\mathcal{O}(\log(m))$, could be enhanced (Conjecture 6.1) to an arbitrarily good approximation $\alpha > 1$ and arbitrarily high success probability $p < 1$, with a space complexity of only $\mathcal{O}(\frac{\log(m)}{(\alpha-1)^2 \cdot (1-p)})$. In an approximative and probabilistic environment, we were able to prove a space complexity of at least $\Omega(\log(m))$ for approximation ratios $\alpha < \sqrt{3/2}$ (Theorem 6.13). For larger approximation ratios, the proven space complexity lower bounds have a log log complexity order, as for the most frequent item problem.

In the following, we will analyze the impact of additional information on the streaming problem $\mathcal{S}_{F_0}$.

Approx. ratio	Succ. prob.	Space bound	Condition	Reference
1	1	$\Omega(m)$	$2n = m$	[AMS99]
1	1	$\leq m + \lceil \log_2(m) \rceil$	—	Theorem 6.2
1	1	$\geq \min\{m,n\} - \log_2(\min\{m,n\})$	—	Theorem 6.3
1	1	$\Omega(m)$	$n \in \Omega(m)$	Corollary 6.1
1	p	$\geq (\min\{n,m\} - \log_2(\min\{n,m\}))\cdot$ $(1 - 1.01 \cdot h(p)) - 1$	—	Theorem 6.4
α	1	$\leq \left\lceil \frac{m}{\alpha^2} \right\rceil + \lceil \log_2(m) \rceil$	$\alpha^2 \in \mathbb{N}^+$	Theorem 6.5
α	1	$\in \Omega(m)$	$\alpha < \sqrt{3/2}$ $n \in \Omega(m)$	Corollary 6.2
α	1	$\geq \frac{1}{\alpha-1} \cdot \log_2(\min\{m,n\} \cdot (\alpha-1))$	$\alpha < \sqrt{2}$	Corollary 6.3
α	1	$\geq \log_2(\log_2(\min\{n,m\}))-$ $\log_2\left(\log_2\left(\frac{3}{2} \cdot \alpha\right)\right)$	$\alpha \geq \sqrt{2}$	Corollary 6.4
α	p	$\mathcal{O}(\log(m))$	$\alpha > 2,$ $p = 1 - \frac{2}{\alpha}$	[AMS99]
α	p	$\mathcal{O}\left(\frac{\log(m)}{(\alpha-1)^2 \cdot (1-p)}\right)$	$\alpha < 2$	Conjecture 6.1
α	p	$\geq \log_2\left(\frac{\log_2(\min\{m,n\} \cdot (\alpha-1))}{\alpha-1}\right) - 4$	$\alpha < \sqrt{2},$ $p \geq 0.505$	Corollary 6.6
α	p	$\geq \log_2(\log_2(\min\{n,m\}))-$ $\log_2\left(\log_2\left(\frac{3}{2} \cdot \alpha\right)\right) - 2$	$\alpha \geq \sqrt{2}$	Corollary 6.7
α	p	$\geq \log_2(m) + \Omega(1)$	$n \in \Omega(m)$ $\alpha < \sqrt{3/2}$	Theorem 6.13

Table 6.1. Summary of general number of distinct items problem

6.2 Hypothesis Verification Analysis

In this section, we will analyze the space complexities of verifying hypotheses.

Verification of All Possible Hypotheses

As we have seen in Theorem 6.2, the exact deterministic general streaming problem $\mathcal{S}_{F_{0,1,1}}$ can be solved with a space complexity of at most $m + \lceil \log_2(m) \rceil$ bits. Of course, the verification of any solution hypothesis can be solved with the same amount of storage bits. Furthermore, we are able to reproduce the proof of Theorem 6.3 with a *hypothesis fooling set*, which implies that the hypothesis verification is, similar to the original problem, almost tight for $n \geq m$.

We use the notation of $\mathcal{S}_{F_{0,1,1}}^{HYP}$, $\mathcal{S}_{F_{0,1,p}}^{HYP}$, $\mathcal{S}_{F_{0,\alpha,1}}^{HYP}$, and $\mathcal{S}_{F_{0,\alpha,p}}^{HYP}$ for the four different settings of the verification of any possible solution hypothesis for the number of distinct items problem.

Theorem 6.14. *The streaming problem $\mathcal{S}_{F_{0,1,1}}^{HYP}$ that has any $n, m \in \mathbb{N}^+$, requires a space complexity of at least*

$$\text{space}\left(\mathcal{S}_{F_{0,1,1}}^{HYP}\right) \geq \min\{m, n\} - \log_2(\min\{m, n\}).$$

Proof. For the two cases $n \leq m$ and $m < n$ we define the hypothesis fooling sets $\mathcal{F}^{HYP,n \leq m} = (\mathcal{F}_L^{HYP,n \leq m}, \mathcal{F}_R^{HYP,n \leq m})$ and $\mathcal{F}^{HYP,m<n} = (\mathcal{F}_L^{HYP,m<n}, \mathcal{F}_R^{HYP,m<n})$ that are very similar to the two fooling sets from the proof of Theorem 6.3. Both test sets are the one from Theorem 6.3 of the general streaming problem. The representatives $I_L^i = (y^i, \tilde{x}^i) \in \mathcal{F}_L^{HYP,n \leq m}$, and $I_L^{i'} = (y^{i'}, \tilde{x}^{i'}) \in \mathcal{F}_L^{HYP,m<n}$, have as input stream parts $\tilde{x}^i$, and $\tilde{x}^{i'}$, respectively, exactly the representatives of Theorem 6.3. The hypotheses y^i, and $y^{i'}$, respectively, are just the cut-value $l_{n \leq m} = \frac{n}{2} =: y^i$, and $y^{i'} := l_{m<n} = \frac{m}{2}$, respectively. In the following, we will justify that we have indeed hypothesis fooling sets and calculate the space complexity lower bound.

As stated in Definition 4.4, we have a hypothesis fooling set if

$$\forall I_L^i = (y^i, \tilde{x}^i), I_L^j = (y^j, \tilde{x}^j) \in \mathcal{F}_L^{HYP} \text{ with } I_L^i \neq I_L^j\colon \; \exists I_R^v \in \mathcal{F}_R^{HYP} \text{ such that}$$
$$\left(y^i = f(\tilde{x}^i, I_R^v)\right) \;\not\Longleftrightarrow\; \left(y^j = f(\tilde{x}^j, I_R^v)\right).$$

For any two representatives $I_L^i = (y^i, \tilde{x}^i), I_L^j = (y^j, \tilde{x}^j) \in \mathcal{F}_L^{HYP,n \leq m}$, or $I_L^{i'} = (y^{i'}, \tilde{x}^{i'}), I_L^{j'} = (y^{j'}, \tilde{x}^{j'}) \in \mathcal{F}_L^{HYP,m<n}$, respectively, there is at least one item $v \in \{1, \ldots, n-1\}$, or $v' \in \{1, \ldots, m-1\}$, respectively, such that v, or v' respectively, is only present in one of the two representatives. We have proven the existence of such an item in previous theorems, as e.g. Theorem 6.3. W.l.o.g, we assume that $v \in \tilde{x}^i$, or $v' \in \tilde{x}^{i'}$. With the test entry $I_R^v = \{v, \ldots, v\}$, or $I_R^{v'} = \{v', \ldots, v'\}$ respectively, we have,

$$\left(y^i = f(\tilde{x}^i, I_R^v)\right) \;\Longleftrightarrow\; \left(\frac{n}{2} = \frac{n}{2}\right) \;\Longleftrightarrow\; \text{true}$$

$$\not\Longleftrightarrow \text{false} \;\Longleftrightarrow\; \left(\frac{n}{2} = \frac{n}{2} + 1\right) \;\Longleftrightarrow\; \left(y^j = f(\tilde{x}^j, I_R^v)\right), \text{ or}$$

$$\left(y^{i'} = f(\tilde{x}^{i'}, I_R^{v'})\right) \iff \left(\frac{m}{2} = \frac{m}{2}\right) \iff \text{true}$$

$$\iff \text{false} \iff \left(\frac{m}{2} = \frac{m}{2} + 1\right) \iff \left(y^{j'} = f(\tilde{x}^{j'}, I_R^{v'})\right), \text{respectively.}$$

Therefore, we have proven that we have a hypothesis fooling set. As the fooling set sizes are the same as in the proof of Theorem 6.3, we have the same general space complexity lower bound. $\qquad\square$

With this theorem, we have the same upper and lower bound for the exact, deterministic setting for both the general streaming problem and the hypothesis verification. Furthermore, we can prove the same lower bound for the exact probabilistic setting as well.

Theorem 6.15. *The streaming problem $\mathcal{S}_{F_{0,1,p}}^{HYP}$ that has any $n, m \in \mathbb{N}^+$ and a success probability $p > \frac{1}{2}$ requires a space complexity of at least*

$$\text{space}\left(\mathcal{S}_{F_{0,1,p}}^{HYP}\right) \geq (\min\{n, m\} - \log_2(\min\{n, m\})) \cdot (1 - 1.01 \cdot h(p)) - 1$$

with $h(p) = -p \cdot \log_2(p) - (1 - p) \cdot \log_2(1 - p)$.

Proof. For this proof, we can use the hypothesis fooling sets from Theorem 6.14 and apply Theorem 4.3. To use Theorem 4.3, we have to verify the minimality of the test sets. As stated after Definition 4.4, we can verify the minimality by checking (4.12) to (4.19), namely,

$\forall I_R^v \in \mathcal{F}_R,$	For all elements of the test set,
$\exists I_L^i = (y^i, \tilde{x}^i), I_L^j = (y^j, \tilde{x}^j)$	there are two different
$\in \mathcal{F}_L, I_L^i \neq I_L^j$	representatives,
s.t. $\left(\left(y^i = f(\tilde{x}^i, I_R^v)\right) \iff\right.$	such that the cache states
$\left(y^j = f(\tilde{x}^j, I_R^v)\right)$	have to be different.
and $\forall I_R^{v'} \in (\mathcal{F}_R \setminus I_R^v):$	And for all other tests,
$\left(y^i = f(\tilde{x}^i, I_R^{v'})\right) \iff$	they are not required
$\left.\left(y^j = f(\tilde{x}^j, I_R^{v'})\right)\right).$	to be different.

We will verify the minimality of the two test sets from the hypothesis fooling sets of Theorem 6.14 for both cases individually.

If $n \leq m$, then, for every item $v \in \{1, \ldots, n-1\}$, or the corresponding test entry $I_R^v = \{v, \ldots, v\} \in \mathcal{F}_R^{HYP, n \leq m}$, respectively, we choose two representatives $I_L^i = (y^i, \tilde{x}^i), I_L^j = (y^j, \tilde{x}^j) \in \mathcal{F}_L^{HYP, n \leq m}$ that have in their input stream parts $\tilde{x}^i$ and $\tilde{x}^j$ exactly $\frac{n}{2} - 1$ items in common from the item set $\{1, \ldots, n\} \setminus \{v, n\}$. The input stream part $\tilde{x}^i$ contains additionally the item v, and $\tilde{x}^j$ contains the item n. Then, we have the inequality from (4.15) and (4.16), i.e.,

$$\left(y^i = f(\tilde{x}^i, I_R^v)\right) \iff \left(\frac{n}{2} = \frac{n}{2}\right) \iff \text{true}$$

$$\iff \text{false} \iff \left(\frac{n}{2} = \frac{n}{2} + 1\right) \iff \left(y^j = f(\tilde{x}^j, I_R^v)\right).$$

Furthermore, for all other $v' \in \{1, \dots, n\} \setminus \{v, n\}$, or their test entry $I_R^{v'} = \{v', \dots, v'\} \in \mathcal{F}_R^{HYP, n \leq m}$, respectively, we have either,

$$\left(y^i = f(\tilde{x}^i, I_R^{v'})\right) \iff \left(\frac{n}{2} = \frac{n}{2}\right) \iff \text{true}$$

$$\iff \left(\frac{n}{2} = \frac{n}{2}\right) \iff \left(y^j = f(\tilde{x}^j, I_R^{v'})\right),$$

if v' is present in both representatives, or,

$$\left(y^i = f(\tilde{x}^i, I_R^{v'})\right) \iff \left(\frac{n}{2} = \frac{n}{2} + 1\right) \iff \text{false}$$

$$\iff \left(\frac{n}{2} = \frac{n}{2} + 1\right) \iff \left(y^j = f(\tilde{x}^j, I_R^{v'})\right),$$

if v' is not present in either representative. Therefore, $\mathcal{F}^{HYP, n \leq m}$ has a minimal test set.

If $m < n$, we can easily verify the minimality of the test set $\mathcal{F}_R^{HYP, m < n}$ from the hypothesis fooling set $\mathcal{F}^{HYP, m < n}$ by exactly the same argument as above by just replacing the variable n with m.

As both test sets are minimal, we can apply Theorem 4.3 on the hypothesis fooling sets. Since these sets have exactly the same sizes as the fooling sets from Theorem 6.14, we have consequentially the same complexity lower bound.   □

Therefore, also for the exact probabilistic setting, we have the same space complexity lower bound as in the classical number of distinct items problems. For the probabilistic deterministic environment, we can solve hypothesis verifications with $\mathcal{O}(\frac{m}{\alpha^2} + \log(m))$ storage bits for any approximation ratio $\alpha > 1$, as described in Theorem 6.5. Furthermore, we can once again prove the same space complexity lower bounds. Here, we will only introduce a proof sketch, as the argumentation is very similar to above proofs.

Theorem 6.16. *The streaming problem $\mathcal{S}_{F_{0,\alpha,1}}^{HYP}$, that has any $n, m \in \mathbb{N}^+$ and some different, 2-sided approximation ratios α, requires a space complexity of at least,*

$$\text{space}\left(\mathcal{S}_{F_{0,\alpha < \sqrt{3/2},1}}^{HYP}\right) \in \Omega(m) \text{ for } n \in \Omega(m) \qquad \text{if } \alpha < \sqrt{\frac{3}{2}} \text{ and}$$
$$n \in \Omega(m),$$
$$\text{space}\left(\mathcal{S}_{F_{0,\alpha < \sqrt{2},1}}^{HYP}\right) \geq \frac{1}{\alpha - 1} \cdot \log_2(\min\{m, n\} \cdot (\alpha - 1)) \qquad \text{if } \alpha < \sqrt{2}, \text{ and}$$
$$\text{space}\left(\mathcal{S}_{F_{0,\alpha \geq \sqrt{2},1}}^{HYP}\right) \geq \log_2(\log_2(\min\{n, m\})) \qquad \text{if } \alpha \geq \sqrt{2}.$$
$$- \log_2\left(\log_2\left(\frac{3}{2} \cdot \alpha\right)\right)$$

Proof. We can prove these three space complexity lower bounds with hypothesis α-fooling sets, that are very similar to the α-fooling sets from the general streaming problem, i.e., as in the proofs of Theorem 6.6 for $\alpha < \sqrt{\frac{3}{2}}$, Theorem 6.7 for $\alpha < \sqrt{2}$, and Theorem 6.8 for $\alpha \geq \sqrt{2}$. We choose as hypothesis α-fooling sets the same test sets, and as input stream parts of the representatives from the hypothesis α-fooling sets simply the representatives of the corresponding original α-fooling sets. As hypothesis, we choose $y^i := \frac{m}{4}$ for $\alpha < \sqrt{\frac{3}{2}}$. For the second lower bound, i.e., for $\alpha < \sqrt{2}$, we choose $y^i := d = \left\lfloor \frac{1}{\alpha^2 - 1} \right\rfloor$. And, finally, we choose for the third lower bound for the approximation ratio $\alpha \geq \sqrt{2}$ as hypothesis $y^i := d(i)$, with the distinctness function that is defined in Theorem 6.8.

Using exactly the same approach as in the proof of Theorem 6.15, we can simply verify the hypothesis α-fooling sets. As they have the same set sizes as the original α-fooling sets from the general number of distinct items problem, we have the same lower bounds as Theorem 6.6, Theorem 6.7, and Theorem 6.8, or their corresponding corollaries Corollary 6.2, Corollary 6.3, and Corollary 6.4 for the 2-sided approximations. $\qquad\square$

Furthermore, we can also verify the same space complexity lower bounds for the approximative, probabilistic setting as for the general streaming problem.

Theorem 6.17. *The streaming problem* $\mathcal{S}_{F_{0,\alpha,p}}^{HYP}$, *that has any* $n, m \in \mathbb{N}^+$, *a success probability* $p \geq 0.505$, *and some different, 2-sided approximation ratios* α, *requires a space complexity of at least,*

$$\mathrm{space}\left(\mathcal{S}_{F_{0,\alpha<\sqrt{3/2},p}}^{HYP}\right) \geq \log_2(m) + \Omega(1) \qquad\qquad \text{if } \alpha < \sqrt{\frac{3}{2}} \text{ and}$$
$$n \in \Omega(m),$$

$$\mathrm{space}\left(\mathcal{S}_{F_{0,\alpha<\sqrt{2},p}}^{HYP}\right) \geq \log_2\left(\frac{\log_2(\min\{m,n\} \cdot (\alpha - 1))}{\alpha - 1}\right) - 4 \quad \text{if } \alpha < \sqrt{2}, \text{ and}$$

$$\mathrm{space}\left(\mathcal{S}_{F_{0,\alpha\geq\sqrt{2},p}}^{HYP}\right) \geq \log_2(\log_2(\min\{n,m\})) \qquad\qquad \text{if } \alpha \geq \sqrt{2}.$$
$$- \log_2\left(\log_2\left(\frac{3}{2} \cdot \alpha\right)\right) - 2$$

Proof. For this theorem, we can use the sketched hypothesis α-fooling sets from the proof of Theorem 6.16. For the first case, if $\alpha < \sqrt{\frac{3}{2}}$ and $n \in \Omega(m)$, we can directly use the hypothesis α-fooling set from Theorem 6.16 and apply Theorem 4.2. Then, we have the same space complexity lower bound as in the original Theorem 6.13, which is at least $\log_2(m) + \Omega(1)$.

For the second case, if $\alpha < \sqrt{2}$, we can once again use the sketched hypothesis α-fooling set from Theorem 6.16. When we apply Theorem 4.2, which does not require the minimality of the test set, and obtain the same lower bound on the space complexity as for the general streaming problem described in Corollary 6.6.

If $\alpha \geq \sqrt{2}$, we can directly apply Theorem 4.3 on the sketched hypothesis α-fooling set from Theorem 6.16. As the test set contains only one entry, it is obviously minimal. Therefore, we get a space complexity lower bound of $\log_2(\log_2(\min\{n,m\})) - \log_2\left(\log_2\left(\frac{3}{2} \cdot \alpha\right)\right) - 2$, as calculated in the proof of Theorem 6.12. $\qquad\square$

With this theorem we have proven the equivalent space complexity lower bounds for both the general streaming problem and hypothesis verification in the approximative and probabilistic setting. This analysis shows that we can repeat all introduced space complexity lower bound proofs from the general streaming problem in any setting for hypothesis verification. Still, we have a gap between these lower bounds and the upper bounds for the general streaming problem. Next, we will study, whether we are able to profit from this gap and find an algorithm, that verifies a hypothesis with a lower space complexity.

Conjecture 6.2. $\mathcal{S}_{F_0}^{HYP}$ *has the same space complexity upper bound order as* $\mathcal{S}_{F_0}$.

In the exact (both deterministic and probabilistic) setting, as well as in the approximative and deterministic setting, we have proven in Theorem 6.14, Theorem 6.15, and Theorem 6.16, that the space complexity lower bounds are exactly the same as for the general streaming problem. For the exact and the approximative, deterministic setting with a 2-sided approximation ratio of $\alpha < \sqrt{3/2}$, we have a lower and an upper bound of the same order. This implies that even if it were possible to profit from the hypothesis, it will have the same complexity order as the general streaming problem.

For the approximative, probabilistic setting, the space complexity lower bounds for both the general streaming problem and hypothesis verification are exactly the same, but nevertheless not very significant. For $\mathcal{S}_{F_0}$ we stated an algorithm in Conjecture 6.1 that solves the streaming problem with any approximation ratio $\alpha > 1$ and success probability $p < 1$ with a space complexity in $\mathcal{O}\left(\frac{\log(m)}{(\alpha-1)^2 \cdot (1-p)}\right)$. For a fixed approximation ratio $\alpha < \sqrt{3/2}$ and a fixed success probability, we have a tight complexity order for both the general streaming problem and hypothesis verification. The factor of $\mathcal{O}\left(\frac{1}{(\alpha-1)^2 \cdot (1-p)}\right)$, that is dependent on the approximation ratio and the success probability, is required to ensure that, e.g., the four possible output values $\frac{f(x)}{\alpha} \pm 1$ and $f(x) \cdot \alpha \pm 1$ are distinguished, because two are within the tolerated approximation ratio, but not the other two. If we want to verify solution hypotheses, we also have to distinguish these cases. Therefore, we may assume that the required factor for $\mathcal{S}_{F_0}$ to solve it with an arbitrarily small approximation ratio $\alpha > 1$ and an arbitrarily high success probability $p < 1$, is also required for $\mathcal{S}_{F_0}^{HYP}$. If we could improve this accuracy factor of $\mathcal{O}\left(\frac{1}{(\alpha-1)^2 \cdot (1-p)}\right)$ for hypothesis verification, it is very likely that it could be applied to the general streaming problem as well.

This conjecture states that it is likely that we are not able to profit from the additional information if we want to verify solution hypotheses.

Justification of One Correct Hypothesis

We can formulate another type of hypothesis verification. In this case, we do not have to verify any possible hypothesis, but just need to justify for every input stream only one correct hypothesis. We can justify the correctness of a certain hypothesis by indicating some argument or proof, why this hypothesis is correct. If this hypothesis would be wrong, the algorithm does not have to indicate any result or can just output a random one. Therefore, this second setting is a non-determinism, where we only have a usable result for a certain correct hypothesis.

In the deterministic setting, a bit map could be used as a solid argument or proof to justify the correctness of a hypothesis, but this would requires m bits.

For the probabilistic setting, we can justify the correctness of the hypothesis by showing that the probability distribution of r_{max} from the algorithm from Theorem 6.10 corresponds to the stated hypothesis. For the exact, probabilistic setting, we can significantly decrease the space complexity. If we have a correct hypothesis of the number of distinct items, we can determine the exact probability distribution of r_{max}. With $\mathcal{O}\left(\frac{1}{1-p}\right)$ computations of the algorithm from Theorem 6.10, we can justify the correctness of the probability distribution with a probability of p, as stated in Conjecture 6.1. Therefore, with a space complexity of $\mathcal{O}\left(\frac{\log(m)}{1-p}\right)$, compared to the proven space complexity lower bound of $\Omega(\min(m, n))$ for the verification of any hypothesis (Theorem 6.15) and the general streaming problem (Theorem 6.4). Similarly, we can justify a correct hypothesis for the approximative and probabilistic setting for small approximation ratios $\alpha > 1$.

6.3 Analysis Conclusion

In the analysis of the general number of distinct items problem, we have seen that we require a linear storage size for an exact result for both a deterministic and a probabilistic setting. While this is also the case for the verification of any possible hypothesis, we can significantly improve the upper bound in the exact, probabilistic setting if we only want to justify a correct hypothesis. This insight leads to the conclusion that in the special scenario of justification of one correct hypothesis in an exact, probabilistic setting, the additional information helps to decrease the space complexity to a complexity order, such that the problem is *efficiently solvable*, because the space complexity is poly-logarithmic in both n and m. In the approximative and deterministic setting, we have a large gap between the upper and the lower bound, but so far it seems to be impractical to close this gap, i.e., to find better upper or lower bounds for either the general streaming problem or the verification of any hypothesis. For the approximative, probabilistic setting, we expanded the algorithm from Alon et al. to a setting where we may have an arbitrarily small approximation ratio $\alpha > 1$ and an arbitrarily high success probability $p < 1$.

Chapter 7

Conclusion

In the final chapter, we first summarize the entire thesis and most important results. Afterwards, we state the resulting conclusion and gained insights. Finally, we list some possibilities how one may improve the stated space complexity bounds and how one may apply the introduced concepts on other streaming problems.

7.1 Summary

In the summary of this thesis, we focus on three different aspects: The introduced concept to prove lower bounds on space complexity and the proven results of the two streaming problems, the *most frequent item problem* and the *number of distinct items problem*.

Lower Bounds on Space Complexity: In Chapter 4, we have introduced two types of *fooling sets* (Definition 4.1 by Ablayev [Abl96] and Definition 4.2 by Hromkovič [Hro97]) based on the communication complexity theory, that prove a lower bound on space complexity for streaming problems in an exact, deterministic setting, as stated in Theorem 4.1. With Theorem 4.2 and Theorem 4.3 by Ablayev [Abl96], we have two concepts to prove a lower bound in a probabilistic setting.

Furthermore, this already known concept has been transmitted to an approximative setting by introducing an α-*fooling set* as defined in Definition 4.3. An α-fooling set ensures, that any two representatives of this α-fooling set lead to different cache states because, for at least one test entry, the function value differ by a multiplicative factor of more than the approximation ratio α. With such an α-fooling set, we can prove a space complexity lower bound on a 1-*sided approximation ratio* of α (Theorem 4.4), or a 2-*sided approximation ratio* of $\sqrt{\alpha}$ (Theorem 4.5), respectively.

Additionally, in Section 4.3, we have introduced a technique to prove space complexity lower bounds for hypothesis verifications. If we want to verify any hypothesis for a given streaming problem, we have to find a *hypothesis fooling set* (Definition 4.4) for the exact, or a *hypothesis α-fooling set* (Definition 4.5) for the approximative setting. Similarly to the general streaming problem, we can prove lower bounds on the space complexity in any exact or approximative, deterministic or probabilistic setting with such a hypothesis fooling set or hypothesis α-fooling set.

With the proven theorems in Chapter 5 and Chapter 6, we have illustrated the usage of these concepts to prove lower bounds on space complexity.

Most Frequent Item Problem: In the analysis of the *most frequent item problem*, we have seen that it is *not efficiently solvable*. We have seen a space complexity upper bound of $\mathcal{O}(m \cdot \log(\frac{n}{m}))$ (Theorem 5.5 and Theorem 5.6) for the exact deterministic setting, which can be further improved by a multiplicative factor of $\frac{p}{\alpha^2}$ for a probabilistic or approximative setting with any success probability $p < 1$ and a 2-sided approximation ratio $\alpha > 1$, respectively. For any problem setting, we proved a linear space complexity lower bound of $\Omega(m)$ (Theorem 5.7, Theorem 5.9, Corollary 5.3, and Corollary 5.6) if the success probability is at least $p > \frac{1}{2}$ and we have a 2-sided approximation ratio of at most $\alpha < \sqrt{2}$. For approximation ratios of $\alpha \geq \sqrt{2}$, we only have weak lower bounds, which are of the complexity order $\Omega(\log(\log(m)) - \log(\log(\alpha)))$ (Corollary 5.5 and Corollary 5.8). For the exact, deterministic or probabilistic setting, we are able to prove a lower bound that is of the same complexity order as the upper bound, namely $\Omega(m \cdot \log(\frac{n}{m}))$ (Theorem 5.8 and Theorem 5.10)

For the hypothesis verification, we can reprove most linear lower bounds (Corollary 5.9 and Corollary 5.11), but not the one that is of the same order as the upper bound (Conjecture 5.1 and Corollary 5.12). Nevertheless, we were not able to design an algorithm that may profit from this gap between $\Omega(m)$ and $\mathcal{O}(m \cdot \log(\frac{n}{m}))$ for the hypothesis verification.

Number of Distinct Items Problem: The *number of distinct items problem* is *efficiently solvable* in an approximative and randomized setting. Alon et al. [AMS99] state an upper bound of $\mathcal{O}(\log(m))$ for the conditional setting with an approximation ratio $\alpha > 2$ and a success probability of $p = 1 - \frac{2}{\alpha}$. We could enhance this limitation such that, for any arbitrarily small approximation ratio $\alpha > 1$ and arbitrarily good success probability $p < 1$, we can efficiently solve the number of distinct items problems with a storage size of $\mathcal{O}\left(\frac{\log(m)}{(\alpha-1)^2 \cdot (1-p)}\right)$ (Conjecture 6.1). For approximation ratios $\alpha < \sqrt{3/2}$, we can prove a lower bound of complexity order $\Omega(\log(m))$ (Corollary 6.2, Corollary 6.3, and Theorem 6.13), that is of the same order as the upper bound for some fixed approximation ratio and success probability.

For the other three settings, namely, the exact deterministic, exact probabilistic, and approximative deterministic setting, we can prove a linear lower bound, namely $\Omega(m)$ ([AMS99], Theorem 6.3, Corollary 6.1, Theorem 6.4, and Corollary 6.2). This lower bound order is only valid for approximation ratios $\alpha < \sqrt{3/2}$. On the other hand, the upper bound is $\mathcal{O}\left(\frac{m}{\alpha^2}\right)$ (Theorem 6.2 and Theorem 6.5), which is almost tight to the lower bound for the exact deterministic setting.

For the hypothesis verification, we reproved the same lower bounds as for the general streaming problem (Theorem 6.14, Theorem 6.15, Theorem 6.16, and Theorem 6.17). Furthermore, in Conjecture 6.2, we argued, why we are not able to find an improved space complexity lower bound for the verification of any hypothesis compared to the general streaming problem.

7.2   Conclusion

Based on this summary, we can conclude that the introduced techniques to prove lower bounds on space complexity are very useful. In most cases, we could prove lower bounds that are of the same order as the identified upper bound, and, e.g., for the exact deterministic number of distinct items problem, we have an almost tight bound. This is not only the case for the different settings of the general streaming problems, but also for the hypothesis verification. Only for larger approximation ratios, namely $\alpha \geq \sqrt{2}$, the technique of fooling sets based on communication complexity reveals some weaknesses. The communication complexity uses as a basis a model of two computers that have unbounded storage and computation resources, but a limited communication. As we have stated in Theorem 5.15 and Theorem 6.9, it is impossible to prove a linear lower bound for the two analyzed streaming problems for approximation ratios of $\alpha \geq \sqrt{2}$ using the technique of communication complexity with the two computer model.

For both streaming problems and approximation ratio of $\alpha < \sqrt{2}$, the upper and lower bounds are close to each other, and, therefore, we can conclude that the described streaming algorithms of the upper bounds are almost optimal.

7.3   Future Work

In this last section, we discuss a few points how one may extend or improve the results and proofs. We structure this with three elements: How one may improve the stated proofs, which further proofs might be possible and a short outlook, for which further streaming problems the introduced concepts could be applied.

Improvement of Stated Theorems: In many space complexity lower bound proofs, we used a fooling set that has a fooling set size of $\binom{k}{k/2}$, as e.g., in Theorem 5.7, Theorem 5.16, or Theorem 6.14. This fooling set size leads to a space complexity of $\log_2\left(\binom{k}{k/2}\right) > k - \log_2(k)$. In some cases, this second order term can be eliminated with a more clever definition of the fooling set. For example, for Theorem 6.3, we can define the fooling set with a cut at $l := n - 1$ and the representatives I_L^i contain any combination of distinct items with a distinctness of $f(I_L^i) \in \{1, \ldots, m - 1\}$. Then, we have not only $\binom{m}{m/2}$ elements in the set of representatives, but

$$|\mathcal{F}_L| = \sum_{i=1}^{m-1} \binom{m}{i} = 2^m - 2.$$

With such a fooling set, we have a space complexity lower bound of $m - 1$, instead of $m - \log_2(m)$. This transformation can be made for some deterministic lower bounds. But it is possible that, for such a fooling set, we might fail to verify the minimality of the test set, which is required for applying Theorem 4.3 on a probabilistic lower bound.

Some streaming algorithms are only space-, but not time-efficient. E.g., the introduced algorithms for the exact deterministic most frequent item problem in Theorem 5.5 or Theorem 5.6 that space-efficiently store the histogram, would require large update times, as the individual frequency counts are not indexed, but only listed one after the other. The update algorithm, that increases the frequency count x_i, would have to parse the entire data-list, until the x_i-th frequency count is found, namely, until $x_i - 1$ delimiters have been counted. In a concrete implementation of this algorithm, one may be interested in using a larger storage size, that enables a faster update procedure.

Further Proofs: For the number of distinct items problem, we could only formulate a conjecture for the approximative, probabilistic setting (Conjecture 6.1), but not mathematically prove the lower bound of the probability gap, which was illustrated in Figure 6.2. If one can show the correctness of this intermediate step and use some better approximations, one has proven the statement of Conjecture 6.1.

For approximation ratios $\alpha \geq \sqrt{2}$, we were only able to design lower bound proofs with a $\Omega(\log(\log(k))$ complexity order for both streaming problems. As we have stated in Theorem 5.15 and Theorem 6.9, it is impossible to prove a lower bound above $\Omega(\log(k))$ with the two-computer model of the communication complexity. Nevertheless, one may probably design a fooling set that leads to an increased lower bound, which is closer to this limit.

Further Streaming Problem: As future work, one may apply these proof concepts to other streaming problems. At the development of this thesis, the two streaming problems *Equality* and *Median* were shortly touched and the main results are summarized in the following for possible future work.

Streaming Equality Problems: The *streaming binary decision problem* (Definition 3.4) *equality* has input streams $x = (x_1, \ldots, x_n)$ that represent two bit-strings $b_1 = (x_1, \ldots, x_k)$ and $b_2 = (x_{k+1}, \ldots, x_n)$ with $k = \frac{n}{2}$, that have to be analyzed, whether they are equal or not, namely,

$$b_1 = b_2 \iff \forall i \in \{1, \ldots, k\} \colon x_i = x_{k+i}.$$

This streaming equality problem can be solved deterministically with $k = \frac{n}{2}$ storage bits that store b_1. We can prove a space complexity lower bound of $k = \frac{n}{2}$ with a *matrix fooling set* (Definition 4.2) that contains all possible bit-strings $b_i = (x_1, \ldots, x_k)$ as rows and columns. This matrix fooling set has a rank of 2^k, as it is the identity matrix. Therefore, we have a space complexity lower bound of $\log_2(2^k) = k = \frac{n}{2}$, which is tight to the upper bound.

With Corollary 4.1 based on Theorem 4.2, we have a space complexity lower bound of $\log_2(\frac{n}{2}) - 4 = \log_2(n) - 5$ for the probabilistic equality problem with a success probability of $p \geq 0.505$. This is almost tight to the 1-sided Monte Carlo algorithm (Definition 3.7) for the equality problem, that requires only $\mathcal{O}(\log(n))$ storage bits, as e.g., explained in detail by Hromkovič [Hro97], in Example 2.5.5.6.

The hypothesis verification will lead to exactly the same lower bounds, when one chooses the same hypothesis for the entire fooling set. Therefore, as the upper and lower bound from the general equality problem are almost tight, it is very likely, that the equality problem does not profit from a hypothesis.

Streaming Median Problems: The *streaming median problem* is a *streaming counting problem* (Definition 3.2) that has to identify the median of the input values. If the input stream length is odd, the median is just the input value in the middle, if one would sort the input stream. Otherwise, if the input stream length is even, the median is defined as the average between the two values in the middle of the sorted input values.

Obviously, this streaming problem can easily be solved with a histogram, as for the *most frequent item problem*, which requires a space complexity of $\mathcal{O}(m \cdot \log(\frac{n}{m}))$. If we have the condition $n \in \Theta(m)$, we can prove a space complexity lower bound of $\Omega(n)$ for the exact, deterministic and probabilistic setting. For the ease of presentation, we assume that n is odd and $n \leq m$. This lower bound complexity is possible with a fooling set that has a cut at $l := \frac{n+1}{2}$. Each representative contains $l = \frac{n+1}{2}$ distinct items from the set $\{2, \ldots, n-1\} \subset \{1, \ldots, m\}$. The test set contains $\frac{n+1}{2}$ entries with different frequencies of the item 1 and m, namely,

$$\mathcal{F}_R := \{\{1, 1, \ldots, 1, 1\}, \{1, 1, \ldots, 1, m\}, \ldots, \{1, m, \ldots, m, m\}, \{m, m, \ldots, m, m\}\}.$$

For any two representatives, if we sort the items of the representatives, we have at least one input value index, such that the two input values are differing. Then, we can cleverly choose a test entry, or its frequencies of 1 and m, such that this differing item is the median. This argument verifies that we have a fooling set. The size of the fooling set is

$$|\mathcal{F}_L| = \binom{n-2}{\frac{n+1}{2}} \in \Omega(2^n).$$

Therefore, for the given condition, we have a space complexity lower bound of $\Omega(n)$. As future work, one can extend this fooling set concept to a more general condition and mathematically prove that it satisfies the properties of a fooling set.

Interestingly, for the median problem, the hypothesis verification is very space-efficient. For any hypothesis, we can just count the number of input values above and below the hypothesis to justify the correctness of a hypothesis. Therefore, the hypothesis verification requires only a space complexity of $\mathcal{O}(\log(n))$, which is from a lower complexity order than the proven lower bound from the general streaming problem.

In this thesis, we have seen that, for several problems and settings, one cannot significantly decrease the space complexity by just verifying a hypothesis instead of computing the solution to a general streaming problem. Nevertheless, the median problem and further streaming problems demonstrate the possible advantage of additional information.

Bibliography

[Abl96]   Farid M. Ablayev. Lower bounds for one-way probabilistic communication complexity and their application to space complexity. *Theor. Comput. Sci.*, 157(2):139–159, 1996.

[Agg07]   Charu C. Aggarwal. An introduction to data streams. In *Data Streams - Models and Algorithms*, pages 1–8. 2007.

[AJKS02]   Miklós Ajtai, T. S. Jayram, Ravi Kumar, and D. Sivakumar. Approximate counting of inversions in a data stream. In *Proceedings on 34th Annual ACM Symposium on Theory of Computing, May 19-21, 2002, Montréal, Québec, Canada*, pages 370–379, 2002.

[AMS99]   Noga Alon, Yossi Matias, and Mario Szegedy. The space complexity of approximating the frequency moments. *J. Comput. Syst. Sci.*, 58(1):137–147, 1999.

[BBD+02]   Brian Babcock, Shivnath Babu, Mayur Datar, Rajeev Motwani, and Jennifer Widom. Models and issues in data stream systems. In *Proceedings of the Twenty-first ACM SIGACT-SIGMOD-SIGART Symposium on Principles of Database Systems, June 3-5, Madison, Wisconsin, USA*, pages 1–16, 2002.

[BFS86]   László Babai, Peter Frankl, and Janos Simon. Complexity classes in communication complexity theory (preliminary version). In *27th Annual Symposium on Foundations of Computer Science, Toronto, Canada, 27-29 October 1986*, pages 337–347, 1986.

[CH09]   Graham Cormode and Marios Hadjieleftheriou. Finding the frequent items in streams of data. *Commun. ACM*, 52(10):97–105, 2009.

[Deu04]   Peter Deuflhard. *Newton methods for nonlinear problems : affine invariance and adaptive algorithms*. Springer series in computational mathematics. Springer, Berlin, Heidelberg, New York, 2004. Autre tirage : 2006.

[Dob10]   Vladimir A. Dobrushkin. *Methods in Algorithmic Analysis*. Chapman & Hall/CRC Computer and Information Science Series, 2010.

[HR88]   Bernd Halstenberg and Rüdiger Reischuk. On different modes of communication (extended abstract). In *Proceedings of the 20th Annual ACM*

Symposium on Theory of Computing, May 2-4, 1988, Chicago, Illinois, USA, pages 162–172, 1988.

[Hro97]   Juraj Hromkovic. *Communication Complexity and Parallel Computing.* Texts in Theoretical Computer Science. An EATCS Series. Springer, 1997.

[IW05]   Piotr Indyk and David P. Woodruff. Optimal approximations of the frequency moments of data streams. In *Proceedings of the 37th Annual ACM Symposium on Theory of Computing, Baltimore, MD, USA, May 22-24, 2005*, pages 202–208, 2005.

[Kel03]   C. T. Kelley. *Solving Nonlinear Equations with Newton's Method.* Fundamentals of Algorithms / Nicholas J. Higham. Philadelphia, 2003.

[KNR01]   Ilan Kremer, Noam Nisan, and Dana Ron. Errata for: On randomized one-round communication complexity. *Computational Complexity*, 10(4):314–315, 2001.

[Kom15]   Dennis Komm. *Eine Einführung in Online-Algorithmen.* Skript zur Vorlesung APPROXIMATIONS- und ONLINE-ALGORITHMEN, ETH Zürich, 2015.

[KS92]   Bala Kalyanasundaram and Georg Schnitger. The probabilistic communication complexity of set intersection. *SIAM J. Discrete Math.*, 5(4):545–557, 1992.

[KSP03]   Richard M. Karp, Scott Shenker, and Christos H. Papadimitriou. A simple algorithm for finding frequent elements in streams and bags. *ACM Trans. Database Syst.*, 28:51–55, 2003.

[MM12]   Gurmeet Singh Manku and Rajeev Motwani. Approximate frequency counts over data streams. *PVLDB*, 5(12):1699, 2012.

[MP80]   J. Ian Munro and Mike Paterson. Selection and sorting with limited storage. *Theor. Comput. Sci.*, 12:315–323, 1980.

[Mut05]   S. Muthukrishnan. Data streams: Algorithms and applications. *Foundations and Trends in Theoretical Computer Science*, 1(2), 2005.

[Pra15]   Ved Prakash. *Efficient Delegation Algorithms for Outsourcing omputations on Massive Data Streams.* PhD thesis, National University of Singapore, 2015.

[PS84]   R. Paturi and J. Simon. Probabilistic communication complexity. In *Proceedings of the 25th Annual Symposium onFoundations of Computer Science, 1984*, SFCS '84, pages 118–126, Washington, DC, USA, 1984. IEEE Computer Society.

[Raz92]   Alexander A. Razborov. On the distributional complexity of disjointness. *Theor. Comput. Sci.*, 106(2):385–390, 1992.

[Rou15]   Tim Roughgarden. Communication complexity (for algorithm designers). *Electronic Colloquium on Computational Complexity (ECCC)*, 22:156, 2015.

[San04]   Paul M. Sant. *Dictionary of Algorithms and Data Structures*. NIST: National Institute of Standards and Technology, 17 December 2004.

[SBB+02]   Josef Stoer, Roland Bulirsch, Richard H. Bartels, Walter Gautschi, and Christoph Witzgall. *Introduction to numerical analysis*. Texts in applied mathematics. Springer, New York, 2002.

[TW12]   Luca Trevisan and Ryan Williams. Notes on streaming algorithms. *CS154: Automata and Complexity*, 2012.

[Yao79]   Andrew Chi-Chih Yao. Some complexity questions related to distributive computing (preliminary report). In *Proceedings of the 11h Annual ACM Symposium on Theory of Computing, April 30 - May 2, 1979, Atlanta, Georgia, USA*, pages 209–213, 1979.

[Yao83]   Andrew Chi-Chih Yao. Lower bounds by probabilistic arguments (extended abstract). In *24th Annual Symposium on Foundations of Computer Science, Tucson, Arizona, USA, 7-9 November 1983*, pages 420–428, 1983.